Septimius Severus
in Scotland

Septimius Severus
in Scotland

The Northern Campaigns of the First Hammer of the Scots

Simon Elliott

Greenhill
Books

To my Dad John Elliott, partner in crime roaming across the Roman Empire!

Septimius Severus in Scotland:
The Northern Campaigns of the First Hammer of the Scots

This edition first published in 2018 by Greenhill Books,
c/o Pen & Swords Books Limited, 47 Church Street,
Barnsley, S. Yorkshire, S70 2AS

www.greenhillbooks.com
contact@greenhillbooks.com

ISBN: 978-1-78438-204-9

A CIP data record for this title is available from the British Library

Typeset in Bembo by Wordsense Ltd, Edinburgh
Maps and line drawings by Paul Baker
Printed and bound in England by TJ International

Contents

Illustrations

Drawings

Maps

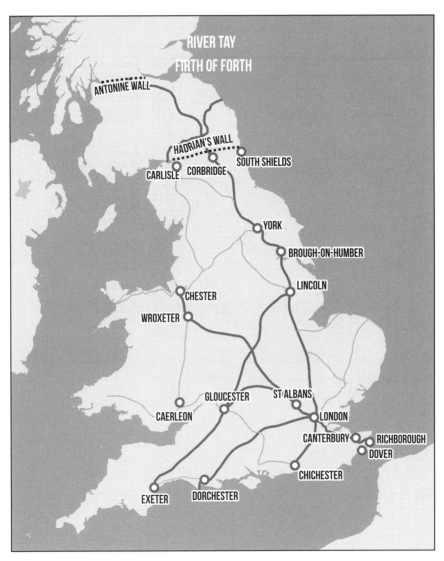

MAP I *Roman Britain AD 200*
[drawn by Paul Baker]

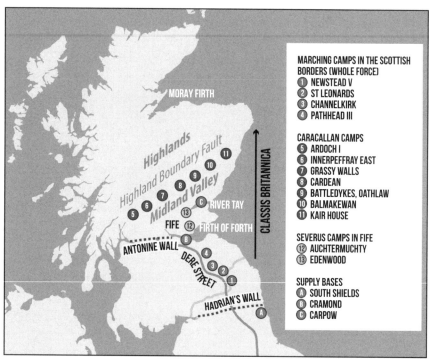

MARCHING CAMPS IN THE SCOTTISH
BORDERS (WHOLE FORCE)
1 NEWSTEAD V
2 ST LEONARDS
3 CHANNELKIRK
4 PATHHEAD III

CARACALLAN CAMPS
5 ARDOCH I
6 INNERPEFFRAY EAST
7 GRASSY WALLS
8 CARDEAN
9 BATTLEDYKES, OATHLAW
10 BALMAKEWAN
11 KAIR HOUSE

SEVERUS CAMPS IN FIFE
12 AUCHTERMUCHTY
13 EDENWOOD

SUPPLY BASES
A SOUTH SHIELDS
B CRAMOND
C CARPOW

MORAY FIRTH
Highlands
Highland Boundary Fault
Midland Valley
RIVER TAY
FIFE
FIRTH OF FORTH
CLASSIS BRITANNICA
ANTONINE WALL
DERE STREET
HADRIAN'S WALL

MAP 2 *The Severan campaigns in Scotland* AD *209 and* AD *210*
[drawn by Paul Baker]

Introduction

No: we are not going to leave a single one of them alive,
down to the babies in their mothers' wombs – not even they must live.
The whole people must be wiped out of existence,
with none to shed a tear for them, leaving no trace.

THESE WORDS, SPOKEN BY AGAMEMNON to his brother Menelaus in Homer's *Iliad* (6.57–9), mark the climax in Roman historian Cassius Dio's narrative regarding the emperor Septimius Severus' attempts to conquer Scotland* in AD 209 and AD 210. Dio (76/77.15.1–4) says they were spoken by the emperor to his soldiers, evidently in acute frustration after the native inhabitants with whom he had negotiated peace revolted yet again. The historian says that Severus used this literary device as a means of ordering his troops to kill everyone they met. To our sensibilities this is an astonishing order as, in effect, he is directing his troops to commit genocide. Given there were evidently eighty years of peace on the northern borders of Roman Britain after Severus' incursions, he appears to have succeeded. This dramatic and gruesome tale is one sometimes tackled in short form, but never previously considered at length. I endeavour to do that with this book, in which all of the issues and the military and political developments of the time leading to this 'shock and awe' *expeditio felicissima Britannica* are set in place, all to allow an informed interpretation to be made of a seemingly brutal campaign – one of the darkest points in the military history of these islands. To achieve this I use not only existing sources, interpretations and data but also new research associated with this book, including physically visiting some of the key sites in Severus' campaigns north of the border to determine their nature, and what they can tell us of the expedition. Additionally the book also contains new interpretations of contemporary portrayals of the Roman military – for

---

* See p. 15 for an explanation of why I use this anachronistic term.

example, the reliefs showing the emperor's campaigns against the Parthians on the Arch of Septimius Severus in the Forum in Rome – to show how an arms race against his eastern opponent was driving a change in military tactics and technology that would have had a major impact on his final campaigns in Scotland.

Lucius Septimius Severus Augustus was one of the great soldier emperors of the Roman Empire. He was born in the heat of North Africa in AD 145 when the Empire was at the height of its power, and he died while on campaign in the freezing north of Britain in AD 211 as the imperial project began its slow, inexorable slide towards the 'Crisis of the Third Century'. He was sixty-five when he passed away, an appreciable achievement for the time, especially given how long he spent on campaign once emperor and in seeing off usurpation attempts. These clearly hardened him, this being reflected on his deathbed in York when he famously told his troublesome sons Caracalla and Geta to 'Be of one mind, enrich the soldiers, and despise the rest' (Dio 76/77.15.3). No doubt he would have then reflected on a lifetime of imperial service and later campaigning on the borders of the far-flung Empire, stretching from modern Iraq and Syria in the east to Hadrian's Wall in north-western Europe. These events form the backdrop to this work, culminating with his attempt to finally bring Scotland into the province of Britain.

The nature of this short but powerfully built hard man will be considered in detail in the conclusion, following my analysis of his life and British campaigns. He was very single-minded, and I set out here some key themes explored in the book to guide the reader as my narrative progresses. In his early senatorial career Severus displayed little martial ardour, following an almost perfect path through the *cursus honorum*, often greatly benefiting from the sponsorship of senior colleagues – many with North African roots. However once in senior positions he was rarely away from the military, ultimately owing his rapid rise to the imperial throne to its allegiance, and then when emperor making sure he was on campaign as much as possible. The enormous *expeditio felicissima Britannica* is the ultimate and final example of this.

Severus also displayed a ruthless streak from early in his career, and once emperor liked to be perceived as an unforgiving character not to be crossed. In that regard it is no coincidence that when he succeeded to the imperial throne he quickly dismissed the Praetorian Guard (recreating it with his own loyal veterans) and created a new legion (the *legio* II *Parthica*) which he based near Rome. Such proximity of military regulars to the imperial capital was unheard of before this. Later, when he built the monumental arch to commemorate his victories against the Parthians, Severus planted it right outside the Senate *Curia* in the Forum. Such moves sent a very clear message to the political classes in Rome: behave or else.

A final consideration for the reader to track as they read the book are Severus' twin obsessions once emperor, which were the military (see above for his alleged final words to his sons) and his imperial *fiscus* treasury (see Chapter 1 for detail). Ultimately, controlling these were the two things he needed to stay in power, and in that regard his strategy clearly worked.

A Brief Note on the Book Title

The subheading referencing Edward I as the Hammer of the Scots is clearly an analogy, and an appropriate one given the particularly brutal nature of Severus' second campaign in the area. In the same way that Edward I sought to subjugate what by his time was known as Scotland, so did Severus regarding the same geographical area, but writ much larger. He in fact led the largest-ever campaign to conquer the far north of the islands of Britain, as he would have known modern Scotland. I obviously realise there were no 'Scots' in northern Britain at the time, nor indeed was there a 'Scotland'. However I have adopted these terms throughout the book where appropriate, given the very clear analogy and – understanding it as that – for the geographical ease of the modern reader.

The Narrative Flow of the Book

In this Introduction to the story of Severus in Scotland I now summarise the book's structure and the events that led to the Scottish campaign, which I briefly touch upon – the aim being to set the scene for the reader. I then detail the sources I have used (both written and otherwise), explain how I will be using certain names given the confusion this can cause (in terms of both people and places), detail the various types of fortifications which will be referenced in the work, explain the various manifestation of the Roman built environment which also feature in the work, and finally explain the chronological history of the political divisions of Roman-occupied Britain (important later in the story).

The remaining chapters in this book are very much designed to provide all the background information needed to understand my analysis of the Severan incursions into Scotland, before going into great detail about the campaigns themselves. Therefore I sequentially cover: the Roman imperial system at the time of Severus (Chapter 1); the Roman military establishment in the build-up to and during his reign (Chapter 2); Roman Britain in the second and early third centuries AD (Chapter 3); and the early and later life of Septimius Severus (Chapters 4 and 5, given an understanding here is particular important regarding the motives behind his *expeditio felicissima Britannica*). The book then concentrates at great length on: the build-up to Severus' arrival in Britain, and its actual occurrence (Chapter 6); the campaigns themselves, which are the central feature of the book (Chapter 7); and finally their aftermath (Chapter 8). The last includes a conclusion in which I review the legacy of this huge military undertaking.

Severus, the founder of the Severan dynasty, was one of a number of leading members of the Punic Septimii family from Lepcis Magna to take full advantage of the integration of North Africa into the Roman Empire (in his case the ultimate example; see Chapter 4 for full detail). As mentioned Severus rapidly advanced through the *cursus honorum* and by the early AD 190s had been a governor, consul and finally a senior border-territory governor, when the Emperor Commodus placed him in charge of Pannonia Superior on the Danube. This was a crucial province to the north of the Balkans, which controlled access to Italy from the east. It always featured a significant military force, and it was this that placed Severus in such a powerful position when Commodus was assassinated on New Year's Eve AD 192. When his immediate successor Pertinax was assassinated in turn, early in AD 193, Severus' troops – initially his *legio* XIV *Gemina Martia Victrix* – proclaimed him emperor. He swooped on Rome in a lightning strike, secured power in a highly successful coup and by the year's end was the ultimate victor in the 'Year of the Five Emperors'.

Severus was to spend much of the rest of his life on campaign: for example, twice in the east against the Parthians and others. He also had to fight to ensure his hold on power. In the last regard the closest he came to defeat was against the challenge of British governor Clodius Albinus, the emperor only just defeating Albinus in AD 197 at the Battle of Lugdunum (modern Lyon). As discussed in Chapter 5, Severus never forgot how close-run this challenge had been to his authority, and Britain remained in his thoughts until an opportunity arose for him to visit the recalcitrant province in person. This came in the form of the famous alleged dispatch in AD 207 from his governor there, declaring the province was in danger of being overrun by the tribes from north of Hadrian's Wall (based on an account by Herodian; see discussion in Chapter 6 regarding the provenance of this note). Herodian requested Severus either attend in person, or send new troops, and he got both. The emperor jumped at the chance to lead an army on campaign and was soon in the field again.

The size of the force Severus gathered for this campaign in Britain is astonishing, numbering up to 50,000 fighting troops plus the 7,000 men of the *Classis Britannica* regional fleet in the province (see Chapter 2 for detail of this calculation). Compare this to the modern British Army's less than 80,000 men and then cross-reference that figure against the size of the population then and now: 3.5 million against more than 65 million. The deployment of such a huge force in these islands (a 'Severan surge' in modern military parlance) must have placed considerable stress on the region's imperial and provincial economies. At that time Britain already featured some 12 per cent of the total Roman military complement in only 4 per cent of the Empire's territory, because of its never-conquered north.

After arriving in AD 208 the emperor then mounted his two campaigns in the following two years before dying in AD 211 in York. With this level of commitment he also didn't travel alone in the imperial entourage. With him came his wife Julia Domna, sons Caracalla (his co-Augustus) and Geta, the imperial *fiscus* treasury, his entire imperial court and retinue (including a praetorian prefect), many of the leading political figures of his day, and crack troops from across the entirety of the Roman military (including the Praetorian Guard). Severus established York, the base for his campaigns northwards, as his imperial capital for the last three years of his life, and vastly increased in size his supply bases at Brough-on-Humber (Roman Petuaria), South Shields (Roman Arbeia) at the mouth of the river Tyne, Cramond on the Firth of Forth and Carpow on the river Tay. The *expeditio felicissima Britannica* was clearly an enormous undertaking, and is detailed in full for the first time in this book.

Data and Sources

In terms of the evidence and sources used in the research for *Septimius Severus in Scotland*, I have accessed the widest possible range. In the first instance this has included my own academic studies over the last fifteen years through my

MA in war studies from King's College London, MA in archaeology from Univeristy College London and PhD in archaeology from the University of Kent. Meanwhile my recently published works on the *Classis Britannica* (*Sea Eagles of Empire: The* Classis Britannica *and the Battles for Britain*) (Elliott 2016a) and the non-military roles of the Roman military (*Empire State: How the Roman Military Built an Empire*) (Elliott 2017) have also proved fertile sources of new information regarding the Severan Scottish campaigns. In addition to that, the specific sources of information and data have included the archaeological record, the historical record (including wherever possible the key primary sources, and contemporary itineraries and epigraphy), analogy and (where appropriate) anecdote.

In terms of the archaeological data, much new information has emerged in recent years, which significantly improves our understanding of Severus' Scottish campaigns. For example, the excavations at South Shields, the publication of the excavations during the 1960s and 1970s at Carpow and more recently at Cramond, together with other recent work on the indigenous Maeatae and Caledonian peoples encountered by the Romans in their offensive, have all greatly added to our knowledge of the *expeditio felicissima Britannica*. Most recently, excavations at the hill fort at Burnswark Hill in Dumfriesshire have dramatically illustrated the brutality of a Roman assault on a native settlement (this dating to the Antonine period but a very useful analogy), while research around Loch Tay in the central Highlands (on the periphery of our area of study and which would have certainly attracted Roman attention) shows settlement ceasing there around the time of the Severan assault. This is perhaps the first direct evidence of the final genocidal policy followed by the Romans, and is discussed in detail in Chapter 8.

Finally in terms of the archaeology, marching camps play an important part in this story, and excavation has helped us track the progress of each Roman incursion into Scotland, and particularly those of Severus given their often huge size. (Note the Severan one at St Leonards Hill in the Scottish Borders, at seventy hectares in area, is the largest in the Roman Empire in Europe.) These and their Severan provenance are discussed at length in Chapters 2 and 7. Meanwhile, in terms of the actual artefacts which provide much of the archaeological data, as always numismatic evidence is important here (there are a number of specific coin and medallion issues related to the campaigns), as are seals of various kinds, pottery and other small finds.

Next, in terms of primary written sources, we have specific accounts of the Severan campaigns in Scotland from two historians, these being Cassius Dio with his *Roman History* (which covers the whole of Roman history in eighty books from the earliest times to his own day) and Herodian with his *History of the Roman Empire* (covering the late second century to mid-third century AD). Although the level of detail in both works is often patchy and inaccurate, their accessibility makes them valuable here, with Birley (2005, 195) usefully providing both accounts back to back in his treatise on Roman government in Britain so they can be cross-referenced. Both were written originally in Greek.

Dio, originating from Nicaea in Bithynia, was a contemporary of Severus. Under Commodus he had been an active senator in the public service, later becoming a consul, governor and proconsul. He was personally acquainted with Severus and had military experience (as governor of Pannonia Superior from AD 226 to AD 228), and so was well placed to illuminate this tale of the emperor's last military expedition. Given he was also hostile in part to Severus (and more so his elder son Caracalla) Dio's views can be thought perhaps more independent than the usual near-contemporary hagiographies which exist of many emperors. On the down side, only excerpts of the key relevant part of his narrative survive in this period in fragments, epitomes and summaries (for Dio's own lifetime only the works covering AD 17 to AD 218 survive in full).

Meanwhile Herodian was an easterner and later perhaps a minor public official in Rome. He wrote a history of the Roman Empire, in the form of eight books which cover the years from the death of Marcus Aurelius in AD 180 until the beginning of Gordian III's reign in AD 238, just after the onset of the 'Crisis of the Third Century'. He provides less information than Dio, and is also sometimes hostile in tone. Commentators view him as notoriously unreliable, with Birley (1999, 172) styling his account of Severus' reign as '. . . riddled with mistakes, omissions and inaccuracies'.

Although not a direct contemporary of Severus, Herodian wrote within living memory of his reign. At the very earliest this was some thirty years after Severus came to Britain, though quite likely not until the AD 240s or AD 250s.

To Dio and Herodian we can also add as a primary written source: the now anonymous *Historia Augusta*. This was a collection of biographies of the Roman emperors between AD 117 and AD 284, and was written later in the Empire. While it provides little regarding Severus' campaigns in Scotland other than recording the place of his death, it is useful as a source of information regarding his earlier life.

Finally in terms of primary sources we can add a number of later Latin chroniclers who briefly mention aspects of the Severan campaign (usually with regard to the 'Severan Wall', see discussion in Chapter 7, or to his death). These include Flavius Eutropius, Aurelius Victor, Jerome and Paulus Orosius. The first three of these (and given their use as sources by the fourth that, too, together with the *Historia Augusta* above) seem to have used as a key resource the so-called 'Kaisergeschichte' hypothetical set of short histories, now lost, which Burgess (1993, 491) argues was probably written between AD 337 and AD 340. Their common wording and phrasing, as well as facts and errors, imply this.

In terms of more modern appreciations of the life of Severus and his *expeditio felicissima Britannica*, we have the early twentieth-century biography of Maurice Platnauer (1918) and also Johannes Hasebroek's (1921) *Untersuchungen zur Geschichte des Kaisers Septimius Severus* study of the narrative on the emperor in the *Historia Augusta* (see above). Birley (1999, 206) calls the latter indispensable. Later, the relevant section of Sheppard Frere's (1974) *Britannia* is invaluable, too. More recently Anthony Birley's (1999) biography of Severus (*Septimius Severus: The African Emperor*, with its excellent family tree of the emperor) is also an useful resource, as is *The Roman Government of Britain* (Birley 2005). Barbara Levick's (2007) study of Severus' empress, *Julia Domna: Syrian Princess,* is insightful in providing a balanced view of the fortunes of the Severan imperial family.

In shorter works Nicholas Reed's (1975) 'The Scottish Campaigns of Septimius Severus' is very useful, as is his critique by Anne S. Robertson (1980). More recently Nick Hodgson's (2014) 'The British Expeditions of Septimius Severus' proved particularly useful given his illuminating discussion regarding the motives for Severus' intervention in Britain. Meanwhile, with regard to some of the key sites in the campaign, Rebecca Jones' (2011) *Roman Camps in Britain* has proved invaluable, as has Paul Bidwell's (2007) *Roman Forts in Britain*.

Among works that focus on Roman Scotland, I have found David Breeze's (2000) *Roman Scotland*, Lawrence Keppie's (2015) *The Legacy of Rome* and Anthony Kamm's (2011) *The Last Frontier* most useful. To this one can add the plethora of works on the military of the time of Severus detailed in the list of references. Finally, in terms of the written record, contemporary or later itineraries (such as the *Tabula Peutingeriana*, *Antonine Itinerary*, *Ravenna Cosmography* and *Notitia Dignitatum*) and a wide variety of types of epigraphy on contemporary stone-built structures and funerary monuments have also proved most useful. In my work, where the data has in any way been contradictory or ambiguous (which is often the case with regard to the primary sources) I have endeavoured to use common sense to make a personal judgement on what I believe to be the truth.

Some Housekeeping Notes

I have tried to keep my use of names (especially with regard to the chief protagonists) as simple as possible: for example, Septimius Severus is always referred to as Severus unless more than one such named member of the Septimii is referenced. Meanwhile his elder son was actually named Lucius Septimius Bassianus for the first seven years of his life, then renamed by Severus as Marcus Aurelius Antoninus (a clear and illuminating attempt by Severus to attach himself to the Antonine dynasty) and was later nicknamed Caracalla after a type of Gallic hooded tunic which he was prone to wear and made fashionable. Often styled Antoninus in some historical appreciations, here I call him Caracalla given this is the name most often used today. Other personal naming issues I cover in the narrative itself.

More broadly, regarding the use of classical and modern names, I have again attempted to ensure that my narrative is as accessible as possible to the reader: for example, I have used the modern name where a place is first mentioned, referencing its Roman name also at that point. Meanwhile, where a classical name for a position or role is well understood, I use that (although referencing the modern name at the first use). Furthermore when emperors are detailed in the main narrative I have listed the actual dates of their reigns when first mentioned.

As well as marching camps, permanent Roman fortifications are also a key feature of this book (some of the most important with regard to the Severan incursions into Scotland are detailed in Chapter 2). For these I have used the size-based hierarchy currently utilised by those studying the Roman military as a means of describing their size. Specifically, these are:

- fortress – a permanent base for one or more legions, some twenty hectares or more in size (which puts into context the enormous Severan marching camps detailed above);
- vexillation fortress – a large fort of between eight and twelve hectares holding a mixed force of legionary cohorts and auxiliaries;
- fort – a garrison outpost occupied by an auxiliary unit or units, some

one to six hectares in size;
- fortlet – a small garrison outpost large enough to hold only part of an auxiliary unit.

The built environment also plays an important role in this book, especially in the context of the progress of the Severan expedition up to the northern border. Therefore, to aid understanding, a framework is required to define different types of settlement. At the top end, for large towns the contemporary convention has been used, with three different kinds each featuring a different legal status. These were:

- *coloniae* – chartered towns of Roman citizens who were often discharged military veterans. Good examples here include Colchester, Gloucester, Lincoln and (later) York;
- *municipia* – also chartered towns but with some kind of mercantile origin, represented in Britain by St Albans among others;
- *civitas* capitals – the Roman equivalent of county towns, which featured the local government of a region. Most often located on the site of their equivalent pre-Roman centres; examples include Canterbury in Kent (the previous principal settlement of the Cantiaci).

Moving down in scale are small towns, which are defined as a variety of diverse settlements often associated with a specific activity: for example, administration, industry or religion. They were also often located at key transport nodes: for example, Rochester at the junction of Watling Street and the river Medway. Next are the villa-estate settlements, these being elite rural domestic and farming sites (although sometimes with another association such as industry). Moving downwards, we next have non-villa settlements where there is an evident lack of display of *Romanitas* (for whatever reason) by the inhabitants, before finally reaching industrial sites (which could be of any size).

The geographical backdrop for the majority of this work is the province of Britannia and therefore an explanation regarding its political organisation is needed. Before the Severan dynasty's reforms of Britain the term references the original single province of Britannia founded after the AD 43 Claudian invasion. After their reforms it then references either Britannia Superior or Britannia Inferior, depending on the context, and sometimes in fact both. While Herodian (3.8.2) claims this division took place shortly after Albinus' defeat, Birley

(2005, 336) makes a strong case that the division was actually carried out under Caracalla shortly into his reign. After the Diocletianic reformation, which established the diocese of Britannia and its four (perhaps later five) provinces, the full name of each is detailed for clarity. The four definite later provinces, as detailed on the *Verona List* of AD 303–314, are Maxima Caesariensis, Flavia Caesariensis, Britannia Prima and Britannia Secunda. These provinces are then listed once more a century later in the *Notitia Dignitatum*, this adding a fifth and problematic province called Valentia. See Chapter 6 for a more detailed analysis of the provincial development of occupied Britain, specifically in the context of York.

For the purposes of this book, I define the Scottish Highlands as I believe it would have been viewed in the classical world, that is as the territory above (to the north and west) of the Highland Boundary Fault; this is fully detailed in Chapter 1. The use in this book of the phrase Highland Line reflects this.

Also important in this book – given Severus' own experiences as his career developed – is an understanding of the social structure of Roman society, especially at the upper end. In terms of the ranking of the aristocracy, at the top was the senatorial class, said to be endowed with wealth, high birth and 'moral excellence' and of which Severus was a member. Next was the equestrian class, having slightly less wealth but with a reputable lineage (Severus' father and grandfather were members of this class), and finally there was the curial class (with the bar set slightly lower again). The last were largely merchants and mid-level landowners, who made up a large percentage of the town councillors in the Empire.

Acknowledgements

Lastly here I thank the many people who have helped make this work on the Severan *expeditio felicissima Britannica* possible. Specifically I would like to thank, as always, Professor Andrew Lambert of the War Studies Department at King's College London, Dr Andrew Gardner at University College London's Institute of Archaeology and Dr Steve Willis at the University of Kent, each for their ongoing encouragement and guidance. Next, my publisher Michael Leventhal at Greenhill Books for his ongoing mentorship of my published historical research. Also Rebecca Jones, Head of Archaeology and World Heritage at Historic Environment Scotland, Sam Moorhead at the British Museum, Dr Ian Betts at Museum of London Archaeology, Meriel Jeater at the Museum of

London, Professor Sir Barry Cunliffe of the School of Archaeology at Oxford University and Professor Martin Millett at the Faculty of Classics, Cambridge University. Next, my patient proofreaders John Lambshead and Nigel Emsen, lovely wife Sara and son Alex, and my dad John Elliott and friend Francis Tusa, both companions in my various escapades to research this book. As with all of my literary work, all have contributed greatly and freely, enabling this work on Severus in Scotland to reach fruition. Finally of course I would like to thank my family, especially my tolerant wife Sara once again and children Alex (also a student of military history) and Lizzie.

Thank you all.

Simon Elliott
October 2017

CHAPTER I

Background

I N THIS CHAPTER I SET out some of the key factors that influenced the progress of the Severan campaigns in Scotland, and also outline the world in which Severus lived. This is designed to help the reader take an informed view about his activities and decisions during the *expeditio felicissima Britannica*. In the first instance I detail the geology and climate of the northern parts of Britain during the Roman occupation given that, according to Dio and Herodian, they both played such a key role in the expedition's planning, execution and outcome. Next, I briefly outline the Principate period in Roman history within which Severus was emperor, with a particular focus on his own dynasty. This is particularly important as it will set the scene for the story of how he became the emperor and also provide the background needed for understanding the legacy of his campaigns in Scotland. I then move on to show how Severus governed his Empire to illustrate how the expedition came about and what transpired once it began, before finally providing a short review of the way the Roman economy worked as this will help explain some of the key decisions made by Severus both before and during the *expeditio felicissima Britannica*.

The Geology and Climate of the Roman North of Britain and Scotland

Both Dio and Herodian say the geology and climate of the north of Britain and Scotland played an important part in the Severan incursions there. Dio (76/77.12.1) states that the native inhabitants who were the target of Severus' ire lived in 'wild and waterless mountains and desolate and marshy plains' while for Herodian (3.14.6) it was too much water that was the problem: 'the land of the Britons becomes marshy, being flooded by the continuous ocean tide'. He adds that because of the mists from the marshes the air in the north is gloomy. In fact both key primary sources paint a very grim picture of the campaigning region and the impact this had on the Roman soldiers there.

These parts of Britain are particularly susceptible to geological and climatic change. Kamm (2011, 14) details that in 1159 BC a volcanic eruption in Iceland produced vast clouds of volcanic ash (experienced in Britain more recently although on a lesser scale in 2010 with the eruption of the Eyjafjallajökull volcano) that caused abnormal weather conditions and many communities to migrate from the Highlands to the Lowlands of Scotland. Noting this linkage between geology and climate, I now consider them in turn.

Geology

Geology has always played a major role in military campaigns in the northern parts of Britain given the impact this has (then and now) on settlement and economic activity, with those during the Roman occupation being excellent examples. To that end one can track through marching campsites and other archaeological data the routes taken by armies campaigning in the region. As I set out in my work on the *Classis Britannica* (Elliott 2016a, 13), the Romans used coastal routes (or lowlands accessible by river from the coast) to avoid the uplands running through centre of the land from the Midlands northwards, in Wales and in the far north. The routes taken by the warrior governor Quintus Petilius Cerialis during his campaigns against the Brigantes in the early AD 70s (see Chapters 3 and 6) are very clear examples of this. They run from the Midlands to the Solway Firth–Tyne Line on both the east and west coast to avoid the Pennines in the centre. Meanwhile, heading further north and with regard to his specific attempts to conquer Scotland, the routes taken in the late first century AD by another warrior governor, Gnaeus Julius Agricola, also focus largely on the east coast (again to avoid the Highlands, this time in central and western Scotland). Severus followed almost exactly the same route as Agricola in the early third century, for the same reasons.

Scotland is unusually varied in its large number of different geological features. The three main geographical subdivisions are:

- The Southern Uplands, lying to the south of the Southern Uplands Fault (and largely composed of Silurian deposits);
- The Central Lowlands, a rift valley mainly comprising Paleozoic formations;
- The Highlands and islands, a diverse area lying to the north and west of the Highland Boundary Fault.

The Highland Boundary Fault played the key geological role in the Scottish campaigns of Severus (and earlier Agricola). Because it runs south-west to north-east from the Isle of Arran to Stonehaven, it delineates the Highlands in the north from the field of campaigning to the south. North of the Clyde–Forth Line this would have principally been in the northern Midland Valley. When one tracks the line of Severan's fifty-four-hectare marching camps there, it is immediately obvious that they specifically follow the fault line, from which glens head north into the Central Highlands and further. This is not to say that campaigning of some kind didn't take place further north than the fault line: for example, over the Grampian Mountains above which sits the Moray and Buchan Lowlands just south of the Moray Firth. Indeed it was in this area that Agricola's famous Battle of Mons Graupius is supposed to have taken place in AD 83 against the 'Caledonians' (and noting that his furthest north marching camp was at Bellie in Moray). However we simply don't have the evidence that Severus went that far north, with his strategy (detailed in Chapter 7) appearing to focus on the isolation of the lowlands of the northern Midland Valley from the Highlands by driving a line of marching camps along the Highland Boundary Fault, and then closing off each glen as they were passed to prevent access to his rear and lines of supply. Perhaps a future campaign might have built on this strategy to head into the far north once the lowlands were secure, but his untimely death put paid to this.

Climate

Almost all the primary sources covering Rome's occupation of Britain comment negatively on the weather in this most north-westerly outpost of the Empire (Tacitus, for example, calls the weather here 'miserable' while Strabo highlights 'the frequent rain and fog'). It is indeed no coincidence that one of the items Britain was best known for in the Roman world was the *birrus* (a rain-proofed hooded cloak). One can muster a rather enigmatic image of the Principate legionaries and *auxilia* along Hadrian's Wall huddling beneath such a garment in the driving rain and snow of a northern winter. It is also no surprise that it was in a freezing February in York that Severus himself died.

In terms of the specific weather conditions for the whole of the British Isles during the occupation (to allow a comparison to made with conditions in the far north) modern scientific research has provided a useful picture. This seems to show that the weather in the province was not too far removed from that which we experience today, excepting that it was perhaps slightly warmer and wetter earlier in the Roman occupation (Grainge 2005, 37). Evidence for this has been found in York where excavations have revealed the remains of insect species that thrive in a warmer climate than that experienced today – the data suggesting a mean July temperature 1°C higher at the time (Ottaway 2013, 16).

The principal type of system dominating weather patterns in the islands of Britain during the occupation were Atlantic lows (as they are today), which led to prevailing winds originating most often from the westerly quadrant. These winds are created by North Atlantic depressions moving east or north-east across the open ocean before meeting the north-western European land mass, usually hitting Ireland and Britain first. Indeed it is this type of system that Julius Caesar describes in his *Conquest of Gaul* and which proved so troublesome to his 55 BC expedition to Britain, and delayed the sailing of his 54 BC expedition (Elliott 2016a, 43). Such weather systems are often modified as they interact with high pressure systems when they approach the continental land mass, and this set of interactions leads to what can at best be described as the cheerfully unpredictable weather conditions that are so much part of the modern British cultural experience.

Both Dio and Herodian make the weather in the far north of Britain sound even grimmer than in the south. Certainly when Caesar (V.135) himself famously described Britain at the time of the 55 BC sortie as being densely populated and heavily cultivated, it was clearly the south he was describing given the more favourable weather conditions there. In that regard Ottaway (2013, 16) highlights that between 1971 and 2000 on the south coast of Britain there was an average of 1,750 hours of sunshine per year, compared to 1,149 in Malham Tarn in north Yorkshire. This differential is even more pronounced as one heads into the far north. Meanwhile, again using Yorkshire as an example in the same time period, Ottaway (2013, 16) adds that in terms of rainfall there is a very pronounced difference in the amount experienced in the upland Pennines when compared to the lowlands: 1,518 mm per annum at

Malham Tarn compared to 600 mm in York. Furthermore the overall picture is one where the northern parts of Britain receive less sunlight than the south, restricting agricultural activity to an extent, with more rain on the upland regions (especially on the western side given the prevailing weather systems detailed above). According to the primary sources, the weather experienced by Severus' troops as their legionary spearheads headed north was particularly grim in AD 209 and AD 210, so overall the climate (as with geology, above) would have had a major impact on the campaign.

The Principate Empire

The Severan incursions into Scotland sit within a time period in the chronology of the Roman Empire called the Principate. This occurred between the accession of Augustus in 27 BC and the end of the 'Crisis of the Third Century' when Diocletian became emperor in AD 284. The name comes from the term *princeps* (chief or master), referencing the emperor as the principle citizen of the Empire.

Though not an official title, *princeps* was assumed by emperors on their accession (Hornblower and Spawforth 1996, 1246) and was a conceit that allowed the Empire to be explained away as a simple continuance of the earlier Republic. It was dropped from the time of Diocletian, after which the name Dominate was used to describe the new, more overtly imperial system (this is based on the word *dominus*, referencing master or lord). Within the Principate period there were a number of distinct dynasties (Kean 2005, 18). These were:

- The Julio-Claudian dynasty, lasting from the accession of Augustus in 27 BC to the death of Nero in AD 68. This period included the beginnings of the Empire and the initial conquest campaigns in Britain from the Claudian invasion of AD 43 onwards;
- The Year of the Four Emperors in AD 69, with Vespasian being ultimately successful;
- The Flavian dynasty, from Vespasian's accession to the death of Domitian in AD 96;
- The Nervo-Trajanic dynasty, from the accession of Nerva in AD 96 to the death of Hadrian in AD 138. This included the campaigns of Trajan, such as his conquest of Dacia in two campaigns from AD 101 to AD 102 and from AD 105 to AD 106;

- The Antonine dynasty, from the accession of Antoninus Pius in AD 138 through to the assassination of Commodus in AD 192. The lengthy twenty-three-year reign of Antoninus Pius was one of relative peace, with the Empire at its most stable;
- The 'Year of the Five Emperors' in AD 193, and the subsequent civil wars. The latter ranged from the accession of Pertinax through to the death of British governor and usurper Clodius Albinus in AD 197;
- The Severan dynasty, from the accession of our protagonist Septimius Severus in AD 193 through to the assassination of Severus Alexander in AD 235. It is this period that forms much of the chronological framework for this book;
- The 'Crisis of the Third Century', from the death of Severus Alexander to the accession of Diocletian in AD 284. This period was a time when the Empire was under great stress, ultimately leading to change within and without its borders and the onset of the Dominate period in Roman history.

How Did Septimius Severus Rule His Empire?

Severus had very clear views about how to rule his Empire, and was autocratic to say the least. This reflects not only his early experiences as he progressed through the *cursus honorum* senatorial career path before he became emperor (see Chapter 4 for detail), but also how he acceded to power during the 'Year of the Five Emperors' and his subsequent struggles to remain in position. His final words to his sons (see p. 14) are testament to this, as he took a rather dim view of any but his family and the military. It is therefore helpful at this point to consider how a Roman Principate emperor exercised his authority, so that we can understand how Severus was ultimately able to gather and sustain such a huge force at the extreme north-western tip of the Empire in his final campaign, while at the same time maintaining his authority elsewhere, up to and including the Parthian frontier in the east.

As set out above, from the time of Augustus the Roman Empire was ruled by the *princeps*, the first emperor also being the first to style himself with the praenomen *imperator* (since 38 BC, being hailed as such twenty-seven times). That aside, Augustus avoided many trappings of authority, quietly removing Republican checks and balances on power and slowly collecting the levers of imperial supremacy while still maintaining the fiction that he was saviour of the Republic. Among the levers of power he gathered were:

- regulation of the Senate, including the means to convene its sessions and also set out the agenda for all its meetings. Emperors also had control over who might be appointed a senator (noting Severus' elevation in that regard by Marcus Aurelius, see Chapter 4); such promotion was based on property qualifications and free birth, as in the Republic. The means used to make senatorial appointments was by the awarding of the *latus clavus* broad stripe. Augustus also first instituted a pre-senatorial service system for eighteen-year-old candidates, who spent a year as a member of one of the four Boards called the *vigintiviri* through which the city of Rome was run (again see Chapter 4 for Severus' experiences in that regard);
- the authority to consecrate temples and to oversee religious ceremonies (as the *Pontifex Maximus*, the leader of the College of Priests), and also to similarly take charge of the appointment of vestal virgins;
- control of the Roman calendar;
- assuming a tribune's legal authority. This included the emperor enjoying the powers of *tribunicia postetas* (the power of coercion) and *sacrosanctity* (legal inviolability through sacred law);
- becoming the supreme commander of the military, in all of its manifestations;
- taking over many of the financial controls of the Empire, through the management of the imperial *fiscus* (see following detail);
- exercising regional authority through the appointment of provincial governors, procurators and the various regional fleet *praefecti classis*.

Using these accrued powers, the emperor exercised his authority through three main bodies:

- The *Consilium Principis* (main council), created by Augustus to be his central advisory body. This was effectively always in session, meeting ad hoc at the emperor's call whenever required to advise on mostly legal and diplomatic matters (Hornblower and Spawforth 1996, 377).
- The *fiscus* (imperial treasury), controlled under the Principate by a *rationibus* (financial officer, later replaced by a *rationalis*), the magnet for the wealth generated in each of the Empire's provinces, which was

used to fund the emperor's activities (including the use of the military). The term *fiscus* is very specific, referring to the personal treasury of the emperors of Rome, and literally translating as 'purse' or 'basket'.

- The famous Praetorian Guard, again founded by Augustus and institutionalised by Tiberius, under the command of praetorian prefects. This body had a monopoly of force within the walls of Rome and was significantly reformed by Severus when emperor (see Chapter 2).

The means by which the emperor then controlled his Empire on a regional basis (until the Diocletianic reformation at least) was through two separate chains of command in each province. The first was the imperial governor, who was the legal and military authority, heading a team that helped him run the province, which from the time of Trajan was regularised in the form of his *officium*. In Britain this comprised an *iuridicus* (legal expert, though not always appointed here), three legionary legates and three senatorial-level military tribunes (Severus' brother Geta holding such a post; see Chapter 4). The remaining staff, by the time of Severus, usually comprised fifteen legionary tribunes and up to sixty auxiliary commanders.

Meanwhile the second chain of command was that of the procurator, always an equestrian, whose role was to ensure the smooth running of the province's finances. His task was to ensure the province contributed to its maximum extent into the imperial *fiscus*, so being worth the conquest. He was supported by a number of lesser *procuratores*, usually other equestrians although with some freed men. These personnel would have been registrars and finance officers, together with the superintendents and specialists who ran major state-sponsored industrial activity such as *metalla* quarries and mining operations, Imperial Estates and other state-run monopolies. Interestingly the *praefectus classis* regional navy commander also resided within the procurator's chain of command. This procuratorial association for the *praefectus classis* reflects the use by the state of the regional navies as effectively an 'army service corps' (Parfitt 2013, 45) in an age before a civil service, nationalised industry or a free market able to raise capital for major construction projects. When carrying out military activities, however, the fleet would then have come under the control of the governor (see Chapter 2 for detail).

A final reflection here regarding this imperial chain of command is the experience of Severus himself. Being a governor at the time he made his power play to become emperor, he fully understood that having reliable imperial representatives running his provinces was the key component to ensure the success of his Empire. Such a view would have been reinforced as he fought to retain control after his success in the 'Year of the Five Emperors', in AD 193 – for example, against the usurper Albinus in AD 196–7 – and it is no surprise that when he mounted his *expeditio felicissima Britannica* he replaced both the governor and procurator here from the moment he arrived (see Chapter 6).

The Roman Economy

To understand how Severus ran his Empire, and specifically funded his *expeditio felicissima Britannica*, it is important to describe the Roman economy. This part of the chapter is therefore divided into three subsections: a brief review of the current theories regarding the Roman economy; detail on the Roman imperial economy (of which the imperial *fiscus* was part); and a review of the provincial economy. The last was based on regional markets, free trade and patterns of consumption (Mattingly 2006, 496), which I broadly refer to as the market economy (though in no way implying this functioned in the manner of a modern manifestation of a market economy).

Current Theories Regarding the Roman Economy

Imperial Rome is often cited as the archetypal 'Empire', a mantle that attracts a wide variety of interpretations of its strengths and weaknesses by commentators from across the political spectrum. At the heart of this debate is the Roman economy itself as this helps to explain the fiscal aspects of maintaining an Empire that enjoyed such longevity (although often experiencing times of financial crisis), and also gives great insight into the lives of those who experienced it. With regard to the latter a wide range of views are evident, from sometimes benevolent to frequently negative. In the former camp Temin (2012, 2) controversially makes the case that the quality of life for an average citizen during the time of the Principate was actually better than at any time before the Industrial Revolution. Meanwhile, at the other extreme, Pollard (2000, 249) in his analysis of Roman Syria talks of an economy where the exploitation of the population through taxation, the requirement to support the army (this was a border territory, so a good analogy for Britain) and the removal of natural resources under imperial control (see below for the imperial economy) outweighed the benefits for the population as a whole: for example, in terms of investment. In the same vein Faulkner (2001, 120) takes this negative experience to the extreme with his contention that the Empire, economically and otherwise, was robbery with violence. All of these themes are considered below, with a specific focus on how similar to the Western premodern economy the Roman economy was (with the 'modernists' seeing more similarities and the 'primitivists' less), and also how integrated the Roman market was in the broadest sense.

Modern considerations of the Roman economy date to the 1950s with a model developed by A. H. M. Jones (1953, 293), which stressed the centrality of agriculture. He argues that most agrarian produce was consumed locally, with the notable exception of the Egyptian/North African grain supply to Rome. He also emphasises the importance of taxes and rents over trade and industry. A seminal contribution to this debate was then made by Moses Finley, who, taking the 'primitivist' position, argues that status was a key factor in the economies of the ancient world (Finley 1999, 45). He hypothesises that these economic systems were embedded in social standing, stating that the ancient world placed so much importance in this regard that there was a clear differentiation between the economic activities in which those in the upper reaches of society could participate and those below them. In this way, such economic systems of the distant past were very different from many of those of today, where there is a general freedom (he contends) for all to participate in commercial enterprises.

An additional contribution was made by Keith Hopkins (1985, xiv–xv), who believes that the Roman economic model also allowed for economic growth, and was not static as others had argued. He sees such growth as being particularly noticeable in the late first millennium BC and the first two centuries AD, with the expanding Empire of the Principate driving surplus production.

Next for consideration was Millett's (1990) dramatic intervention with *The Romanization of Britain*, his watershed appreciation not only of the Roman economy but also of Roman Britain more broadly, its main focus being on cultural change. His work had its earliest roots in Francis Haverfield's (1906) *The Romanization of Roman Britain*, then being incubated through Finley's (1999) conception of the Roman economy and the subsequent academic debates on the subject through the 1970s and 1980s.

Millett's (1990) central contention was that the integration of a province into the Roman Empire was a two-way social acculturation process rather than the one-way domination by the latter over the former. This involved complex patterns of interaction between the incoming world of Rome and native population, with the impact of the arrival of the former sometimes minimised. Millett suggests this was more of a 'change at the top' with a new Roman upper tier being added, combined with a form of 'light touch' imperialism, and adds (Millett 1990, 8): 'The net effect of this was an early imperial system of loosely decentralised administration which allowed overall control by Rome while leaving the low-level administration in the hands of the traditional aristocracies.' This certainly set him against the views of Hingley (1982, 17) and others who had argued in favour of a province such as Britain being an administered economy – Hingley (2005, 49) later emphasising its exploitative nature.

More recently Erdkamp (2005, 2), continuing this imperial exploitation position, used the grain market of the Empire as a cipher through which to understand the wider Roman economy, with a particular focus on market integration. Basing his research on philological and epigraphic evidence, Erdkamp takes a 'modernist' position, believing that Roman society was not dissimilar to that of premodern Europe (he uses the analogy of imperial Russia). This included the dominance of agriculture, the high cost of transportation and (where there is a sophisticated-enough level of commerce and supply) market integration. Erdkamp (2005, 14) specifically separates out wealthier farms from those of the peasantry, arguing that the latter less frequently participated in the capital market and often had the poorest land, which was regularly overworked. In the latter case this led to a pattern of diminishing returns, as more of the output was consumed by those working the land than the return (Erdkamp 2005, 15). This was, he says, in juxtaposition to the larger, wealthier farms which found it much easier to generate a larger surplus.

Regarding the market integration identified as an important factor in the success of the Roman economy by Erdkamp, Bonifay (2014, 557) has most recently expanded on the idea, using Roman Africa as an example (useful here given the focus on Septimius Severus and his family) and basing his conclusions on ceramic data. He argues that Mediterranean patterns of consumption were only visible along the strip of coastline adjoining the sea, adding that in inland regions local production and markets substituted for more recognisable Mediterranean products. Again the differential cost of transport is the key factor, a major element defining the provincial and indeed imperial economy (see below). In this regard Hingley (2005, 106) argues that the Roman market system certainly seemed to be at its most integrated in the areas that had maritime access.

The Roman Imperial Economy: Making the Province Pay

Roman provinces were always challenging to finance, although simple subsistence wasn't their purpose, with each imperial procurator under great pressure to ensure it contributed substantially to the imperial *fiscus*. Mattingly (2006, 491), in his stark assessment of Britain's experience of the occupation of Rome, is clear about what the economic drivers of the Roman state were in this regard: 'The economy of Britain was profoundly affected by the desire of the Roman state to extract resources from the province and this was a constant of Roman Imperialism.'

Hingley (2005, 49) also emphasises the exploitative nature of the Empire, directly linking imperial expansion with the exploitation of human labour in the form of slavery. Both he and Mattingly stand in stark contrast in their interpretation of the experience of the provinces to Roman rule when set against that of Millett (1990). In the context of this debate between those with the latter's positive view of Romanization and the more negative post-Romanization focus on experience, identity and community, others more recently have not taken such a bleak view as Mattingly (2006) and Hingley (2005). For example, Millett himself (2015, 558) recently highlighted the strong appetite for the symbols of the new culture as shown by data from the excavations along the Roman road from Brough-on-Humber to York (the importance of this for the Severan campaigns in the north is discussed in Chapter 6) as it traverses Hayton and Shiptonthorpe in the East Riding of Yorkshire. Meanwhile Willis (2008) in his earlier review of Mattingly's (2006) work speaks of continuities enduring from the Late Iron Age (LIA).

In terms of the imperial economy, in the first instance economic exploitation in a given province was quickly evident immediately after the campaigns of conquest, given the need to utilise the brutally gained spoils of war to offset the expensive costs of conquest. Such spoils included the private possessions of the indigenous elites in the form of portable wealth and the redistribution of their land. Once the conquest was complete, however, and a given territory settled into the Empire, the primary demands on the imperial economy would be:

- paying for the army, in terms of their pay, bonuses, materials, equipment, supplies and discharge bounties. To provide some context here, the total costs annually of the salary and discharge bounties for the army in the second century AD were 150 million denarii (Mattingly 2006, 493);

- the provincial government's own infrastructure, noting as an example that the annual salary for the governor alone in Britain was around 200,000 denarii (Mattingly 2006, 493);
- transport costs, especially where this activity was facilitated by the state;
- capital investments such as the costs of running imperial properties and public lands;
- diplomatic subsidies, always a consideration in Britain given the unconquered far north and very relevant to the story of Severus' campaigns in Scotland (especially in the preceding decade, see Chapter 3).

Such demands were clearly huge in terms of the burden they placed on the province, especially early in the occupation, and were magnified in Britain given the always exponentially large military presence (and especially during Severus' enormous expedition). In this regard Mattingly (2006, 493) estimates that the overall cost of running the province of Britain would have been in the region of 'some tens of millions' of denarii, and that outside the spikes in military campaigning activity.

Continuing this hardline view of the exploitation of provinces such as Britain by the Roman state and imperial household, the various options then available to the state through the imperial economy to ensure that the province paid its way included:

- the property of the landed classes – this always being at risk of appropriation and redistributed by the state when an opportunity presented itself. Individual fortunes in this regard were also equally at risk of any sudden change in the providence of the owner (certainly the case for many members of the elites in Britain after the failure of Albinus' usurpation attempt against Severus);
- the landed property itself which was also vulnerable to state exploitation through rentals, sales, legacies and disposals;
- land that was controlled directly by the state – in its most extreme in the form of Imperial Estates;
- the exploitation of the wider population through taxation (see below), tribute demands, liturgies, military recruitment, labour requirements and slavery;
- with specific regard to rural populations, the use of exploitative tools such as rents, dues, requisitioning, price fixing and once again tax;

- the exploitation of natural resources: for example, through the *metalla*;
- any profit derived from the existence of harbours, markets and trade;
- the system of military supply (incorporating a number of aspects of the above), which in a given province had a marked effect on the economy involving peaks and troughs in the required output and often featuring long distances for such goods to travel.

As can be seen, a key theme running through all was taxation. For much of the Principate this was based on a periodical census, which listed the resources in a given province, thus allowing two direct taxes to be levied. These were the *tributum soli* (a land tax) and the *tributum capitis* (based on capitation). Such *tributa* direct taxes were ultimately paid to the procurator through his fiscal officials, who used tax-farmers (working under state contracts) and local authorities to act as middlemen. Meanwhile *vectigalia* indirect taxes such as the harbour dues were collected by officials such as *publicani* contractors.

It is specifically regarding the subject of taxation where we see the first major change taking place within the imperial economy during the Principate, and one instituted by Severus himself. This was his establishment of the Empire's first full *annona* tax-in-kind system, which would later dominate Roman taxation from the reign of Diocletian (see below). The term originated with the *Cura Annonae* grain supply to the citizens of Rome, coming to represent any type of ad hoc taxation in kind, which was occasionally levied in times of crisis but now became the norm.

Kulikowski (2016, 5) has recently argued that the roots of these Severan economic reforms are actually to be found much earlier in the Principate. He argues that the causational event was the displacement over time of power away from the leading, hierarchical senatorial classes in Rome in favour of the leading noble families from elsewhere in the growing Empire (note the later rise in influence of such families from North Africa when Severus was emperor); the equestrian classes broadly (see below for the Severan experience in this regard); and a new nouveau riche class of meritocrats who had benefited when the Empire expanded early in the Principate.

Thus, by the time that Severus had acceded to power, he was in a much better position to institute major political and economic changes than his predecessors earlier in the Principate. Once in control of the financial institutions of the Empire he quickly realised that the economic system he had inherited was struggling to keep up with demand, particularly the cost of the military of whom he was so fond (see Chapter 2 for detail regarding the extra pressure he himself placed on the economic system of the Empire through increasing the pay of the military). To alleviate this financial pressure he firstly increased the number of government officials (including more procuratorial staff), particularly on the Danube frontier, in the east and in North Africa. This followed a similar pattern with regard to the Senate, where he had also favoured the promotion on non-Italians – a deliberate move designed to water down opposition from the traditional Italian senatorial classes after his accession (thus accelerating the process already detailed above). Severus also further increased the importance of the equestrian nobility (again accelerating the process described above), with more members being incorporated from this class into his *Consilium Principis*. Finally he regularised the ad hoc use of the *annona* as a means of raising taxes in times of crisis, instituting it across the entirety of the Empire (including Italy which had previously had some privileges of exemption from such types of taxation). He specifically opted for this new 'official' layer of taxation as it was protected to some extent from the effects of the inflation which was beginning to gather pace in the early third century AD (the denarius had already been devalued as early as AD 194).

The Severan *annona* was managed by the wealthiest *decuriones* (municipal councillors) within the key cities and towns throughout the Empire, who were financially responsible for the levying and collection of the taxes, with new *boulai* (municipal senates) being set up to facilitate their activities in provinces such as Egypt. The actual day-to-day running of the *annona* was performed by a new '*annona* service' of civil servants instituted by Severus, which took over some of the administrative tasks previously managed by the military.

However this original full *annona* itself came under pressure as the third century progressed, principally because of the turbulence caused by the multifarious challenges of the 'Crisis of the Third Century'. The imperial response to this challenge was threefold:

- The state began to confiscate long-established city revenues (such as local tolls, taxes and endowments), from the middle of the century.
- The currency was debased again (by reducing the silver content in the denarii with which the troops were paid).
- At times of extreme crisis (frequent in this period), additional emergency taxes were raised.

Further economic stress was then caused when Aurelian attempted to mark his reunification of the Empire by launching new gold and silver coinage, apparently aiming to replace much of the money then in circulation. The result was to almost demonetise the Empire because of the poor quality of the coinage.

It was in such dire circumstances that Diocletian, as part of his wider political, economic and social reformation, instituted a fully systemised taxation system on all economic production. This was called the *annona militaris*, and it replaced all that had existed previously (including the Severan *annona*).

The Roman Provincial Economy

Running parallel to the imperial economy detailed above was the local provincial economy, often difficult to distinguish from its imperial counterpart. Its nature was heavily influenced by the preconquest economy of a region, especially at the beginning of a territory being integrated into the Empire. Thus in Britain the market economy in the south-east was more sophisticated than elsewhere, which was not surprising given the existing links with northern Gaul.

Continuing the use of Britain as an example, from the point of conquest it seems the provincial economy grew extensively, particularly during the early years of the Principate. Ultimately it catered for the top-down needs of the state and also for the downwards-up demand from a new consumer class feeding on new ideas and innovations. With regard to the latter, Hingley (2005, 108) has highlighted the subordinate cultures of merchants, craftsmen and freed men who drove a marked increase in trade and industry. On the same topic, Mattingly (2006, 497) says: 'If measured in simple terms across the period AD 50–350, there is plenty of evidence for the evolution of urban markets and the integration of rural territories with them, of an increase in coin use, of expanded manufacturing activity and increased consumption of a wide range of goods across a broad spectrum of sites (military, urban and rural).'

Specifically on the issue of coin usage, Mattingly (2006, 497) adds that this was in the first instance part of the imperial economy (given the need to pay the administration and military). Hingley (2005, 108) earlier said that the movements of groups including the troops themselves created a system of contacts quantitatively significant, thus proving highly influential in the provincial economy within which they resided. Nevertheless coin use only slowly became part of the provincial economy – in a British context not reaching levels similar to that seen in the imperial economy until later in the second century AD. The availability of coinage was then understandably disrupted during the 'Crisis of the Third Century' when supply was dislocated and when poor-quality forgeries entered circulation.

The key components of the provincial market economy were the markets themselves, which were mostly located in urban centres and needed to be officially sanctioned by the state (showing the ever-present proximity of the imperial economy). Such markets acted as emporia for the distribution of manufactured products, and in a British context introduced many innovations of the occupation.

Now, having considered the relevant background detail to some of the key issues that influenced the Severan *expeditio felicissima Britannica*, I move on to review the military machine Severus was able to deploy in his attempt to conquer Scotland.

CHAPTER 2

The Roman Military Machine at the Time of Septimius Severus

Although the armies and navies of Rome at this time were broadly similar to those of the earlier Principate (following the significant reforms of Augustus), they had already begun the process of change that was to see the armed forces of the later Empire being very different in nature to their predecessors. Severus himself was the first of the great reformers of the Roman military, and this is evident in the huge force he deployed in his Scottish campaigns. To enable the reader to track these early changes, and more generally develop an understanding of the military prowess deployed by Severus in Britain against his opponents (a very asymmetrical match-up indeed), this chapter looks specifically at the military reforms initiated by Severus, then sequentially at the key components of the Roman armed forces of the time (namely legionaries, auxiliaries and naval *milites*) before finally detailing some of the key fortifications that played such a crucial role in the campaigns of Severus.

The Severan Reforms of the Roman Military

For the majority of the Principate the legions in the west were stationed on the frontiers of the Empire. Barriers such as the river Rhine created a natural frontier, in this case later to be fortified as the *limes Germanicus* (D'Amato, 2016, 6). The military units so deployed were within easy reach of such borders, with the few permanently garrisoned camps positioned further back fulfilling other functions (such as facilitating administration) rather than being the defence-in-depth-type deployment seen in the later Empire. Meanwhile, not relevant to this narrative of Severus in the west but useful as context, in the east this pattern of legionary deployment was slightly different, with the majority of military formations often deployed near major urban centres (although it should be noted these were often closer to the imperial frontiers than many of their western counterparts, and were for the most part larger too). However in both west and east it was common for detached units of the legions to be sent elsewhere on a variety of duties, including joining large campaigns. In that regard, the various vexillations of the Rhine and Danube legions, which joined Severus for his *expeditio felicissima Britannica*, are an excellent example.

Broadly these patterns of deployment in the west and east started a gradual process of change from border defence to the later defence-in-depth pattern from the time of Severus, and specifically with his creation of legions I, II and III *Parthica*. These three new legions were founded in AD 197 for use in the emperor's eastern campaigns, but while I and III *Parthica* remained in the region after the completion of military operations there, II *Parthica* went back directly to Italy. Once there it was based at Albanum, thirty-four kilometres from Rome (Elliott 2016a, 156). This was a very iconoclastic move on the part of Severus given it had been centuries since a legion had been permanently based in Italy, and clearly one of the reasons to position it so close to Rome was as a classic Severan reminder to the elites there to behave. However it also, for the first time, provided the emperor with a strategic reserve at the heart of the Empire, which could be deployed by him on campaign, exactly as happened in his *expeditio felicissima Britannica* when vexillations from the legion certainly accompanied him (and possibly the whole legion, see Chapter 7). In this sense *legio* II *Parthica* actually appears to have become the centre of a critical mass around which what would later be called a field army coalesced.

Thus when Severus set out for Britain he was joined by elements of his Praetorian Guard (this was his first military reform, in which he disbanded them and then reformed them with his own men as soon as he became emperor, see Chapter 6), the Imperial Guard cavalry and even perhaps one of the urban cohorts of Rome (see Chapter 7 for discussion on the make-up of his overall force). Such a strategy of maintaining important reserves and defending in depth later came to dominate Roman military thinking from early in the Dominate, through the military reforms of Diocletian (he creating more new legions than any preceding emperor from the time of Augustus) and later Constantine. This change was ultimately dramatic, with the legionaries and *auxilia* of the Principate later replaced by *comitatenses* field army troops (featuring a much larger proportion of mounted troops than previously) and *limitanei* border troops. In this sense, one could perhaps argue that through the basing of *legio* II *Parthica* near to Rome, and then building a new campaigning force around it, Severus' *expeditio felicissima Britannica* was the first embryonic use of the later field armies.

Severus was concerned not only with reforming the military capabilities of his troops, but also with their welfare. For example, he increased the annual salary of his legionaries to 450 denarii, from the 300 they were paid at the start of his reign, and at the same time raised the pay of the auxiliaries from 100 to 150 denarii (note that Speidel 1992, 106, and others have challenged this level of *auxilia* compensation, arguing their pay from the reign of Augustus through to that of Maximinus Thrax was much closer to that of the legionaries). Similarly the cavalry of the legions had their pay increased from 400 to 600 denarii, while auxiliary cavalry had a rise to 300 denarii from 200 if they belonged to a cohort, or from 333 to 500 denarii if they were based on the wing of a combat formation. Caracalla, taking his father's deathbed advice to heart (see p. 14), later increased the pay of the military even further, such that by the end of his reign it was double the figure it had been under Commodus in the late second century. This process was of course economically destabilising (even though long overdue) and is a factor that has already been discussed in Chapter 1, particularly with regard to the reasons behind the introduction of the Severan *annona*.

The Legionaries

The military machine of Rome was a professional and permanent institution by the time Augustus died in AD 14. Always at its core during the Principate were the legions, the first emperor having inherited around sixty after the lengthy civil wars from which he had emerged as the victor. He reduced this number to twenty-eight (which fell to twenty-five after the loss of three legions in Germany in AD 9). The total hovered around thirty for the next two hundred years: for example, twenty-nine existed at the time of the accession of Marcus Aurelius and Lucius Verus in AD 161 (Cowan 2003b, 6).

Throughout our period of interest regarding Severus' *expeditio felicissima Britannica*, the Principate legion still numbered some 5,500 men, organised into ten cohorts. Of these, the first had five centuries of 160 men (interestingly *legio* II *Parthica's* first cohort had six such centuries), with the remaining nine having six centuries of eighty men each (Connolly 1988, 217). Each normal century was broken down into ten eight-man sections, which were called *contubernia* (whose men shared a tent when on campaign, and two barrack-block rooms when in camp). Additionally the legion also featured 120 auxiliary cavalry (Goldsworthy 2003, 50), which acted as dispatch riders and scouts, and also support staff.

The numbering and naming of the legions seems rather confusing to us today, reflecting their being raised by different Republican leaders (especially at the time of the civil wars of the Late Republic; Connolly 1988, 217) and emperors, and at different times. After this many shared the same legion number (always permanent; D'Amato 2016, 8) but had different names: for example, there were five third legions. Others shared the same name but with different numbering: for example, our Severan foundings I, II and III *Parthica*. The longevity of this numbering, and the clear differential in the naming, suggest there was a strong sense of identity within these most elite of military units. As Goldsworthy (2003, 50) explains: 'Legionaries were proud of their unit and contemptuous of others. The standards and the symbols on men's shields . . . made each unit unique.'

Legionaries could be volunteers or conscripted (under a levy called the *dilectus*), depending on the circumstances, although by the time of Marcus Aurelius they were increasingly enrolled as conscripts. This was usually on a regional basis as with *legios* II and III *Italica* (Cowan 2003b, 6). Those recruited (by either means) were exclusively Roman citizens for most of the Principate, originally being all Italian at the end of the Republic, although increasingly from Gaul and Spain as citizenship spread.

The Principate legionary term of service was initially twenty years, set by Augustus as part of his military reforms, with the last four as a veteran excused fatigues and guard duty. This length of service was later extended by Augustus to twenty-five years, with five as a veteran – this term of service to last until the end of the Principate. Connolly (1988, 218) says the increase was due to a shortage of recruits, and adds that the strain placed on the imperial economy to pay the *praemia* retirement gratuity for retiring legionaries was also a factor (given the very large number of troops Augustus inherited). These gratuities were in the form of money (3,000 denarii in the late first century BC, rising to 5,000 denarii by the time of Severus) or land – in the latter case often *centuriated* land parcels or in *colonia* settlements. Such retired legionaries often settled near to their former legionary bases, and these settlements then developed into *coloniae* towns as happened with Gloucester (Roman Glevum), Lincoln (Roman Lindum Colonia) and York (Roman Eboracum, see Chapter 6 for detail on the latter).

Roman legionaries were for the most part specialist heavy infantry whose arms and armour were always geared towards defeating their opponents through the shock of impact and discipline (although see p. 51 regarding legionary *lanciarii*). Their arms, armour and tactical deployment were beginning to change by the time of Severus – and not just because of the reforms he initiated. In that regard, another key factor was that the Roman military by this time had begun adapting to a change in the nature of their opponents. Previously the legions had most often faced a similar infantry-heavy force (excepting the Parthians in the east), but were now tackling a multitude of threats, many of a differing nature which required a more flexible response. This change is shown in real time on three of the monuments set up in Rome by three great warrior emperors: the Column of Marcus Aurelius and the Arches of Septimius Severus and Constantine. The first and last are referenced in the commentary below regarding the changes taking place with the legions of Rome as the Principate matured, but the Severan monument (built in the early third century to celebrate his eastern campaigning, principally against the Parthians) contains imagery and epigraphy which provides vital insight into the troops later deployed in his British campaigns. Its four large relief panels are detailed here:

- Relief 1 on the left Forum-facing panel shows preparations for the first of the two wars, a battle scene featuring a large number of troops, and the liberation of the besieged city of Nisibis in AD 195, the enemy leader fleeing to the right. Sadly it has been much worn but is still a useful source of data.

- Relief 2 on the right Forum-facing panel is also damaged and is thought to show the revolt of a Roman ally, perhaps Osrhoene. In the upper register, we see how Severus later announced the annexation of Osrhoene and Nisibis.

- Relief 3 on the left Capital-facing panel is better preserved and shows the second campaign, specifically against Parthia at the end of the second century AD. Here we see the Roman attack on Seleucia-on-Tigris, with Parthian troops fleeing left and right. The upper part also shows the citizens of the town surrendering.

- Relief 4 on the right Capital-facing panel shows the last battle of the war, namely the siege and sack of Ctesiphon, the Parthian capital. A siege engine is shown employed to breach the walls and the city then surrenders. In the upper register we can see how Septimius Severus declares Caracalla as his co-ruler, with Geta named as the crown prince.
- Other reliefs on the arch include images of winged Victory flying in the spandrels, four statues of the four seasons, and prisoners of war on the pedestals. Importantly for us we also see how the loot is being transported, these images including representations of the legionaries.

The principal missile weapon of the front-rank troops for the majority of the Principate was the *pilum* – a weighted javelin of which two were carried, one heavy and one light (Cowan 2003b, 30). These had barbed heads on long, tapering iron shanks whose weighted socket attached it to the wooden shaft. This provided the driving force needed to hammer the weapon through enemy shields and armour. In terms of their specific use, the lighter weapon was used as the legionaries approached the enemy, while the heavier one was then brought into play immediately prior to impact (the long iron shafts being designed to bend after impact to disable the use of the opponent's shield).

As the Principate progressed into the third century, however, there is evidence to suggest that such *pila* were being replaced by a thrusting spear (of 2–2.7 metres in length), and this change is evident on the three monuments detailed above. Thus on the Column of Marcus Aurelius legionaries in classic *lorica segmentatata* armour (of banded iron, see p. 50) are mostly armed with *pila*, while on the Arches of Severus and Constantine they seem to have been replaced by spears – even when held by troops in *lorica segmentatata*, although confusingly here some of the relief panels on the Constantine arch were reused from an earlier and now lost arch to Marcus Aurelius (Scarre 1995b, 116). In this regard Paul Elliott (2014, 93) says that, while spears were more often associated with *auxilia* (see below) in the second century AD, by the third century they had become more common as part of a legionary's equipment mix. This was almost certainly a response to the experiences in fighting mounted opponents more frequently. In this regard, Rome had long engaged with Parthian heavy shock cavalry and supporting horse archers in the east, but in the Marcomannic Wars under Marcus Aurelius and Lucius Verus the legionaries had also found themselves fighting against the Iazyges Sarmatian tribe, who were also cavalry based and with a higher proportion of mounted shock troops. Thus a legionary spear wall would have made more sense when engaging such opponents than the use of *pila* impact weapon. Paul Elliott (2014, 94) indicates that this change was in its early transitional phase at the time of Severus' *expeditio felicissima Britannica*:

> . . . [the] shock throwing weapon had been part of the legion's armoury since its earliest days and it continued in use throughout the third century. The spear did not eclipse it, but instead may have replaced it for certain types of battlefield engagement. It was the pilum, not the spear, that remained the essential weapon of front rank legionaries of this period.

Once the *pila* had been expended, the legionary then drew his sword, worn on the right-hand side for the rank and file troopers for much of the Principate.

At the beginning of the Principate this sword was the famous *gladius*, a weapon that originated in Spain as the *gladius Hispaniensis* (*gladius* was actually a generic name for 'sword' from the Mid-Republic onwards). Rather than this weapon being the short stabbing sword of popular legend, it was actually a cut-and-thrust weapon of medium length, up to sixty-nine centimetres long and five centimetres in width, featuring a tapering sharp stabbing point. This sword developed during the reign of Augustus into the Mainz-type *gladius*, broader and shorter in shape with a longer stabbing point. A further development, dating to the end of the first century AD, was the Pompeii-type *gladius*, slightly shorter than Mainz type with a shorter, triangular stabbing point. All of these weapons used a very similar cut-and-thrust combat technique, which dominated Roman fencing methods in the early and mid-Principate.

By the time of Severus a great change seems to have taken place. According to Paul Elliott (2014, 71), from around AD 200 the longer cavalry-style *spatha* (up to eighty centimetres in length) had replaced the shorter sword for all Roman foot soldiers. This is a bold statement and it seems more likely that, while a transition was taking place at this time, some of the earlier swords did remain in use (although the switch was far more advanced than that from the *pilum* to the spear). The new sword was suspended from a baldric on a Sarmatian-type scabbard slide, and it came to dominate Roman military equipment in the west until its end, and continued in use in the east afterwards. It seems likely that the adoption of this weapon had its origins in a need for more reach to tackle armoured mounted opponents (just as with the spear), and its deployment also seems to have played a role in a further significant change in legionary equipment, namely with regard to the shield.

From the early to mid-Principate the legionary was equipped with the curved, rectangular *scutum* (a development of the Republican example, which had been more oval in shape). This shield was around 83 centimetres wide and 102 centimetres long, comprising planed wooden strips laminated together in three layers. Given its sturdy nature, at up to ten kilograms in weight, it was held by a horizontal grip using a straightened arm. Rather than being used simply for protection, the *scutum* was also used as an offensive weapon in its own right to smash into opponents and push them over, forming a lethal combination alongside the *gladius*.

As the Principate progressed, a change began to take place. According to Cowan (2003b, 31) by the mid-second century AD the traditional *scutum* was in the process of being replaced by a large, flat (sometimes slightly dished), oval shield, confusingly still called a *scutum*. This new design superseded the expensive triple laminate construction of the earlier *scutum* with a form of simple plank construction with stitched-on rawhide, strengthened with iron bars. The two types appear to have been used side by side for some time, in the same way a transition is seen from the *pilum* to the spear and *gladius* to *spatha*, with examples of both having been found at the fortified frontier trading town of Dura-Europos in Syria, both dated to AD 256. This transition is also very evident on the three monuments detailed above. Legionaries in *lorica segmentatata* on the Column of Marcus Aurelius carry the highest proportion of *scutums*. Meanwhile, legionaries on the Arches of Septimius Severus and Constantine –in *lorica segmentatata*, *lorica hamata* (chain mail) and *lorica squamata* (scale mail) – have the highest proportion of oval or round shields.

Once again this change, as with that of the *pilum*/spear and *gladius*/*spatha*, seems associated with the type of opponent more commonly being faced – the round variety perhaps being more suited to dealing with the threat from the mounted archers (likely being easier to wield) and also providing great freedom of movement for the new weapons coming into use with their greater reach (P. Elliott 2014, 77). I also believe that the new, rounder shields would have been cheaper to produce in the state-run *fabricae* manufactories across the Empire – an important factor considering the pressure the Roman economy was under as Severus took office.

The legionaries of the Principate wore a wide variety of types of full body armour. The most commonly depicted in imagery, and also found in the archaeological record in the early to mid-period, is the *lorica segmentatata* mentioned above, made from articulated iron plates and hoops. This was highly effective, although a complicated set of armour to make and maintain, and as time progressed the armoured suit was simplified for ease of use by the legionary. In that regard one example found at the *principia* at Newstead in 1905 featured simple rivets to replace earlier bronze hinges, a single large girdle plate to replace the two previous ones, and strong hooks instead of earlier and more complicated belt-buckle fastenings (Warry 1980, 191). Such simplification of this armour continued through to its demise in the Dominate. We know of its extensive use at the time of Marcus Aurelius given its widespread depiction on his column; its lesser use at the time of Severus by it appearing as a smaller proportion of amour types shown on his arch; and finally as an even smaller proportion (although still appearing) on the Arch of Constantine (although these last images could have originated in the earlier Arch of Marcus Aurelius, see above). Interestingly, on the Severan arch the armour appears on troops associated with what seems to be the handing over of tribute to the emperor, indicating they might be Praetorian Guards. Given the expense of the *lorica segmentatata* compared to the other legionary armour types considered below, this would make sense at a time when frontline troops were also being equipped with seemingly cheaper-to-manufacture shields, as above.

Other armour types were also worn by the legionaries: for example, the *lorica hamata* (a long, chain-mail shirt), which had its roots in the armies of the Republic. This weighed around fifteen kilograms and was actually the predominant legionary armour of the later Republic and early Principate. It was superseded to a large extent by the ubiquitous *lorica segmentatata* in the mid-Principate period but then came back into full favour in the third century AD, when it largely replaced the *lorica segmentatata*. This transition can be seen on the Arches of Severus and Constantine, where chain mail is the predominant armour type visible. Meanwhile another variant of such body armour was *lorica squamata* scale mail, which is also visible on the two arches. Additionally, when fighting certain types of opponent, extra armour was fitted, including the articulated iron *manicae* arm guards, thigh guards and greaves visible on some of the legionaries depicted on Trajan's Column in Rome in the context of his early second-century AD Dacian campaigns.

Certain troop types within the legions were also often differentially equipped with armour: for example, officers are frequently shown wearing iron and bronze muscled cuirasses, with centurions and standard bearers in chain mail, even when their legionaries wore *lorica segmentatata*. Meanwhile a new legionary type may also have made its European combat debut during

Severus' *expeditio felicissima Britannica*. This was the *lanciarii* – a light trooper armed with a quiver of javelins and lighter armour than their front-rank, line-of-battle equivalents. Such troops, which seem to have operated like the *velites* of the mid-Republican legions (Cowan 2003b, 24) by skirmishing forward to deter mounted bowmen and other lightly armed missile troops, are attested for the first time in gravestone epigraphy in the ranks of *legio* II *Parthica* in the context of Caracalla and Macrinus' AD 215–18 Parthian War. It is unclear if they were an innovation of this particular conflict, or had been created earlier and in time for Severus' campaign in Britain five years earlier.

The helmet of the legionary also evolved during the Principate. The traditional Republic Roman Montefortino type was a Celtic design, featuring a domed conical crown and neck guard, and was still in use in the first century AD. By this time, however, two new types had begun to appear: the Coolus type with a round cap of bronze and small neck guard (this disappearing in the middle of the first century AD); and the iron port type, which featured a deep neck guard and was named after the site-type location of Port bei Nidau in Switzerland. The latter type developed into the classic 'imperial' Gallic helmet often associated with the Roman legionary of the first and second centuries AD, which featured an even larger neck guard. Meanwhile a final 'imperial' type was the Italic design originating in Italy, which Connolly (1988, 231) calls a bronze compromise between the Celtic and more traditional Roman types. All of these helmets had prominent cheek guards and often a reinforcing strip on the front of the cap to deflect downward sword cuts. Ear guards were added by the AD 50s. Meanwhile, as the Principate progressed, legionary helmets became increasingly substantial, with the Italic 'imperial' type disappearing in the early third century AD, by which time many legionaries were being equipped with heavier, single bowl designs (Cowan 2003a, 41) reinforced by cross-pieces and fitted with deep napes, meaning only a minimal T-shaped face opening. It seems that by the time of Severus' *expeditio felicissima Britannica* a variety of these helmet types – old and new – were in use, with the heavier, single-bowl design, which provided exceptional levels of protection, beginning to appear in numbers.

For non-military kit, when on the march each legionary carried non-essential equipment on a T-shaped pole resting on his shoulders, with his shield held in place on his back. Helmets were normally strung from the neck across the front of the chest. The marching kit itself of the legionary would normally have included a *paenula* (a hooded, bad-weather cloak made from thick wool), which fastened with toggles or a button on the centre of the chest. This would have been vital for the troops on Severus' *expeditio felicissima Britannica*, given the very poor weather attested by the primary sources. It may well be that some legionaries were actually equipped with the *birrus* (the even heavier, hooded, woollen cloak for which Britain was famous in the Roman world) detailed on p. 27. Officers would have worn the shorter rectangular *sagum*, which fastened on the right shoulder using a brooch, although again practicality on this campaign would have seen many wearing their heavier counterparts.

Another very important piece of kit for the legionary was his hobnailed *caligae* (sandals), especially given the huge distance he was expected to march during his military career. Connolly (1988, 234) says that a typical piece of the legionary footwear featured a leather upper made from a single piece sewn at the heel, being stitched to a multiple-layer hide sole shod with many iron studs. Each sandal could weigh up to one kilogram.

The legionary would also have a sturdy, cross-braced satchel for his personal effects, a *patera* bronze mess tin, a water skin in a net bag, a cooking pot and canvas bags for grain rations and spare clothing (Windrow and McBride 1996, 26). Furthermore every legionary in the Principate had to carry a sickle, saw, basket, pickaxe, chain, two stakes and a leather strap, which enabled him to do engineering and fortification work (Connolly 1988, 239). The overall marching load of the average legionary was therefore an impressive thirty kilograms.

In terms of command structure, the legions from the early Principate were led by a senatorial-level *legatus legionis* (Goldsworthy 2003, 50). Severus himself performed this role with the *legio* IV *Scythica* in Syria. The second-in-command, called the *tribunus laticlavius*, was also of senatorial level. He would have been a younger man gaining the experience needed to command his own legion in the future (Severus' elder brother Geta performed this function with the *legio* II *Augusta* in Caerleon). Third in command was the *praefectus castrorum* (camp prefect), a seasoned former centurion responsible for administration and logistics. Below him were five younger, equestrian-level tribunes, called the *tribuni angusticlavii*, who were allocated tasks and responsibilities as necessary.

The actual control of each cohort in the legion was the responsibility of the centurions (six to a normal cohort), who had specific titles reflecting their seniority based on the old manipular legions of the Mid-Republic. These names, their seniority in ascending order, were:

- *hastatus posterior;*
- *hastatus prior;*
- *princeps posterior;*
- *princeps prior;*
- *pilus posterior;*
- *pilus prior.*

An army, of course, marches on its stomach and the legions of Rome were no different. In terms of diet, Vegetius (3.3) in his late fourth-century AD military manual says that troops should never be without corn, wine, vinegar and salt. This was the same for Roman troops of all periods, with bread, beans, porridge, eggs and vegetables forming the core diet of the legionary. Meat would be eaten on feast days – the wider diet then being supplemented by local produce and hunting. When on campaign, as with Severus in Britain, the daily staples were hard tack and wholewheat biscuits, together with bread baked at the end of the day's march after the marching camp had been built (note on p. 147 the care taken in the Severan campaigns in Britain with regard to granaries to ensure these supplies).

Finally, regarding the Principate legions of Rome, Table 2.1 (overleaf) details all known such formations for reference.

The *Auxilia*

The legions of the Principate were only part of the military power emperors were able to deploy in war and peace. In that regard, a significant proportion of the empire's martial might during the Principate was made up of the auxiliary infantry and cavalry. These troops were recruited from non-Roman citizens, often those recently conquered in the new provinces as the empire expanded. The *auxilia* also provided the majority of the specialist troops of the Roman military formations: for example, archers, slingers and javelinmen (later joined by staff slingers and even crossbowmen).

The idea of recruiting auxiliary infantry to complement the legionaries originated in the armies of the Republic when allied formations of troops regularly supported the citizen armies of Rome. Such troops fought in their own formations and under their own commanders, and it wasn't until the accession of Augustus that they were professionalised as a regular component of the Roman armed forces. The *auxilia* were certainly the junior partners to

TABLE 2.1 *The Roman Legions*

Legion	When Founded	Destroyed/disbanded
legio I *Germanica*	Later Republic	disbanded AD 70 after Civilis Revolt
legio I *Adiutrix pia fidelis*	provisionally recruited by Nero, then made a regular legion by Galba	
legio I *Italica*	under Nero	
legio I *Macriana*	under Nero	civil war legion, disbanded AD 69/70
legio I *Flavia Minervia pia fidelis*	under Domitian	
legio I *Parthica*	under Septimius Severus	
legio II *Augusta*	Later Republic/under Augustus	
legio II *Adiutrix pia fidelis*	under Nero	
legio II *Italica*	under Marcus Aurelius	
legio II *Parthica*	under Septimius Severus	
legio II *Traiana fortis*	under Trajan	
legio III *Augusta pia fidelis*	Later Republic/under Augustus	
legio III *Cyrenaica*	Later Republic	
legio III *Gallica*	under Caesar	
legio III *Italica concors*	under Marcus Aurelius	
legio III *Parthica*	under Septimius Severus	
legio IIII *Flavia felix*	under Vespasian	
legio IIII *Macedonica*	under Caesar	disbanded AD 70
legio IIII *Scythica*	under Mark Antony	
legio V *Alaudae*	under Caesar	destroyed under Domitian
legio V *Macedonica*	Later Republic	
legio VI *Ferrata fidelis constans*	under Caesar	
legio VI *Victrix*	Later Republic	

Legion	When Founded	Destroyed/disbanded
legio VII *Claudia pia fidelis*	under Caesar	
legio VII *Gemina*	under Galba	
legio VIII *Augusta*	Later Republic	
legio IX *Hispana*	Later Republic	possibly destroyed in the reign of Hadrian during the Bar Kochba rebellion in Judea
legio X *Fretensis*	Later Republic	
legio X *Gemina*	under Caesar	
legio XI *Claudia pia fidelis*	Later Republic	
legio XII *Fulminata*	under Caesar	
legio XIII *Gemina pia fidelis*	Later Republic	
legio XIV *Gemina Martia Victrix*	Later Republic	
legio XV *Apollinaris*	under Augustus	
legio XV *Primigenia*	under Caligula	disbanded AD 70
legio XVI *Flavia Firma*	under Vespasian	
legio XVI *Gallica*	under Augustus	disbanded AD 70
legio XVII	under Augustus	destroyed in AD 9 in Germany
legio XVIII	under Augustus	destroyed in AD 9 in Germany
legio XIX	under Augustus	destroyed in AD 9 in Germany
legio XX *Valeria Victrix*	under Augustus	
legio XXI *Rapax*	under Augustus	possibly destroyed under Domitian
legio XXII *Deiotariana*	under Augustus	possibly destroyed under Hadrian
legio XXII *Primigenia pia fidelis*	under Caligula	
legio XXX *Ulpia Victrix*	under Trajan	

Source: After Goldsworthy 2003, 51

their legionary counterparts (P. Elliott 2014, 26), their pay being 100 denarii if infantry from the later first century AD and 200 denarii if cavalry; those based on the wing of a battle formation were paid 333 denarii. Terms of service were similar to those of the legionaries after the later reforms of Augustus – this being twenty-five years. Upon retirement the trooper was given a diploma granting Roman citizenship to himself and his heirs, the right of legal marriage to a non-citizen woman, plus citizenship for existing children. There is no evidence that auxiliary veterans received any gratuity; and from AD 140 Antoninus Pius abolished the citizenship for children already born before discharge.

Despite their lower status when compared to the legionaries, *auxilia* were still a formidable fighting force and it was very rare for a campaigning army to comprise only legionaries (*auxilia* made up a significant component of the force Severus deployed for his *expeditio felicissima Britannica*). Furthermore, even when legionary forces were present, it might often be only the *auxilia* who engaged in combat: for example, at the Battle of Mons Graupius in AD 84, when Agricola finally managed to bring the Caledonians to battle south of the Moray Firth in the Grampians (Tacitus, xxxvi.1–2).

The infantry formations of the *auxilia* were based on a single quingenary cohort of 480 troops, or a double-sized milliary cohort of 800 troops. Auxiliary cavalry (which made up by far the largest mounted component of Principate military formations) were organised into quingenary *alae* of 512 men or milliary *alae* of 768. *Auxilia* could also be fielded in units that featured both infantry and mounted troops, their organisation being less well understood (Goldsworthy 2003, 58). Such infantry cohorts, cavalry *alae* and combined units were very flexible and could easily be moved around the Empire as needed in the same manner as vexillations of legionaries – hence the large number being gathered by Severus for his British campaign.

Auxilia infantry cohorts (both the small and large) were divided into centuries of between 80 and 100 men, under the command of a centurion; they clearly replicated the similar structure in a legionary formation. The centurions, however, unlike the auxiliary troopers, were sometimes Roman citizens appointed from the legions (by the governor of a province or even the emperor). Others were drawn direct from the rank and file of the auxiliary unit. Above this level, the command of the overall cohort was given over to equestrians: a *praefectus* for a quingenary unit and a *tribunus* for a milliary unit.

The majority of auxiliary foot troops were close-order infantry who fought in a similar manner to the legionaries. They were armed with short, throwable spears called *lancea* (rather than *pila*) and a sword similar to the legionary *gladius* (Connolly 1988, 239), which was later replaced by the *spatha* – as with the legionaries. *Auxilia* are never depicted in *lorica segmentatata*; instead they were most frequently shown wearing chain-mail or scale-mail hauberks, which were shorter and less sophisticated that the equivalents worn by their legionary counterparts. Their helmets also seem to have been cheaper bronze versions of those used by the legionaries, while auxiliary infantry shields are most often shown as an oval and flat design. Troops carrying this military panoply are certainly shown on the Arch of Septimius Severus.

For most of the Principate, including during the campaigns of Severus in Scotland, auxiliary cavalry seem to have been armed in a similar way to their infantry counterparts with chain-mail shirts (shorter than those of the infantry to allow greater movement in the saddle; such armour weighed around nine kilograms), flat hexagonal or oval shields and spears (longer than those of their infantry counterparts). They also carried the *spatha* (Connolly 1988, 236) from a much earlier point, and indeed it was from the auxiliary cavalry that the weapon's use was later transferred to the legionaries and foot *auxilia*. The armour and equipment of the auxiliary Roman cavalrymen did begin to change as the Principate progressed, becoming increasingly either heavier (ultimately as the *equites cataphractarii* and *clibanarii* of the later Empire) or specialised: for example, the javelin-armed *equites illyriciani* and bow-armed *equites sagittarii* skirmishing light cavalry. Some of these types, or at least troops equipped like them (particularly the light horse), may have accompanied Severus in Scotland, but the majority would have been the traditional auxiliary cavalry of earlier in the Empire.

The Regional Fleets

Here I consider the regional navies of the Roman armed forces and their naval *milites*. These fleets originated once again with the Augustan reforms of the Roman military, as before this date the fleets of the Republic were more often than not ad hoc in nature, designed to fight symmetrical engagements against opponents such as Carthage, Macedon or civil war rivals in the Mediterranean. As with many other aspects of Roman military power, the fleets were professionalised under Rome's first emperor, and on a regional basis to reflect the Empire's expanding geographical reach. By the end of the first century AD there were ten such regional fleets, each with a very specific area of territorial responsibility. Table 2.2 details them, and is particularly instructive in that the size of the annual stipend for each fleet's commander gives an indication of their seniority in the wider military framework of the Empire.

TABLE 2.2 *Regional Fleets of the Roman Principate*

Fleet	Annual Stipend (in sesterces)
Classis Ravennas	300,000
Classis Misenensis	200,000
Classis Britannica	100,000
Classis Germanica	100,000
Classis Pannonica	60,000
Classis Moesica	60,000
Classis Pontica	60,000
Classis Syriaca	60,000
Classis Nova Libica	60,000
Classis Alexandrina	60,000

Source: Ellis Jones 2012, 61

The manpower complement of the *Classis Britannica* and its 900 ships (Elliott 2016a, 63), which are most relevant to this work, can be inferred from the size of the wider Roman fleet, and its regional components, over time. The original Roman war fleets created to fight the First and Second Punic Wars were extensive, given the nature of the conflict across the western Mediterranean, numbering up to 60,000 men in terms of crew for the second iteration. Most of these would have been rowers: for example, 30,000 such specialists were needed for the 203 BC invasion of Africa to man 160 warships, according to Pitassi (2012, 61). He believes that the 60,000 overall figure would have fallen to around 30,000 by the reign of Augustus at the turn of the first century BC, then rising to around 50,000 again by the reign of Hadrian in the second century AD as the regional fleets reached maturity. Key factors in this increase over 140 or so years would have been the formation of the *Classis Germanica* (incorporated very late in the first century BC) and creation of the *Classis Britannica* in the later first century AD.

As can be seen above, based on the stipend paid to their commanders, these two were jointly the third most important fleets in the Empire after the Italy-based

Classis Misenensis and *Classis Ravennas*. It is from the complements of these last two fleets, the former 6,000 and the latter 10,000 strong during the reigns of Otho and Vitellius in AD 69, that we can start to infer the size of the *Classis Britannica*. For this, Mason (2003, 31) bases his calculation on the number converted for legionary land-based warfare during the civil war of that year. Mason (2003) then looked at the military mission of the *Classis Britannica*, arguing that it would need at least three squadrons to fulfil the various roles detailed below. Finally he researched the known *Classis Britannica* bases at Boulogne, where he says the fort would have accommodated 3,500, Dover (640 men) and other bases such as Richborough, Lympne and Pevensey (the last two presumed to have featured *Classis Britannica* forts). Based on all of these factors Mason (2003) calculates that the complement of the *Classis Britannica* would have been around 7,000 men.

Command of the fleets was also reformed under Augustus, who did away with the single naval command structure of the Republic. This had been led by a single consular-level officer, perhaps with a *praetor* commander from the army beneath him. Instead, to provide greater flexibility, this arrangement was replaced with a devolved structure featuring an equestrian-level *praefectus classis*, who was appointed directly by the emperor for each individual fleet and who reported to a province's procurator rather than the governor (although clearly falling under the latter's command for military operations). Birley (2005, 298) emphasises this importance, saying that in Britain through to the mid-third century AD the *praefectus classis Britannicae* was second only to the procurator in terms of importance within the province's military and civilian chains of command.

As the Principate progressed the post of *praefectus classis* grew into a very senior position. Initially it was occupied by a senior former legionary or auxiliary officer, and epigraphic evidence suggests that it was common for the *praefectus classis* to switch between land-based military and naval command, and also between both of these and senior civilian posts. Later in the first century AD, as part of Claudius' rationalisation of the civil and military branches of the administration of the Empire, the role of the *praefectus classis* was opened up to allow freed men of the imperial household to hold the post. This situation reverted after the 'Year of Four Emperors' in AD 69, when sea power played a key role in the eventual victory of Vespasian, and the post once again was reserved for members of the equestrian class.

As part of his headquarters organisation, the *praefectus classis* had a specialist staff to help manage his regional fleet. This featured his second-in-command, called the *subpraefectus* (an executive officer and aide-de-camp), together with a *cornicularius* acting as third-in-command and chief of staff. Other key members of the team included staff without a specific portfolio called *beneficiarii*, *actuarii* (clerks), *scribae* (writers) and *dupliarii* (leading ratings) attached from the naval component of the fleet.

Below the headquarters staff, the hierarchy of the regional fleets relied heavily on Hellenistic nomenclature, adapted following Rome's contact with the Greek world in the later Republic. Thus the commander of a squadron of ships was called the *navarchus* (the most senior being called the *navarchus principes*), with the captain of an individual vessel being a *trierarchus* (which referenced the name's origins with the commander of a trireme). As the hierarchy progressed downwards, land-based Roman military nomenclature was added, with the *trierarchus'* executive team including the *gubernator* (the senior officer who was responsible for the steering oars), the *proretus* 2nd lieutenant and the *pausarius* rowing master. Other junior officers on the staff of the *trierarchus* included the *secutor* (master at arms), some *nauphylax* officers of the watch and specialists such as the *velarii* (with responsibility for the sails) and the *fabri* (ships' carpenters).

The ship's company itself, below the level of the executive team, was called a century, reflecting the preference of the Republican Roman navies for close action based on the expertise of their land-based counterparts. The century was commanded by a centurion, again a direct transference of terminology from the legions. He was assisted by his own team, which comprised an *optio* (second-in-command), a *suboptio* (junior assistant), a *bucinator* (bugler) or *cornicen* (horn player) and an *armorum custos* (armourer).

The rest of the ship's complement was composed of marines – *ballistarii* (artillery crew), *sagittarii* (archers) and *propugnatores* (deck soldiers) – *velarius* (sailors) and plenty of *remiges* (oarsmen). The oarsmen were always professionals, not slaves as depicted in popular culture (Goldsworthy 2014, 167). The whole company was styled *milites* (soldiers; the singular is *miles*), again reflecting the original Republican preference for maritime close action.

At the beginning of the Principate, service as a naval *miles* was less well regarded than serving as a legionary or *auxilia*, although this did change over time as the regional fleets began to make their presence felt. The initial recruits for the navies came from local communities with maritime experience in each fleet's area of responsibility. This recruiting base expanded as the Empire grew, and by the second century recruits were being sourced from communities further afield. The terms of service for all of the ranks in the regional navies (up to the *trierarchus*) was twenty-six years, which was then rewarded with Roman citizenship. Only the *navarchus* could achieve citizenship within this twenty-six-year service period. Perhaps reflecting recruitment issues, after AD 160 this term of service was increased to twenty-eight years.

Each naval *miles* received three gold pieces or seventy-five denarii upon enlistment, with basic annual pay at the onset of the Principate for the lower ranks being a hundred denarii, putting them on a similar level to the *auxilia*. Crew members with greater responsibilities were paid an additional amount: for example, those paid 1.5 times the normal salary were called *sesquiplicarii* and those paid twice the amount were *duplicarii*.

The actual vessel types utilised by the fleets differed chronologically and geographically during the Principate, although by this period the ram and ballista-equipped *liburnian* bireme war galley had by and large replaced the giant polyremes of the Mid- and Late Republic. The regional fleets also utilised a variety of different *myoparo* and *scapha* cutters and skiffs, and transport vessels of all types.

In this period, the regional fleets had specific military roles (Elliott 2016a, 75):

- blue-ocean sea control of the regional oceanic zone;
- control of the coastal littoral zone in the region of responsibility (very important during the Severan incursions in Scotland, see Chapter 7 for a new analysis in this regard);
- intelligence gathering and patrolling;
- transport, supply and amphibious warfare;
- general maritime supply;
- communications.

The regional fleets also fulfilled a variety of civilian functions, and in this regard Parfitt (2013, 45) is explicit, using the British regional navy as an example: 'The *Classis Britannica* seems to have (often) functioned . . . as some kind of army service corps, supporting the government and provincial army, rather than (just) as a navy in the modern sense.'

Clothing for the naval *milites* differed between the regional fleets, reflecting differing climatic and operational conditions. Taking the *Classis Britannica* as an example, an essential item of clothing in the northern waters at the edge of Empire would have been the *birrus* (see p. 52). Other key clothing items here would have been the *pilos* conical felt hat, a belted tunic with trousers, and either sandals or felt stockings with low-cut leather boots rather than the legionary *caligae.* The short *sagum* military cloak (see p. 52) would have been worn when on formal duty. For weaponry the marines of the regional navies were armed and equipped in a similar fashion to land-based auxiliaries. The principal missile weapons, in addition to artillery, would have been the bow, sling, javelin and dart. *Pila* armour-penetrating javelins as used by the legionaries would also have been adopted at close range, while for hand-to-hand work the marines would have been armed with boarding pikes, the *hasta navalis* (naval spear), various types of sword and the *dolabra* (boarding axe). Armour would again mirror that of the *auxilia*, with a hip-length shirt of chain mail or scales, while in sculpture the *navarchus* and *trierarchus* are often depicted wearing a muscled cuirass. Helmets ranged from those of a standard military pattern made at state-run *fabricae* to simple *pilos* conical types. For a shield the marines used the auxiliary wood and leather oval design, which when at sea would have been stowed along the sides of the *liburnae* over the oar ports.

Key Fortifications of the Severan Campaigns

To conclude this chapter on the Roman military of the time of Severus I consider the fortifications, both permanent and temporary, which played such a key role in the Severan campaigns in Scotland and its aftermath.

Fortifications had already played a major role as the Roman military headed north into Scotland in the 130 years before Severus. Some were significant in size and complexity: for example, the short-lived Antonine Wall of the mid-second century AD along the Clyde–Forth Line, and the Flavian (and possibly Antonine) Gask Ridge system of eighteen known signal stations/watchtowers. The latter is particularly interesting as it does highlight the extent of forethought given to the siting of such networks. It ran along a spine of land heading (broadly) north-east, beginning at the fort at Ardoch and ending with the fort at Bertha, with views north along the line of the Highlands and south back into the hollow of Strathearn (Keppie 2015, 166). As such it would have performed an early warning function as Agricola's marching camps progressed up the Highland Line, and allowed rapid communications from these back to reserves in the south.

The use of such fortifications and fortified networks came into their own during the Severan incursions into Scotland, which is not surprising given the size of force he deployed in that regard. He already had wide experience of upgrading border defensive networks, especially at the conclusion of his various campaigns. Examples include the *limes Arabicus* after his second eastern campaign and the *limes Tripolitanus* in North Africa after his campaign there (see Chapter 5 for detail on both). Later, in Chapter 6, I consider Roman infrastructure in Scotland in the discussion there on the regional background to the campaign, but given their specific importance I here detail the most significant examples. These include generic site types and specific locations, in the first instance focusing on marching camps given their vital importance to us in tracking the Severan campaigns. I then (heading south to north) detail the fort and supply base at South Shields on the river Tyne, then Hadrian's Wall on the Solway Firth–Tyne Line, then the Antonine Wall on the Clyde–Forth Line, then the fort and supply base at Cramond on the Firth of Forth and finally the fort and supply base at Carpow on the river Tay.

Marching Camps

Marching camps are a key feature of all Roman military campaigning, from the mid-Republican period through to the end of the Dominate. To that end, and in normal circumstances, at the end of each day's march in enemy territory the military force in question would build a marching camp, largely through the labour of the legionaries (including specialist pioneers) and *auxilia* – and even, especially during the Severan campaigns in Scotland, the naval *milites* of the regional fleets. The marching camp was constructed in a few hours after the day's march, with the camps coming in a variety of sizes based on the mass of the force needing protection. The typology of such camps largely tracks that for permanent fortifications detailed in the Introduction, excepting that at their upper limits they far outstripped their permanent counterparts in size: for example, that at St Leonards Hill in the Scottish Borders was a massive seventy hectares (the largest in Europe in the Roman Empire). Another factor to consider here is that the marching camps were often built on the same sites as other more permanent fortifications, which may (or may not) have been abandoned by the time the camp was erected. Newstead provides one good example where a sixty-seven-hectare Severan marching camp sits beside the earlier Agricolan and Antonine fort, while others can be seen at Inveresk near the Dere Street crossing of the river Esk, and at Ardoch in Perth and Kinross. Such fortifications were often abandoned after a few days' use, although later reoccupation was common.

While temporary by their very nature, these marching camps required substantial amounts of trained military labour in their construction. Always playing card in shape, each generally featured a deep ditch between one and two metres wide, with the spoil used to create an internal rampart. Atop this ran a palisade created by stakes carried by the soldiers as part of their specialist engineering equipment. A regular part of Roman military training was designed to enable the rapid raising of such fortifications (Oleson 2009, 702). The palisade atop the rampart was either a continuous wooden barrier, or one created by the stakes being lashed together to form large caltrops. The camps also featured various kinds of protected gateway to ensure their resilience against any aggressor.

Within this barrier the camp would be set out for the night, effectively recreating the interior layout of a Roman permanent fortification. Cowan (2003a, 45) says that after a night's rest (noting up to 20 per cent of the soldiery would have been on guard duty at any given time), or longer if the formation was staying in place for an extended period of time, the camp was then rapidly struck. As Cowan explains: 'In the early morning, camp was struck as quickly and in as orderly a way as it had been constructed. The first trumpet call signalled the striking of the tents; the second to ready the pack animals and destroy the camp; the third to fall into marching ranks.'

Even though the camps were often deliberately slighted to deny their use to any enemy after being abandoned, their substantial nature is clear in that even today their remains (as crop marks at the very least) are an enormously valuable source of data to the archaeologist and historian attempting to understand a specific campaign. In a Scottish context, given the wide variety of different periods of campaigning north of Hadrian's Wall during the Roman occupation of Britain, their dating has largely relied upon coins and pottery (and more recently radiocarbon dating), although anecdote is acceptable here too given that we are fairly clear on the size of the forces that campaigned at various periods. In Chapter 3 I discuss those of Agricola and during the reign of Antoninus Pius, but here specifically concentrate on the marching camps used by Severus and his sons.

Hodgson (2014, 38) says that it is traditional to associate two of these recognisable marching camp sequences in Scotland with the campaigns of Severus, these being the twenty-five-hectare and fifty-four-hectare groups, to which can also be added the extremely large camps (at around sixty-seven hectares, that at St Leonards Hill being slightly larger) running up Dere Street in the Borders of south-east Scotland (Jones 2012, 134). The two northern sequences follow a similar route, from the Forth crossing perhaps at North

Queensferry near Edinburgh or further upriver (see discussion in Chapter 7 regarding the type and location of this crossing), via Strathmore and to the Mounth (the range of hills on the southern edge of Strathdee in north-east Scotland, the eastern extent of the Highlands that reaches the sea at Stonehaven), transiting through the heartlands of the Maeatae and Caledonians (see discussion in Chapter 6 regarding their exact location) and often along the Highland Boundary Fault as detailed in Chapter 1. Two camps from this period also occur in Fife, on a route leading up to the river Tay crossing point at the legionary fort and supply base at Carpow (see below). In the past the dating of all of these camps as Severan has been questioned, but to my mind the size of the fifty-four-hectare and sixty-seven-hectare sequences anecdotally can only place them during his early third-century campaigns. Hard evidence in this regard comes in the form of the superimposed series of camps at Ardoch on the south-western end of the Gask Ridge where the fifty-four-hectare camp is the latest of all.

This sequence of large camps of the two sizes (setting aside the twenty-five hectares initially suggested given size is the key determinant for the Severan association here) seems to show the actual campaign routes of the Severan incursions, with the 50,000-strong army as one unit advancing up Dere Street from Hadrian's Wall to Cramond on the Forth, using the enormous camps such as St Leonards Hill and others in the sixty-seven-hectare sequence, then splitting into a group shown by the fifty-four-hectare camps sealing off the Highland Line, and with a smaller force crossing to Fife and then heading for Cramond and the river Tay crossing. Hodgson (2014, 41) does say that radiocarbon dating has now definitively ruled out a Severan date for the series of camps, forty-four hectares in size area, that run from the Mounth to the Moray Firth (specifically, Raedykes to Muiryfold), they now being identified as Agricolan and as setting a northern limit for the campaigns of Severus at Kair House on the Bervie Water some thirteen kilometres south-west of Stonehaven. Here his advancing army would have seen the Highland Line converging with the sea, and it is presumably at this point that Severus would have claimed to have 'approached the extremity of the island' as detailed by Dio (76/77.13), although clearly one cannot rule out maritime raiding and reconnaissance further north by the regional fleet.

Given the above hypothesis regarding the identification of the Severan marching camps in Scotland based on size, I now list them below, starting with the sixty-seven-hectare sequence in the Scottish Borders running south to north along Dere Street (Jones 2011, 103):

- Newstead V;
- St Leonards (the largest at seventy hectares, which could hold at least 40,000 men);
- Channelkirk;
- Pathhead III.

Above this, after the line of Dere Street traverses Cramond towards the Forth crossing, are the fifty-four-hectare sites running south–west to north–east, tracking the Highland Boundary Fault to seal off the Scottish Highlands (Jones 2012, 113):

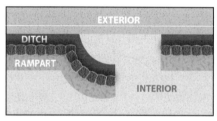

Internal clavicula

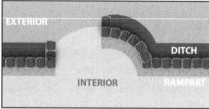

External clavicula

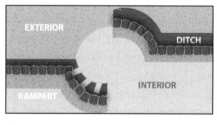

Cuspate *entrance*

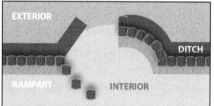

Stracathro-type gate

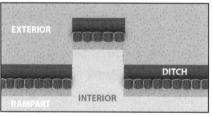

Titulus

Types of Roman marching camp entrances
[drawn by Paul Baker]

- Househill Dunipace near Falkirk, presumably the stopping-off point before crossing the Forth;
- Ardoch I at the fort site on the south-western end of the Gask Ridge;
- Innerpeffray East;
- Grassy Walls;
- Cardean;
- Battledykes, Oathlaw;
- Balmakewan;
- Kair House.

Finally, there are the two sites in Fife related to the river Tay crossing point at Carpow:

- Auchtermuchty;
- Edenwood.

South Shields

The original Roman fort, supply base and fortified harbour at South Shields, sitting on the south side of the mouth of the river Tyne, dates to the AD 120s around the time of Hadrian's visit to Britain. It developed into a maritime supply station for the troops based on Hadrian's Wall, and from its inception contained permanent stone-built granaries; it remaining occupied until the early fifth century AD. The site plays a key role in the story of the Severan incursions into Scotland as it was vastly increased in size at the time to provide the necessary levels of support for the huge undertaking. In particular the granaries were increased in area by more than a factor of ten (Elliott 2016a, 157), twenty-one being added to the original two. This enabled 2,500 tonnes of grain to be stored there, which was enough to feed the whole Severan force for two months.

South Shields was first recognised as a Severan supply base in the 1930s, with archaeologists more recently drawing attention to the series of rare lead sealings that portray Severus and his sons with the legend showing Severus and Caracalla as joint Augusti; these finds are dated between AD 198 and AD 209. Hodgson (2014, 37) says this establishes that supplies for the Severan expedition were definitively passing through the supply base before the autumn of AD 209. More recently a sealing has been found that shows Geta elevated to Augustus. This is likely dated to the autumn of AD 209 at the earliest – these supplies presumably being stored for use in the final campaign in AD 210.

Meanwhile other stratified lead sealings found at the site indicate that the military unit managing the supply base in the build-up to, and possibly during (see reference to Carpow below), the Severan campaigns was the auxiliary *cohors* V *Gallorum*. Their identification adds to our existing knowledge that in the fourth century AD the site was home to a unit of *barcariorum Tigrisiensum* (Tigris boatmen), who were operating a long way from their home on the river Tigris (Hodgson 2007, 24).

Hadrian's Wall

The origins of Hadrian's Wall along the Solway Firth–Tyne Line is discussed in Chapter 3 in the context of the Emperor Hadrian's visit to Britain in AD 122. However its military context is considered here, given the important role it played in the province for much of the occupation (including being the effective jumping-off point for the Severan campaigns in the far north). At 117 kilometres long, the fortification ran west to east from Bowness-on-Solway (site of the Roman fort of Maia) on the Irish Sea to Wallsend (Roman Segedunum) on the river Tyne. Building began in AD 122 (Fields 2003, 9), and was an effective Hadrianic acknowledgement that the imperial expansion of the early years of the Principate had come to an end.

As constructed, Hadrian's Wall was threaded with watchtowers and milecastle fortlets (commonly two of the former between each of the latter), with the western part initially constructed from compacted turf blocks (which were later replaced with stone). This was the section built first, and quickly (hence the original use of turf), giving insight perhaps into the direction of the principal threat at the time of Hadrian's visit (see discussion in Chapter 3). Meanwhile the eastern section was constructed as new from stone, the line of the overall wall being chosen to the north of the already existing Stanegate military road, which ran west to east. Ultimately 3.7 million tonnes of sandstone and limestone were needed just for the facing of the wall. It featured a north-facing fore-ditch (where this was possible), and a large vallum constructed to its immediate south. This latter included a broad flat-bottomed ditch up to 2.96 metres deep, 5.4–5.9 metres wide at the top and 2.1 metres wide at the bottom, with a mound 5.92 metres wide on either side. This provided rearward defence for the wall and has led to speculation that the north at the time of its construction was suffering from agitation among the Brigantian natives in the region (see Chapter 3).

The construction of Hadrian's Wall and its associated infrastructure, which took at least six years to complete, provides great insight into how the Roman military themselves were utilised in completing such projects. Breeze and Dobson (2000, 66) say that all three British-based legions at the time were used in this regard: *legio* II *Augusta*, *legio* VI *Victrix* and *legio* XX *Valeria Victrix*. Units of the *Classis Britannica* regional fleet also helped construct elements of the wall: for example, the granaries at the cavalry fort at Benwell (Elliott 2016a, 107) and also possibly at other sites including Halton Chesters and Rudchester (Breeze and Dobson 2000, 66). At least one, and probably more, units of *auxilia* were also involved in the building of the wall, particularly the vallum (Breeze and Dobson 2000, 67). The local population either side of the wall would also have been at risk of forcible recruitment into service to support the building operation: for example, as indentured workers (Elliott 2016a, 125). In this regard Field (2003, 32) highlights research showing that for every ten military personnel used for the construction work, around ninety additional individuals would have been needed to help in the supply and transport of raw materials.

Evidence for the deployment of troops from the above legions comes in the form of numerous examples of epigraphy, with one of the best-known coming from milecastle number 38 at Hotbank (RIB 1638). This recorded the names of Hadrian and the governor and was set up by legionaries of *legio* II *Augusta*. Similarly we know of the deployment of *milites* of the *Classis Britannica* at Benwell through epigraphy (RIB 1340), which again references Hadrian and the governor on an inscription set up in the portico of the granary.

The scale of the construction task faced by the military in building Hadrian's Wall is highlighted by an experimental archaeology project carried out by the Royal Engineers in 1966 at Lunt Roman fort in Coventry. Here it was estimated that to build a simple 283-metre circuit with a rampart revetted with turf up to a height of 3.6 metres and with a base width of 5.4 metres, some 138,000 turf blocks would have been required. This project concluded that it would have taken a labour force of around 300 men, working ten hours a day in good conditions, up to twelve days to finish the task (which also included a double ditch).

Another consideration here is the identification of Hadrian's Wall as the so-called 'wall of Severus' fortification referenced by a number of primary sources (for example, the *Historia Augusta*, Aurelius Victor and Eutropius) in the context of the emperor's early third-century campaigns in the north of Britain. The descriptions are all fairly consistent and state that the wall ran from 'sea to sea' and was around 212 kilometres long. We now know, of course, that the wall was built by the emperor whose name it carries today, but a number of antiquarians actually believed that Hadrian's Wall was indeed the one that the primary sources referenced Severus building. One of the reasons for this was that while in Britain, as part of his northern campaigns, Severus carried out a major renovation of both the wall and the fortifications along its length. The military units so engaged once again made their presence known through the use of epigraphy. Despite the discrepancy in the length of the wall, the reference to the fortification running from sea to sea, and its substantial nature, seem to indicate that the latter is precisely what the primary sources are describing, namely Severus' extensive repair of Hadrian's Wall (although confusingly Severus also repaired and remanned the Antonine Wall, see below).

A wall cutting the island in half is also referenced by Dio (77.12.1–4) when describing where the Maeatae was based in Scotland. While some have suggested this was Hadrian's Wall, placing this tribal confederation in the Scottish Borders, a more likely interpretation is that it references the Antonine Wall.

Antonine Wall

The origins of the Antonine Wall along the Clyde–Forth Line is discussed in Chapter 3 in the context of the campaigns in Britain during the reign of Antoninus Pius, but its military context is considered here given (as detailed above) that it was repaired and remanned during the Severan campaigns in the far north.

The wall (called the *vallum Antonini* during the occupation) was a turf fortification built on stone foundations, and it represented the northernmost frontier barrier in the whole Roman Empire. It was around sixty-three kilometres in length, some three metres in height overall and five metres in width. The wall featured a deep ditch on the northern side, while the turf wall itself was topped with a wooden palisade.

Construction of the Antonine Wall began in AD 142 and took about twelve years to complete, with the final wall protected by sixteen forts (two of which were, at least in part, stone built). There were small fortlets between them in a similar manner to the system used along Hadrian's Wall. The wall was abandoned after only eight years of occupation, with the garrisons for the most part then relocating back to Hadrian's Wall. Its renovation during the Severan campaigns is discussed in Chapter 7.

Cramond

The Roman fort, supply base and fortified harbour at Cramond is one of only two permanent Roman bases in Scotland known definitively to have been occupied during the Severan campaigns in the north (the other being Carpow, see below). At 2.43 hectares (making it a fort rather than a fortress), the site was ideally located as a supply base, fronting onto the Firth of Forth from the south shore with the river Almond delineating the location to its immediate west and providing fine sheltered harbourage.

The stone-built fort originated in the Antonine period as part of the Antonine Wall construction programme (it is unclear if it was preceded by a Flavian site), and may have continued in use into the AD 160s or even later. It reached the zenith of its use at the time of Severus, when a very large annexe was constructed against the eastern side. This featured manufacturing activity and a high-status building – the latter evidence by the fine window frames found there. Within the fort itself excavations have revealed the *principia* headquarters building, workshops, barracks, granaries and a latrine (Keppie 2015, 124). An altar there was dedicated by the commander of the auxiliary *cohors* V *Gallorum* we last referenced in South Shields, and it is possible that this unit was tasked with managing the important maritime supply link between South Shields, Cramond and even further north to Carpow, with Hodgson (2014, 41) suggesting that the contemporary accommodation at South Shields was insufficient for the whole unit.

A mention should be given here to Cramond's best-known Roman artefact – the Cramond lioness sculpture found in 1997 at the mouth of the river Almond. This large design depicts a bound male prisoner being killed by a lioness; the rather graphic interpretation shows the beast sinking her teeth into his head. Likely to have been imported to this location in the far north of the Empire, it has been interpreted as part of the tomb of a Roman military commander or official with a connection to the fort, and most probably dates to the Antonine period rather than its later Severan use.

Carpow

This Roman fort, supply base and fortified harbour played a major role in the Severan incursions in the north. The site lies on the south bank of the river Tay near modern Newburgh, with its confluence with the river Earn a kilometre to the west. The identification of this eleven-hectare legionary fortress as being part of the Severan campaigns was established in 1961–2 by R. E. Birley and later confirmed by the subsequent excavations of J. D. Leach and J. J. Wilkes (taking place between 1964 and 1979, being finally published in 1999).

The fortress walls were built from turf, with stone being used to construct the gates and principal internal buildings. These included a fine *principia*, bathhouse and granary. More than 200 stamped roof tiles indicate that the *legio* VI *Victrix* from York was present at this site, as was the *legio* II *Augusta*, whose motifs have been found on carved stone from the east gate, which also features a few letters from the title of an emperor, probably Caracalla. The latter indicates that the fort here could have remained in use slightly later than other sites north of Hadrian's Wall after the end of the Severan campaigns (see Chapter 8). In that sense it could be seen as a key fortified regional evacuation point, and also as a shipping point for the captives and slaves generated by the campaigns (see discussion in Chapter 8).

Hodgson (2014, 42) says that the fortress here was preceded by two earlier large enclosures: one possibly Flavian associated with Agricola's campaigning; and the other with the initial arrival of the first season of Severan campaigning. The site is also important in the narrative of the Severan campaigns in that many (for example, Reed 1975, 95, and Robertson 1980, 131) have argued it was the site of a bridge crossing the Tay, either permanent or a bridge of boats (based on coin evidence, see detailed discussion in Chapter 7) in the context of the campaigns themselves.

CHAPTER 3

Roman Britain in the Second and Early Third Centuries

I N ORDER TO FULLY UNDERSTAND the Severan *expeditio felicissima Britannica*, and the reasons behind it, a firm grasp of the situation in Britain in the later second century AD is essential given the complex series of issues and interactions that eventually drew Severus to the province early in the third century AD. Therefore I briefly outline the initial Roman conquest in the first century AD (at the same time detailing the geographical spread of native tribes across Scotland), before considering the chronological narrative of Roman Britain in the second century AD, all building up to the crisis that eventually attracted the attention of the emperor.

The Roman Conquest of Britain

The Roman Empire had had designs on the islands Britain well before Claudius' invasion in AD 43. For example, Julius Caesar famously made two incursions in 55 and 54 BC, although these were more like armed reconnaissances than a full attempt at conquest. Augustus himself, the founder of the Principate, planned at least three invasions – in 34 BC, 27 BC and 25 BC. The first and last were abandoned because of issues elsewhere in the Empire, while the second was cancelled after successful diplomacy. Such false starts were certainly viewed negatively at the time with, for example, the first-century BC poet Horace (*Odes*, III.v) reflecting that: 'Augustus will be deemed a god on Earth when the Britons and the deadly Parthians [also targets for early Imperial Roman expansion, and later Severus] have been added to our Empire.'

Next, in AD 40 the emperor Caligula also abandoned a planned invasion of Britain while actually on the beaches of northern Gaul. To support a full invasion he had gathered the legions to do so, built 900 ships which were to later become the basis of the *Classis Britannica*, and fully stocked warehouses along the length of the continental coast of the English Channel and southern North Sea. Three years later such planning proved useful to Claudius, when the pretext was presented to him to achieve what no emperor had done before – the conquest of far-off Britain – as the ships and supplies were still in place.

Prompted by opportunities presented when the Catuvellauni tribe displaced the Trinovantes as the main kingdom in the south-east, the Claudian invasion marked a huge watershed in the story of Britain. The most likely landing areas would have been the east Kent coast, with the shelter of the then Wantsum Channel and the expanse of beaches from Sandwich to Deal being particularly inviting to the invading Romans. These landing places in eastern Kent would later be marked in monumental fashion, when a fine quadrifrons triumphal twenty-five-metre-high arch was built during the reign of Domitian at Richborough.

From that point the conquest commenced, although it wasn't until around the time of the raising of the above arch in the AD 90s that the northern border of the province settled on the Solway Firth–Tyne Line. The initial conquest included the drive to the Medway, where the famous river-crossing battle took place shortly after the Claudian landing. Then the campaign moved northwards and across the Thames, with Claudius (famously only here for sixteen days) taking the surrender of his native opponents at the Catuvellauni capital of Camulodunum (modern Colchester), from where the province of Britain was declared. Aulus Plautius, who had actually commanded the Roman forces during the initial conquest campaign, became its first governor.

The legionary spearheads then began to spread out across Britain, expanding the territory of the province year by year with, for example, Vespasian dramatically conquering the south-west in a series of lightning campaigns – his legionaries and *auxilia* being supported by the fleet. Sequential governors then continued Plautius' work: for example, Ostorius Scapula, Didius Gallus, Gaius Suetonius Paulinus (who defeated the Boudiccan Revolt), Marcus Vettius Bolanus (who may have campaigned as far as the Scottish Borders, see Chapter 6), Cerialis (as detailed in Chapter 1, against the Brigantes in the north) and Sextus Julius Frontinus. However it is the next warrior governor who takes the plaudits for coming the closest until Severus to actually conquering the whole of the main island of Britain – namely Agricola, with his ambitious attempts to conquer Scotland. He arrived in AD 77 and then fought five fierce campaigns up to the Moray Firth, finally defeating the native Caledonians (used by primary sources here as a catch-all term for the tribes of Scotland, so including others in addition to the regional Caledonii tribe) at the Battle of Mons Graupius somewhere in the Grampians. Under Domitian, however, the Empire lost interest in the far north of the province (see Chapter 6 for discussion in that regard) – hence the northern border settling on the line between the Solway Firth and Tyne.

I now consider the tribes of Scotland at the time of the Roman conquest. Some of these may have been engaged during the campaigns of Bolanus, while many certainly fought Agricola. This provides the background to understanding the change that had taken place by the time of Severus' incursions in the early third century when much broader confederations were evident. Jones and Mattingly (1990, 21 and 45) use the second-century AD geographer Ptolemy and others to detail these tribes:

- Votadini in the eastern Borders;
- Selgovae in the central Borders;
- Novantae in the western Borders;
- Dumnonii around the Clyde;
- Epidii in the Mull of Kintyre;
- Creones and Carnonacae above the Clyde on the west coast, going south to north, and Caereni (at the far north-western tip of Scotland);
- Caledonii (in a specific context) broadly throughout the Grampians;
- Venicones on the east coast around the river Tay;
- Vacomagi and Taexali in Aberdeenshire, going south to north;
- Decantae, Lugi, Smertae and Cornacii above the Moray Firth, again going south to north.

Roman Britain in the Second Century AD

I now turn to the history of the province between the campaigns of Agricola in the late first century AD and those of Severus in the early third century AD, taking in the extensive military activity in occupied Britain during the reigns of Hadrian, Antoninus Pius, Marcus Aurelius and Commodus.

First, I briefly touch on the size of the 'normal' military presence in the province in the second century AD, as this gives some idea of the level of threat the forces of Rome normally faced in Britain.

Mattingly (2006, 131) argues that at this time the army numbered (at most) an astonishing 55,000 for the land forces alone, to which one can add the 7,000 personnel of the *Classis Britannica* regional fleet, giving a huge total of 62,000 military personnel operating in and around the islands of Britain. This would represent one-eighth of the entire imperial military complement at the time – a figure large enough to prompt Herodian (2.15) to comment on its size and power. Put another way, this is 12 per cent of the total military complement in the Empire at the time, in a province comprising only 4 per cent of its territory. Such a figure is also outside the context of the Severan expedition in the early third century, when he was able to field a single force of 50,000 men for his two campaigns north of the border (indicating that large numbers of troops were still required elsewhere in the province, the latter still perhaps in some kind of lockdown after the usurpation attempt of Albinus; see Chapter 5 and Chapter 6 for discussions).

Back to the narrative of the second century AD province, as the first century AD ended the mood in Britain was one of stability as the process of Romanization accelerated, with new towns growing rapidly and villa estates proliferating, especially in the south and east. Meanwhile, to the west and (particularly) the north, military garrisons settled into the regular routine of patrolling these most northerly borders of the Roman Empire. Such forces included: forward-deployed vexillations of legionaries from the main garrison fortresses such as those from *legio* II *Augusta* based at Caerleon in Wales; and auxiliaries (making up the majority of the border defence forces) and units from the *Classis Britannica* regional fleet. The latter forged up the west coast from bases such as Chester and up the east coast from Wallsend, aiming to protect the maritime flanks of the Solway Firth–Tyne Line.

Economically, the province had already begun to take on the geographical appearance that was to dominate its structure for most of the occupation. To that end, below a line drawn from the Severn to the Humber was much of the growing urban and agricultural development detailed above, while north of it was the exponential military presence detailed in Chapter 2, with the whole regional economy there turned over to supporting this border military presence.

In the very early second century AD there appears to have been little imperial interest in offensive military activity in Britain, with Trajan, for example, targeting the eastern frontier following his Dacian campaigns rather than the darker, wetter prospect of campaigning in the far north of his Empire. It is around this time that some of the principal legionary fortresses in Britain began to replace their turf and timber defences with those built of stone (Southern 2013, 170), indicating that the military presence in the islands of Britain was settling in for a long stay. In that regard, it was from this point that the three principal legionary fortresses in the province settled on Caerleon (as above), Chester and York – a situation that was to remain for the next 200 years (see Chapter 6 for specific detail on the legionary presence in York).

It is at the beginning of the reign of Hadrian that we see military action in the province of Britain on a scale that registers with the primary sources. This is in the context of evident trouble here at the beginning of the new emperor's reign in AD 117, with the *Historia Augusta* (Hadrian, 5.1–2) saying: 'When he took over the Empire, Hadrian reverted to an earlier policy, devoting his energies to keeping the peace throughout the world. The people subdued by Trajan had rebelled, the Moors were launching attacks, the Sarmatae making war, and the Britons could not be kept under control.'

There is only one other near-contemporary primary source reference to this apparently traumatic event in Britain – from the Roman rhetorician Marcus Cornelius Fronto. Writing in the AD 160s to his former pupil Marcus Aurelius, he said that casualties suffered by the then emperor in conflict with the Parthians in the east were comparable to those suffered at the beginning of Hadrian's reign in Britain (Birley 2005, 118). The primary sources give little further detail about the actual nature of this apparently dramatic event, which appears to be part of the pattern later repeated many times, with the native tribes of Scotland taking advantage by raiding across the northern border whenever the attention of Rome was diverted elsewhere (excepting for eighty years after the Severan campaigns, see Chapter 8).

Any insurrection early in the second century AD may also have involved the disgruntled Brigantes of the occupied north of the province, given that this region was effectively a militarised border zone. In this regard, one of the key references in the famous writing tablets from the fort of Vindolanda dating to this period is also of particular interest. Specifically, tablet number 164 refers to 'nasty little Britons' (*Brittunculi*), certainly showing there was no love lost between Rome and the natives of northern Britain at this time. Meanwhile a cavalry prefect named Titus Haterius Nepos also features on contemporary epigraphy carrying out a census in Annandale in Dumfries and Galloway, a move seemingly designed to put the stamp of Rome on an unenthusiastic local populace (see p. 38 for discussion on how such censuses played a key role in the Roman system of taxation).

Whatever the nature of this crisis in the north of Britain, the situation had stabilised by AD 119 when commemorative coins were struck to record a victory (though some argue they may be of a slightly later date). These coins are noteworthy as they show for the first time an image of Britannia, the now-famous female warrior armed with a shield and spear. The incident was certainly serious enough to have made an impression on the new emperor as he chose to visit Britain shortly after, in AD 122. Hadrian was taking no chances, for an honorific inscription from Ferentinum in Italy records how Titus Pontius Sabinus, *primus pilus* (senior centurion) of the *legio* III *Augusta*, had been put in command in the *'expeditio Britannica'* (this clearly referring to Hadrian's visit) of vexillations from the *legio* VII *Gemina*, *legio* VIII *Augusta* and *legio* XXII *Primigenia*. This indicates Hadrian was accompanied by reinforcements. Such troops, totalling more than 3,000 men from the *limes Germanicus* and Spain, give real context to events in Britain at that time – the last occasion such reinforcements were required being in the wake of the Boudiccan Revolt. It is worth noting here that Hadrian's Wall had not yet been built and that the frontier was held along the Solway Firth–Tyne Line by a number of vexillation fortresses and smaller forts built along the Stanegate military road. Such fortifications included Vindolanda (as mentioned above), where a centurion from the first Auxiliary Cohort of Tungrians (originating in modern Belgium) was killed during the fighting at the beginning of Hadrian's reign and commemorated on a tombstone there. Hadrian headed north immediately on arrival, to view the situation himself. All was clearly not well as he next tasked the new governor, Aulus Platorius Nepos, to seal off this most northerly border of the Empire with the wall that still carries his name (see Chapter 2 for full detail).

Hadrian died in AD 138, with matters in the long term in the north of Britain clearly unresolved because within a year his successor, Antoninus Pius, had ordered renewed campaigning in the province. Thus within a year the new governor, Quintus Lollius Urbicus, was in the north, to oversee a significant upgrading of the logistical infrastructure in the region to support a new northern campaign. This included the refurbishment of key fortifications at sites such as Corbridge (see Chapter 6 for detail), Risingham and High Rochester. We have little visibility of the campaigns north of Hadrian's Wall that followed but they were over by AD 142, when coins were minted to commemorate a famous victory.

The route taken in this campaign above the Solway Firth–Tyne Line can be tracked through the rebuilding of the old Flavian forts (for example, Newstead near Melrose) and the additional building of new ones – the advance clearly being rapid and decisive. Any native opposition was easily overcome, perhaps indicating that the reason behind this particular venture north was more for imperial aggrandisement than because of a dangerous and renewed threat. This advance northwards was also accompanied by the renovation of the Flavian military harbours, which had supported the campaigns of Agricola, and again also the construction of new ones. In the Clyde these included Dumbarton on the north shore and Lurg Moor and Bishopton on the south shore, while on the Forth they included Inveresk, Cramond and Carriden.

Inveresk, where Dere Street crosses the river Esk before heading westwards to Cramond, is particularly important in the context of this campaign as two contemporary pieces of epigraphy in the form of altar dedications have been found there, placed by Quintus Lucius Sabinianus, the British procurator at the time (one altar was to Apollo Grannus, the deity of mineral and thermal springs, who was associated with healing). The presence there of the official tasked by the emperor with making the province pay is important in that it could indicate a desire to maintain a permanent presence in the north of Scotland. Indeed it is at this time that the Antonine Wall was constructed on the Clyde–Forth Line (taking twelve years to complete), bringing at least the Scottish Borders within the province of Britain.

The events of the campaign and the building of the wall were significant enough to have an entry in the *Historia Augusta* (Antoninus Pius, 5.4), which states that the emperor: '. . . defeated the Britons through his legate Lollius Urbicus, and having driven back the barbarians, he built another wall, of turf'.

The wall seems to have been constructed in haste, with the whole of the *legio* II *Augusta* and vexillations from the *legio* VI *Victrix* and *legio* XX *Valeria Victrix* involved (see Chapter 2 for detail of its construction). Once completed, 7,000 troops remained in the north to garrison the new frontier, while Hadrian's Wall on the Solway Firth–Tyne Line was abandoned for the most part.

In the AD 150s trouble erupted again and once more reserves were urgently summoned to the province from the legions and *auxilia* of Upper and Lower

Germany. We know of this military activity in the north from dedications these troops erected to the emperor in a shrine next to the bridge over the river Tyne – they also mentioned vexillations of the three resident British legions. Such trouble in the north is also attested by the minting of coins in Rome dating to AD 154–5, which show Britannia in mourning. Greek geographer and traveller Pausanias (*Guide to Greece*, 8.43.4) also mentions Antoninus Pius depriving the Brigantes of territory. This may indicate that the trouble in the north at this time was from a threat at least partly much further south than the Antonine Wall. Perhaps this reflects native discontent that the regional economy was bent to support the exponentially large military presence there, though some argue that this was a misunderstanding by Pausanias, with the Brigantes he references actually being located in Raetia near modern Bregenz in Austria.

While we have no further sight regarding the military activity at this time, we do know that by AD 158 the Antonine Wall had been abandoned, only sixteen years after its construction had begun and seemingly acknowledging Pausanias' southern threat. The evacuation of the north above the Solway Firth–Tyne Line was carried out by the governor Gnaeus Julius Verus, who re-established the northern border along the line of Hadrian's Wall, which was extensively renovated at this time. Interestingly, during the governorship of Verus' next-but-one replacement, Sextus Calpurnius Agricola, the vallum to the rear of Hadrian's Wall was filled in, indicating that the internal threat from the Brigantes had been removed.

Some military presence did remain further north for a while, as happened in the immediate period following the post-Agricolan Scottish withdrawal. Some of the forts perhaps remained garrisoned as late as the AD 190s, when it has been argued troops from the *legio* VI *Victrix* dedicated an altar to the god Mercury at the fort at Castlecary on the line of the old Antonine Wall (although this dating is hypothetical).

Further military activity is evident in AD 169 at the time of the death of co-emperor Lucius Verus, with the *Historia Augusta* (Marcus Aurelius, 22.1) again referencing trouble in Britain, although giving no further details. However six years later we have information showing the *Classis Britannica* transporting 5,500 Sarmatian heavy cavalry to the province, perhaps indicating that reserves were required once more.

Finally, and an immediate precursor to the events early in the third century which brought Severus to Britain, trouble erupted along the northern border again in the AD 180s and AD 190s. Dio (77.12) explains that by this time there were two main 'races of Britons': the Maeatae north either of Hadrian's Wall or the Antonine Wall; and the Caledonians to the north of them (see Chapter 6 for full detail of both including discussion on their exact locations). The Caledonians, and almost certainly the Maeatae, breached Hadrian's Wall in AD 182 and headed south along Dere Street, destroying the forts at Halton, Chesters, Rudchester and Corbridge, with a Roman general being killed in the process. The new emperor, Commodus, responded decisively, ordering the British governor Ulpius Marcellus to counterattack in force. The campaign seems to have been successful as three epigraphic inscriptions (one at Corbridge and two from Carlisle) mention successful military action beyond Hadrian's Wall at this time (Southern 2013, 229). Confirmation of this success comes in AD 184, when Commodus received his seventh acclamation as imperator and took the title Britannicus.

Events again gather pace less than a decade later, following the assassination of Commodus on New Year's Eve in AD 192, which ushered in the 'Year of the Five Emperors' (see Chapter 5 for full detail). This led to a series of events culminating in the British governor Albinus launching a usurpation attempt against Severus in AD 196, in the process taking significant elements of his three provincial legions with him to ultimate defeat in south-western Gaul in AD 197. As detailed in Chapter 5, Severus' response was to send military legates to Britain to bring the military back under his full control, and also to install his supporter Virius Lupus as the governor. Southern (2013, 237) says that when the latter arrived in AD 197 he found the province in chaos and quickly set about restoring order. However the Caledonians, soon to be joined by the Maeatae, lost no time in causing even more trouble and began agitating along the border yet again. They clearly sensed an opportunity given the diminished Roman military presence. With a new invasion across Hadrian's Wall now in prospect (and with no reserve troops to call upon given the emperor's current focus on Parthia in his second eastern campaign), Lupus had few options so opted to secure peace along his northern borders with massive payments of money (Dio 76.5). However this bought only a short period of stability, and the next developments as this paid-for peace collapsed fall within the remit of the direct build-up to the Severan incursions detailed in Chapters 6 and 7.

CHAPTER 4

Septimius Severus: Early Life

The future emperor and imperial strongman Septimius Severus was born in the North African city of Lepcis Magna, Tripolitania, on 11 April AD 145, seven years into the reign of Antoninus Pius. Thus he was born into an unusually long period of imperial stability, which played a key role in his later world view. Of this time in the Principate, Birley (1999, 1) says: 'The Roman Empire was then at the height of its prosperity. Antoninus Pius . . . gives his name to an era synonymous with peace and affluence.'

Severus was also fortunate to be born in what was one of the most prosperous regions of the Roman Empire, parts of North Africa having long been very fertile. The area was also far less prone than the provinces in Europe and the Levant to incursions along its borders, which stretched across the entirety of the North African provinces from the Red Sea to the Atlantic Ocean (Scarre 1995a, 104). In this chapter I firstly detail the region of Severus' birth; he never forgot his North African roots throughout his career as he ascended the imperial career ladder to become emperor and beyond. I then look at his early life given the clues they can give us to help interpret his later activities and achievements as emperor.

Africa Proconsularis, Tripolitania and Lepcis Magna

The region of Tripolitania was called such after its three principal cities: Lepcis Magna and its two western neighbours, Oea (modern Tripoli) and Sabratha. At the time of Severus' birth Tripolitania lay along a strip of Mediterranean coast in modern Libya in the province of Africa Proconsularis, with the provinces of Numidia to its west and Cyrenaica to its east (Kean 2005, 108). The region as part of the Roman Empire had its origins in the Republican period, specifically in the context of the later Punic Wars. Following the final destruction of Carthage in 146 BC the whole of north-western Africa fell under Roman rule, with the coastal area of western Libya later being incorporated into a Roman province (confusingly, initially called Tripolitania, a provincial name to return to the region in the early fourth century after the Diocletianic reformation). The new province was governed from the region's major trading port, Lepcis Magna, and marked Rome's first permanent footing in the area after the centuries of brutal conflict with the Carthaginian Empire. It was joined as a province by Cyrenaica in 74 BC, to which Crete was added in 20 BC (replicating Ptolemaic Egypt's earlier domination of the eastern Mediterranean). This latter heritage of Cyrenaica was to prove an interesting point of difference between it and Tripolitania as the two provinces evolved within the Roman sphere of dominance, given that the former persevered to a large extent with its former Hellenistic Greek heritage (despite being incorporated into the Republic). The few Romans residing there were organised into a *Conventus civium Romanorum* to help preserve their own distinct Roman cultural heritage.

In contrast, the lands of the Libyans to the west reflected the cataclysmic demise of Carthage, with Roman culture finding it much easier to gain a footing in Tripolitania. Birley (1999, 29) says that this was because after the defeat of Carthage in the Second Punic War, which concluded in 201 BC following Hannibal's defeat at the Battle of Zama the previous year, Tripolitania was left largely to its own devices. Therefore, by the time of the ultimate defeat of Carthage at the end of Third Punic War in 146 BC, the region had had more than fifty years of effective independence, with the three key cities able to gather vast swathes of territory under their control – in the case of Lepcis Magna more than 5,000 square kilometres. Thus, by the time Rome turned its full attention to prosperous Tripolitania, its principal city was already one of the richest in the Mediterranean.

Despite being under official Roman control after Tripolitania was declared a province, its independent outlook continued such that, even though the cultural roots of the three principal towns were clearly Punic, *Romanitas* found it much easier to gain a foothold there than in Cyrenaica (where Greek culture continued to dominate). Indeed, by the time of the onset of the Principate in the reign of Augustus, Tripolitania was considered by contemporary sources markedly more 'Roman' than its eastern neighbour. It became one of the most stable parts of the Empire, the fertile coastal strip spreading further south than today, although the Sahara Desert to its south remained a permanent barrier to most – then as now.

While, as mentioned above, the border was far more stable than elsewhere in the Empire, it did suffer from infrequent raiding: for example, during the rebellion by the Libyan Nasamones tribe (originating to the south of Lepcis Magna) during the reign of Domitian in the later first century AD. During this extreme event a Roman force from the *legio* III *Augusta pia fidelis* led by their legionary legate Gnaeus Suellius Flaccus was decisively defeated. This was the only legion in the province, and had originally been placed there by Augustus to protect the grain supply to Rome. Once Flaccus was able to deploy significantly more troops he was able to secure a decisive victory with ease, to the extent that the emperor was able to report to the Senate that the tribe had ceased to exist – an interesting precursor to Severus' later treatment of the Maeatae and Caledonians.

The province of Tripolitania had actually been incorporated into the new, wider province of Africa Proconsularis about 27 BC. Its territory roughly comprised modern-day Tunisia, the north-east of modern Algeria and the western Libyan coast along the Syrtis Minor. Scarre (1995a, 104) says that the lands there were among the most fertile in the Empire, with a more agreeable climate than today, and Roman agricultural techniques and technology allowed vast swathes of land to be taken under intense cultivation. Indeed many of the Empire's agricultural Imperial Estates were located there.

The principal crops were cereals and olives, both widely exported around the Mediterranean, and it is in Tripolitania that we see some of the best examples of market integration anywhere in the Empire (see Chapter 1 and the discussion on the Roman economy). Scarre (1995a, 104) puts this into context: 'Roman North Africa was second only to Egypt as the supplier of grain for Rome, and such was the abundance of olive oil that only the poorest households were unable to afford oil lamps to light their homes.'

The emporia of the region were also major ports of transit for goods from the south and elsewhere in the Empire: for example, gold and slaves in the case of the former; and wines, drugs and horses from Cyrenaica to the east. Merchants and artisans from across the Empire established themselves across the region, while major construction and engineering projects were carried out, largely under the auspices of the military, to build dams and cisterns to irrigate the province and to regulate against flash floods. This all peaked, unsurprisingly, during the reign of notable local Septimius Severus.

Despite the stability of the southern border (note the single legion based here compared to the multiple legions on the Rhine and Danube, for example), a *limes Tripolitanus* was still constructed principally to protect the cities in Tripolitania, given their huge wealth, from raiding by the Garamantes Berber tribe. This *limes* had its origins under Augustus, although the first fort to be constructed along its length at Thiges wasn't completed until AD 75. For much of its length it was simply an east–west trunk road, with fortifications (such as that at Thiges) built at key choke points, where nomads from the south could access the coast to mount raids. However it was significantly expanded first under Hadrian, then under Trajan and finally under Severus, in the last's reign by *legio* III *Augusta pia fidelis'* legate Quintus Anicius Faustus. Between AD 197 and AD 202 Faustus considerably increased the number of fortifications along its length: for example, by building the substantial forts at Garbia and Golaia. A particular feature of the *limes Tripolitanus*, dating from the reign of Trajan onwards, was the use of *centenaria* (fortified farmhouses) along the *limes* in which veteran troops were settled after leaving the army. Some 2,000 of these are known in the southern peripheries of Lepcis Magna and Sabratha alone, with examples including those at Gheriat esh-Shergia and Gasr Banat.

The province was also famous within the Empire for its academic literacy, with many important literary and legal figures originating there. It proved fertile territory for the early spread of Christianity too, with an advanced episcopal structure developing in the second and third centuries AD.

Cornell and Matthews (1982, 118) state that, following the formation of the wider province of Africa Proconsularis, urbanisation in the fertile areas was rapid and fairly even, though clearly the prosperous towns and cities were the main foci of settlement. In that regard, aside from the three cities of Tripolitania along its eastern coast, other great urban centres included Tacapae (modern Gabès), Neapolis (modern Nabeul), the rebuilt Carthage (following its destruction in 146 BC, and now the provincial capital) and Utica (modern Utique). Lepcis Magna clearly stood out among these to contemporary audiences as the shining jewel along the Tripolitanian coast, even before its elevation after Severus' accession to emperor.

Although little is known about the early history of the city except its Punic founding in the second half of the seventh century BC, its wealth is evident early in the written records, which reference it giving one talent a day in taxation to its initial Punic overlords. Later it was able to pay an annual fine of three million Roman pounds of olive oil imposed by Julius Caesar for the part it played in North African resistance to him.

The first major manifestations of *Romanitas* appeared about the time of Augustus, when Lepcis Magna was classified as a *civitas libera et immunis* (free community) over which the regional governor had total control. Many monuments built under the sponsorship of the local aristocracy date to this time, and they went on to be key features of the Roman town through to the end of the Empire in the West and beyond. Golvin (2003, 106) says that as part of this process of transforming itself into a Roman city the original town square was expanded and turned into a forum, around which a *basilica* (great aisled hall) and several temples were built. Meanwhile a hippodrome was also erected, which, at 450 metres by 100 metres, was one of the largest in the Roman world, with an equally impressive 100-metre by 80-metre amphitheatre being constructed nearby. Later a new marketplace and theatre were put up in the city's south-west corner, around which a new urban quarter developed.

The city became a *municipium* (see p. 21 for detail on the various kinds of towns and cities in the Roman Empire) about AD 75 under Vespasian (Birley 1999, 16) and a *colonia* under Trajan about AD 110 (taking the title *Ulpia Traiana fidelis*). There was probably some link between this latter development and the first appearance of the *centenaria* as part of the *limes Tripolitanus* at this time. Golvin (2003, 106) says that under Trajanic and Antonine patronage archaeological data shows an evident increase in the importation of luxury goods, reflecting the further increasing status of Lepcis Magna. Fine-quality marble was used in the restoration of existing buildings and also in new construction projects including the grand Baths of Hadrian and Arch of Antoninus Pius.

This coincided with the birth of Severus, and indeed it was under him when emperor towards the end of the century that the city reached its peak in splendour. It is very evident that Severus favoured his home town above all of the other major regional cities, lavishing new buildings and wealth on it to the extent that it rivalled Carthage in terms of its prominence across the whole of the southern Mediterranean. Golvin (2003, 106) explains that: 'Under the guidance of a childhood friend of the emperor, a massive expansion programme began. An extension of the southern quarter was designed, a luxurious [new] forum and *basilica* built, a superb avenue with porticoes laid out, and a nymphaeum [a monument consecrated to nymphs, particularly those of springs] and triumphal arch [dedicated to Severus] were erected.'

The surrounding countryside was also extensively landscaped, with a new 200-metre dam and canals being built to re-route the Wadi Lebda around the city. An artificial port was also constructed, which contemporaries said rivalled that of Carthage in size and grandeur (this today being the best preserved Roman port anywhere in the world). New residential areas also sprang up, with the city's population by the end of Severus' reign being around 100,000. By this time the city had grown to some 435 hectares.

Decline after such a heady elevation was inevitable, beginning with the dissolution of the *legio* III *Augusta pia fidelis* by the emperor Gordian III in AD 238. This led to an increase in Berber raiding, compounding economic problems caused by a decrease in regional trade during the 'Crisis of the Third Century'. Thus by the late third century the city was a shadow of its former self, although Diocletian did make it the capital of the newly reformed province of Tripolitania after his reformation. The city then fell to the Vandals in AD 439 as part of their conquest of the whole of Roman North Africa, and in AD 533 it was recaptured and incorporated into the Eastern Empire during the reconquest of the region by Belisarius under Justinian I. By this time, it was suffering from extensive Berber raiding, eventually being overrun as part of the Arab Conquest in AD 647; it was then abandoned.

The Early Life of Septimius Severus

Septimius Severus was the son of Publius Septimius Geta (called Geta from this point in this chapter) and Fulvia Pia. The Septimii were a wealthy and distinguished family of largely equestrian rank (although with some senatorial pedigree, see below), and with some experience of the world of Rome from the mid-first century AD. Severus' mother was a member of the wealthy Italian Fulvia family with land in Tuscany.

Geta was a minor provincial official who never seems to have held high public office, which is surprising given the growth of the city at that time as there would have been plenty of opportunity for advancement in the imperial system. Severus' grandfather on Geta's side, Lucius Septimius Severus (called L. Severus in this chapter), after whom the future emperor was named, had been a notable character in Rome as one of its leading equestrians when a young man. He then became Lepcis Magna's leading public figure on his return to his home town (this story detailed below). Meanwhile two of Geta's older first cousins, Publius Septimius Aper and Gaius Septimius Severus (Birley 1999, 216), had risen to senatorial rank and served as consuls under Antoninus Pius. The picture we get here of the Septimii family to which Severus was born is one on the rise, making its breakthrough in the high politics of both the imperial capital Rome and Lepcis Magna, but with Severus' father perhaps being a bit of an underperformer compared to others in the family. Birley (1999, 1) speculates this may have been due to ill health.

The story of the rise of the Septimii to the highest levels of Roman power is the ultimate analogy to help understand the gradual integration of provincial elites into Roman political structures as the Empire grew to its maximum extent, incorporating peoples from across the known world. In terms of the aristocracy of Lepcis Magna, the key transition of these elites from styling themselves as Punic to presenting themselves as fully Roman (for example, in the way they named themselves on epigraphy) seems to have taken place towards the end of the first century AD after Lepcis Magna had become a *municipium* (under the Emperor Vespasian as he cast his gaze around the Empire to identify new sources of revenue). This was a key development for Lepcis Magna as it automatically conferred Roman citizenship on those annually elected as magistrates (this later being expanded to include all the citizens of the city), and it seems to have prompted an outbreak of desire among the local elites to display their *Romanitas*. As an example, it was around this time that the nobility of the city began changing their family names from the original Punic to Roman. As Birley (1999, 17) says: 'Within a few years the (Punic) Annobals, Balsillechs, Balithos, the Bodmelqarts, Magos and Ithymbals disappear from public records, to be replaced by (the Roman) Claudii and Flavii, Marcii, Paccii, Cornelii and Plautii.'

The Septimii seem to have been early starters in this regard, with two family members being the first to style themselves Roman through their names, by taking the Roman *gentilicium* Septimius. The first is a senator from Tripolitania called Septimius, who is recorded taking a son called Septimius Severus to Italy, with the boy then being raised in Rome. It seems likely that the elder Septimius here is Septimius Macer (interestingly retaining the Punic Macer), Severus the emperor's great-grandfather, this then identifying the boy as Severus' grandfather L. Severus. The second candidate is one Septimius Flaccus, recorded with the same *gentilicium* around the same time. He has been associated by some as being the same legionary legate Gnaeus Suellius Flaccus, who led the *legio* III *Augusta pia fidelis* against the Nasamones tribe (see p. 84).

He is also recorded in epigraphy adjudicating a boundary dispute along the coast in the AD 80s.

In terms of the family wealth of the Septimii, its origins are unclear but certainly they possessed extensive North African olive plantations, and they may also have been involved in trans-Saharan trade (in gold and perhaps slaves). As they began to establish themselves in Italy in the mid- to late first century AD, they began to acquire land, and by the time L. Severus was being raised in Rome they owned property in three specific areas:

- near Veii to the north of Rome, along the Via Cassia and perhaps at a place called Baccanae;
- further to the north-east, near the Via Salaria at a place called Cures Sabini;
- to the south-east of Rome, possibly at Anagnia along the Via Latina in formerly Hernician country.

Once in Rome L. Severus began his education, which would have been to the uppermost standards of the day, alongside the offspring of the Empire's highest-ranking great and good. Any trace of his Punic accent would soon have been stamped out, and his grasp of Latin and Greek tightened until the reading of literature in these languages became second nature to him. Schooling for the children of the Roman nobility, even arrivistes such as the young L. Severus, was onerous, repetitive and always prone to corporal punishment for the slightest mistake. L. Severus seems to have been part of a golden generation, however, as the Principate matured. He completed his studies under the great master of Roman rhetoric Quintilian (the first holder of an imperially endowed chair of rhetoric). Meanwhile his classmates included the future senator Vitorius Marcellus and other notables, while Quintilian could also count as a former pupil Pliny the Younger. This was heady stuff indeed for the young boy from North Africa.

As he grew to manhood L. Severus could have acquired the 'broad stripe' of a senator (as with his father), although he instead settled on the 'narrow stripe' of an equestrian. He trained and then practised as a barrister in Rome, also turning his hand to verse as a pastime. In that regard he counted as a close friend the noted poet Publius Papinius Statius, author of the *Thebaid* (a Latin epic poem in twelve books written in dactylic hexameters covering the then famous Theban Cycle of stories about the assault of seven champions from Argos against Thebes). Most usefully for us given the insight it provides,

Statius also wrote a poem in honour of L. Severus. The ode of fifteen four-line stanzas emphasises that his 'sweet' friend Severus spoke like an Italian, not with a Punic accent, and equally dressed like a Roman (the expensive education clearly having done its job). Noteworthy here is the age difference between the young man and the poet – Statius having been born in AD 45 and dying in AD 96. Thus he may also have been a patron for the young man making his way in Roman aristocracy. Another such patron seems to have been the city prefect Rutilius Gallicus, who had met Septimius Macer in Lepcis Magna in the early AD 70s. Therefore L. Severus was ideally placed in Roman society as new pathways opened up roads for advancement in the highest Roman political circles for non-Italians for the first time, with consuls of non-Italian birth serving by the end of the Flavian period. Birley (1999, 19) says that in this society a rich family from Lepcis Magna would have felt very much at home.

We next hear of L. Severus around the time of Domitian's assassination in AD 96, when he was appointed an *iudex selectus* (select judge). After this he seems to have travelled back to his native Lepcis Magna as we hear of him in the context of the high-profile trial of the governor of Africa Proconsularis and his legate (in this case a civil office holder), who were both accused of bribery (the city in some way being involved). This long-lasting event concluded about the time Trajan became emperor in AD 98.

Now back in the family home, L. Severus continued to prosper, and Birley (1999, 22) paints a fine picture of his rise to become the city's leading man. He was already a *sufes* (the old Punic name for a high-ranking civil administrator) of the *municipium* by the time of Trajan's accession, and when the latter conferred *colonia* status on Lepcis Magna he automatically became one of the city's first two *duoviri* (magistrates) – he was already a Roman citizen, the first in the family.

L. Severus also married, although we do not know his wife's name; in fact Birley (1999, 23) says he may have married more than once. He had two children that we know of: a son Geta (Severus' father) and a daughter called Septimia Polla. Geta is an unusual name to choose (originally being a slave name), and it seems that L. Severus selected it because his old Italian school friend and now Senator Vitorius Marcellus back in Rome had so named his son. In this context the naming of L. Severus' son was therefore a clear nod that his allegiance was now with Rome.

We have little other detail of the lives of L. Severus and his less successful son Geta (also of equestrian rank) until the latter married Fulvia Pia. Meanwhile other members of the Septimii also seem to have been making their mark in Lepcis Magna, given one Gaius Claudius Septimius Aper (possibly the brother of L. Severus) dedicated a new statue of Cupid in the Chalcidicum. The next we hear of the Septimii is with the birth of Geta's three children: an elder son called P. Septimius Geta; a younger son whom we know as Septimius Severus (the protagonist of this book, his birth specifically dated to 11 April AD 145 as set out above); and a daughter called Septimia Octavilla.

There are few details available to illuminate the early life of the future emperor, although apparently his favourite game was 'judges', in which Severus made his friends act as *lictors* carrying imitation rods of office before him. This is rather grand behaviour for the son of a relatively minor provincial official, although one shouldn't forget the influence his grandfather would have had across the entire Septimii family.

For his schooling the primary sources say that Severus excelled at Latin and Greek, although he is also thought to have been fluent in the Punic of his family (and indeed, unlike his grandfather, apparently retained his Punic accent throughout his life). At the age of seventeen he is recorded as giving his first speech in public – a declamation which marked the ending of his formal schooling. Meanwhile in terms of his physical appearance at this age, he is said to have been fairly short but very powerfully built.

It is likely that by this time his elder brother Geta had already left Lepcis Magna to begin his own career in imperial service, for we know that shortly afterwards he became senatorial tribune (as the *tribunus laticlavius*) of the *legio II Augusta* based at the legionary fortress of Caerleon in south-eastern Wales. One can perhaps see their grandfather's influence here again, especially as the British governor at the time was Sex. Calpurnius Agricola, a native North African from Numidia. This was an individual later to appear in the context of Severus' own association with Britain, as we shall see in Chapter 6.

Severus himself, having finished his schooling, set out for Rome to make his way in the world, with Kean (2005, 111) saying he travelled on his eighteenth birthday (April AD 163). By this time Antoninus Pius had died and the Empire was being ruled by its first diarchy under his adopted sons and successors, Marcus Aurelius and Lucius Verus. Birley (1999, 37) describes the imperial capital in the AD 160s as having an atmosphere of urgency as the long years of calm under Pius came to an end (with the Parthians almost immediately agitating on the eastern frontier). It was in these circumstances that we see North African aristocrats rising to multiple positions of authority across the

Empire: for example, with Geminius Marcianus from Cirta commanding the *legio* X *Gemina*, which was transferred from the Danube to bolster the eastern frontier; with Antistius Adventus from Thibilis being given command of the *legio* II *Adiutrix* from Budapest in addition to the *legio* VI *Ferrata fidelis constans* when Geminius arrived in the east to join him in Palestine; and with the governor in Britain as we have seen being Sex. Calpurnius Agricola. It was also at this time that Severus' elder brother was serving as a tribune at Caerleon with *legio* II *Augusta*.

Once in Rome Severus studied law under the noted jurist Q. Cervidius Scaevola. According to some of the Latin sources and the *vitae* of Caracalla and Geta in the *Historia Augusta*, he went on to hold the equestrian post of *advocatus fisci* – established under Hadrian, with the holder tasked with helping look after the imperial treasury. The original source for this information was seemingly the 'Kaisergeschichte'; see p. 20. The claim regarding this posting remains unproven, however.

Severus was clearly ambitious, and from an early age had set his eyes on the broad purple stripe of senatorial rank as worn by his father's cousins Publius Septimius Aper and Gaius Septimius Severus (who as we have seen had already served as consuls in AD 153 and AD 160 respectively) rather than the narrow equestrian stripe of his father and grandfather. Indeed it was the latter second cousin who took Severus under his wing and petitioned Marcus Aurelius to admit the future emperor into the senatorial ranks. Severus must already have caught the eye of the emperor as this was quickly granted. He now began his journey along the pathway of the *cursus honorum* – the sequence of public offices held in a Roman aristocrat's political career, reformed by Augustus early in his reign and staying the same for the rest of the Principate (Birley 2005, 3; see also Chapter 1 above). Severus seems to have first served as a *vigintivir* before being allowed to enter the Senate itself. The career path thereafter in the *cursus honorum*, in positions both at home and abroad, was usually as follows:

- *quaestorship* (the lowest-ranked magistrate) – twenty-four years old;
- tribunate of plebs/*aedileship* (with responsibility for public buildings/ festivals) – when he was twenty-five and twenty-six years old;
- *praetorship* (military commander or senior elected magistrate) – when he was twenty-nine years old;
- consulship (effectively now, under the Principate with its emperor, an honorific title) – when he was forty-one years old.

Severus held his first (urban) *quaestorship* in AD 169/170. Becoming a *quaestor* also meant he was now able to style himself *vir clarissimus* (the Right Honourable). He then gradually made his way through the various positions in the *cursus honorum*, although one point of interest here – given the martial nature evident in his later life – is that he didn't follow his elder brother in a senatorial military career, evidently making no move to become a military tribune. Kean (2005, 111) argues that this was because his network of connections in Rome by this time was good enough for him not to have had to go down this route (usually seen as a means of building up such a network in the first place). Next we hear of him returning to Lepcis Magna for a short time, possibly coinciding with his brother Geta becoming the *quaestor* to the proconsul in the province of Crete and Cyrenaica. Birley (1999, 45) says he may then have spent time in Carthage before returning to Rome.

Geta and Severus continued to progress along the *cursus honorum* – the former serving for a time as the *curator* of the key port town of Ancona on the eastern coast of Italy around AD 170. By this time only Marcus Aurelius was emperor (as Lucius Verus had died in AD 169) and the north-east of Italy was under serious threat after a major incursion across the Danube from AD 166 by the Marcomanni, Juthungi, Quadi and Sarmatian Iazyges. This invasion began the so-called Marcomannic Wars, which were to last until AD 180 (Kean 2005, 96). Perhaps because of Geta's responsibilities there, it was Severus and not Geta who returned to Lepcis Magna in the early AD 170s to settle family affairs after the death of their father. This move prevented Severus from taking up his first foreign *quaestorship* in Hispania Baetica (the province of southern Spain centred on modern Cordoba). By the time he was free to take up the post, Moorish pirates had started ravishing the province, so instead he was appointed to the more peaceful province of Sardinia. It appears that his lack of military experience might have counted against him in Hispania Baetica while his Carthaginian roots might have proved a useful qualification in Sardinia, given that Punic was still spoken there. Severus stayed on the island for a year.

His family connections then offered him the chance of another rapid boost along the *cursus honorum* when his second cousin and earlier champion Gaius Septimius Severus became the proconsul of Africa Proconsularis in AD 173. He chose Severus to be one of his civilian *legati pro praetore*, the young man returning once more to North Africa – this time to Carthage. Birley (1999, 51) says that while in post he deputised for the proconsul: for example, in the settling of legal disputes. He also travelled to his home town of Lepcis Magna again, and one story of his time there during this visit is clearly meant to show that he had outgrown his native roots and was now a man of authority in the Roman political system. The tale goes that when he was travelling through his home town, attended by his *lictors* with their *fasces* of office (an interesting image in its own right given the games he used to play as a boy, see p. 91), he had an old *plebeian* acquaintance flogged after the man hugged him in public greeting. This story is perhaps the earliest we have which gives some real insight into the ruthless streak the future emperor was developing as he progressed along the *cursus honorum*. He was now clearly styling himself a leading public figure, and it was on his return to Rome in late AD 174 (approaching his thirtieth birthday) that we begin to see the serious upturn in career opportunity that was eventually to open up the pathway for ultimate greatness and glory.

CHAPTER 5

Septimius Severus: Imperator

WE REJOIN SEVERUS ON THE verge of senior office in the *cursus honorum*, with him casting his gaze back on Rome once again. In this chapter I firstly consider the career path that led to him being in position to mount his assault on the imperial title. Then I trace the year AD 193, the 'Year of the Five Emperors', and Severus' subsequent career as emperor prior to his arrival in Britain in AD 208 (including his civil wars and foreign campaigning), before finally considering his impact on the imperial capital once emperor. Thus the narrative builds up to the next chapter's specific focus on the beginning of his *expeditio felicissima Britannica*.

The Pathway to Power

Severus was beginning to make real traction along the *cursus honorum*, and as his time as one of the *legati pro praetore* in North Africa was coming to an end he would have been encouraged by his family and peers to take a wife. He chose a North African girl by the name of Paccia Marciana, whose family name indicates Punic rather than Italian heritage – her ancestors gaining Roman citizenship through association with first century AD proconsuls in the province. Very little is known of her background or even her and Severus' life together, although Birley (1999, 52) indicates there were no children (the *Historia Augusta* mentions two daughters but historical convention has interpreted this as a literary convention to explain away later claimed events; Kean 2005, 111). Paccia and Severus were to remain together until her death a decade later. Given that Severus later had statues erected in her memory it seems the future emperor was at least fond of his first wife.

In AD 174 Severus returned to Rome, no doubt relieved once more to be at the centre of political life – a marked contrast to his later negative view of the imperial capital. He quickly took his next step in the *cursus honorum*, and a big one too, being appointed tribune of the plebs. This indicates he'd once again attracted the attention of the emperor Marcus Aurelius. Severus began his term on 10 December AD 174 and married Paccia Marciana the following year – she having travelled back to Rome with him.

Severus performed his tribunate duties well, and indeed may have been involved in the preserving of public order in Rome during a failed usurpation attempt after false rumours spread that the emperor was dead. Marcus Aurelius, actually at the front with his northern legions, certainly took note of the trouble in the imperial capital and whisked his thirteen-year-old heir, Commodus, away to join him, investing him with the *toga virilis* in July AD 175. Because Rome would have been depleted of guard units at the time with the emperor on the northern frontier, perhaps Severus made an impression on the young Commodus, given the favour the latter was later to show him. The conflict keeping the emperor at the front was the Marcomannic Wars mentioned in the last chapter, which began in AD 166 and lasted until AD 180 (Kean 2005, 96). By this time the fighting was focused on the Danube frontier, with the emperor based at Sremska Mitrovika (Roman Sirmium, capital of Pannonia Inferior) in modern-day Serbia, from where he launched his successful campaign against the Sarmatian Iazyges.

It is in the context of this conflict that we next see evidence of the Septimii prospering – this time with regard to Severus' elder brother Geta. This was because in later AD 175 Helvius Pertinax, son of a freed man and former schoolmaster, was made a consul (alongside Didius Julianus, both to play a greater role in the narrative of Severus' rise to power later in this chapter) and appointed initially as governor of Moesia Superior and then also of Moesia Inferior, with Geta serving under him as the legate of *legio* I *Italica*.

Meanwhile Severus continued his public service career in Rome. He was designated praetor (senior elected magistrate) at the beginning of AD 177, joining in the festivities when Commodus accompanied his father in celebrating a joint triumph on 23 December that year. By then the emperor's son had been granted the title *Imperator Destinatus* (heir apparent) in a move designed to smooth his accession to power given his father's ill health. Commodus was then made a full Augustus in January AD 178, just one step away from being sole emperor. It seems likely this planned transition made a big impact on Severus, given his later promotion of both his sons, once emperor.

Imperial favour continued to follow Severus and before his praetorship was over he was posted to his first top-level position in the provinces, as the *iuridicus* (legal expert) on the staff of the governor of Hispania Tarraconensis (northern and eastern Spain). This was the most senior position in a governor's *officium consularis*, the post holder being the key legal adviser to the governor. Meanwhile Marcus Aurelius died on 17 March AD 180, thereby issuing in the reign of Commodus, which was ultimately to lead to Severus claiming the throne thirteen years later.

Severus' next posting, shortly after Marcus Aurelius' death, gave him his first real taste of direct engagement with the military, a relationship that was to define the rest of his professional and indeed personal life, to the extent that his dying words referenced keeping the troops happy above all else except family. Intriguingly, up to this point the discerning reader will have noticed that Severus' career path along the *cursus honorum* had been distinctly lacking in frontline military experience. In fact, given that he hadn't chosen to go down the legionary legate route early on (unlike his elder brother), and then hadn't taken up his post in Hispania Baetica when this was under attack by Moorish pirates, a harsh interpretation would be that he had dodged the opportunity for conflict (even given the critical nature of the coverage of his life by the principal primary sources). All that was now to change, and from this point Severus never looked back from immersing himself in all matters military.

The posting that began this relationship with the military was a real case of being dropped in at the deep end; he was sent from the far west to the far east of the Empire to become the legionary legate of *legio* IV *Scythica* in Syria. This famous legion had been founded by Mark Antony in 42 BC to campaign against the Parthians, and had remained a bulwark against the enemies of Rome in the east ever since. It was also the most senior of the three regional legions, being based closest to Antioch, usually at Zeugma on the Euphrates.

It seems highly probable that Severus would have experienced combat of some kind for the first time here – probably against the Parthians. His journey east to take up his post would have been an experience too, taking him through some of the richest parts of the Empire, cultural and otherwise, including Greece and Asia Minor. Then once in post he found himself following in his brother's footsteps by serving under Pertinax, who by this time was governor of Syria. This led to a relationship that was to play a pivotal role in the 'Year of the Five Emperors' in AD 193. It is from Pertinax that Severus would perhaps have learnt for the first time in detail of military command in the far-off province of Britannia (assuming he hadn't met his elder brother since the latter had served with *legio* II *Augusta* in Caerleon). Pertinax had previously served as one of the five equestrian tribunes of the *legio* VI *Victrix* in York (where Severus was to die in AD 211), and he later served on Hadrian's Wall in command of an auxiliary unit. Birley (1999, 69) speculates that during his time as legate of his legion, controlling the most direct access routes to Antioch from the east, Severus would have inspected his main garrisons along the frontier, including Dura-Europos, which since its capture in AD 162 was Rome's furthest outpost on the Parthian frontier.

When Severus left this command is unclear, though it may have been associated with the recall of Pertinax to Rome in AD 182, after which the latter spent three years on his family property in Liguria in disgrace. We do not know the reason for this, but by AD 185 Pertinax was back in imperial favour.

Severus is next recorded being promoted to the senior post of *legatus pro praetore* in the province of Gallia Lugdunensis (modern north-western France including Brittany and Normandy). This was his first governorship and a mighty elevation in rank along the *cursus honorum*. He acquitted himself admirably and proved an efficient administrator of an important if not frontline province (although it did have a military presence: for example, the auxiliary cavalry Ala Asturum unit, and of course his urban cohorts). Severus would also have had his first personal experience of Britannia (although there is no evidence he actually visited), since the most north-westerly province of the Empire lay to the direct north of his own. Indeed his principal interaction with the military while there would have been with the *Classis Britannica*, given that one of the tasks of the British regional fleet would have been keeping the English Channel clear of piracy.

He would also have renewed his acquaintance with Pertinax now that his former superior in the east was governor of Britannia (from AD 185 to AD 187). This was to prove an unhappy experience for Pertinax, who had been tasked with bringing the exponentially large military presence there into line after some sort of major incident. However he was unsuccessful, with one legion rebelling against him and attacking his bodyguard, leaving him for dead. Pertinax recovered and dealt with the rebels very severely, which led to his growing reputation as a strict disciplinarian. However he was forced to resign in AD 187, given the continuing hostility of the legions – a lesson not lost on Severus, who later as emperor viewed the military in Britain with deep suspicion, especially after the later usurpation attempt by Albinus. In Chapter 6 this is discussed as a potential factor in his decision to mount his *expeditio felicissima Britannica*.

Sadly for Severus, while in this posting at Gallia Lugdunensis his wife Paccia Marciana passed away, apparently soon after they arrived (Birley 1999, 75). However close they had been, Severus doesn't appear to have spent much time mourning. Ever practical, he quickly turned his attention to finding a new wife. This may seem a little callous to modern sensibilities, but as a leading aristocrat he was clearly concerned with his family legacy (he being over forty and apparently childless).

We know from the primary sources that Severus was a great believer in astrology and apparently heard at this time of a woman in Syria whose horoscope had predicted she would marry a king, with the sources saying he therefore sought her out (this is the first reference to him having imperial ambitions). This was to be his second wife, Julia Domna, the youngest daughter of Gaius Julius Bassianus, the high priest of the cult of the sun god Heliogabalus in the Syrian city of Emesa. The family is said to have had enormous wealth, being promoted into Roman senatorial aristocracy. Julia Domna herself owned substantial wealth in her own right, having inherited the estate of her paternal great-uncle Julius Agrippa, a leading Syrian nobleman from the original royal family of Emesa.

This story, with its astrology references, sounds fanciful, especially since Severus had been based in Syria as the senior legionary legate and would certainly have visited Emesa. One could argue that it seems likely he had already met Julia Domna, and perhaps even developed some sort of relationship, but we have no record of that. Levick (2007, 124) says Severus came to know a variety of oriental cults during his time as the legate there, and such a meeting might have taken place in that context. Whatever the truth, a proposal of marriage was quickly on its way from the Rhone Valley to Syria, and events developed rapidly from there.

Julia Domna was considered a great catch for Severus by contemporary audiences, being not only wealthy but very attractive too. Given her family background she was very well read and a patron of philosophy (when empress she developed a reputation as a protector of philosophers and helped the social sciences to flourish in Rome).

The marriage took place in summer AD 187 (the proximity to the death of Paccia Marciana is again noteworthy here), almost certainly in the provincial capital of Lyon (Roman Colonia Copia Claudia Augusta Lugdunum) (Levick 2007, 31). It proved to be a happy marriage, with Severus clearly cherishing his wife and valuing her political counsel. The couple had two sons, Caracalla in AD 188 and Geta in AD 189. Also worthy of note here is how well the wider family of Julia Domna flourished from this point, with her elder sister Julia Maesa being grandmother to two later Severan emperors, Elagabalus and Severus Alexander (both having unhappy ends).

Moving back to Severus' career development, after helping suppress the *bellum desertorum* rebellion of Maternus, he left Gaul in AD 188 and moved back to Rome, where his name went into the ballot for another governorship; he was subsequently appointed to the important proconsulship of Sicily. Birley (1999, 77) indicates that his brother Geta may have preceded him in this post. Here Severus seems to have courted controversy by 'consulting magicians', which Platnauer (1918, 46) says left him exposed to impeachment by his imperial rivals. This indicates the heady heights to which he had risen along the *cursus honorum*. The impeachment was quashed, however, and the accuser crucified, again testament to Severus' growing power – his unforgiving nature perhaps visible too.

The next natural step for Severus was a consulship in Rome itself and this he received on 1 April AD 190 (as *consul suffectus*), serving alongside a fellow noble called Apuleius Rufinus. Their time in this very senior position in Rome seems to have passed unremarkably. In Severus' case this is probably understandable as in short order he received yet another appointment, and it is at this point that the wheels of fate really began to turn in his favour as later on in AD 190 he was appointed governor of the very important province of Pannonia Superior. This appointment was as much political as a reflection on his undoubted administrative (and emerging military) capabilities, being at the suggestion of the praetorian prefect Quintus Aemilius Laetus (a fellow North African) to Commodus. It placed him at the heart of the imperial defensive (and occasionally offensive) network – the province having three legions spread out along the Danube to cover the north-eastern approaches to Italy and the Balkans. With his headquarters at Carnuntum (the Roman legionary fortress and headquarters of the *Classis Pannonica* Danubian regional fleet) on the Danube, he set about settling a province which had been much disrupted during the Marcomannic Wars. He seems to have done a good job too, given the loyalty of the elites there when Severus was presented with the ultimate imperial opportunity three years later.

Before moving onto the specifics of the 'Year of the Five Emperors', it is worth briefly reflecting on how militarily well placed Severus was in that fateful year. This was because his province was not alone in providing the northern Danubian defences of the Roman Empire. As Paul Elliott (2014, 14) says:

> This set of provinces (Raetia, Noricum, Pannonia and Moesia) bound both the eastern and western halves of the Empire together. They formed, along with their legions, a vital bulwark against which the belligerent tribes of Dacia and Germany crashed. Its legions were motivated and battle-hardened, and crucially for the fate of any would-be emperor, there were a lot of them.

The military was indeed heavily represented in the region, with a string of legionary fortresses stretching from Regensburg (Roman Castra Regina) in modern Bavaria to Novae in modern Bulgaria, with each province having its own set of legions, all veterans of the Marcomannic Wars. The regional Danubian fleet was on hand as well. Dacia, still a province standing proud of the Danube to the north of Moesia Superior and Moesia Inferior at this point, was also heavily manned by the military. It would have greatly suffered in the Marcomannic Wars. For two reasons this overall situation gave Severus an exponential advantage over his opponents once the scramble for power emerged:

- the numbers and experience of his troops as frontline warriors in the Roman military machine, always engaged in military action of some type and most recently being the bulwark of Empire in the Marcomannic Wars;
- their proximity to Rome in large numbers compared to any of the other potential candidates with military support.

One can imagine how Severus, ever the pragmatist, must have sensed his opportunity once it became clear there was trouble in the imperial capital, so I now turn to the story of the 'Year of the Five Emperors' and his ascent to ultimate imperial power.

The 'Year of the Five Emperors' and Severus as Emperor before AD 208

By AD 192 Commodus had become a very unpopular emperor, having always struggled in the shadows of his illustrious father Marcus Aurelius, the earlier political stability under Antoninus Pius and Hadrian and the martial might of Trajan. Commodus had always, in his pronouncements and iconography, stressed his unique god-like status to counter this, and many commentators consider he became mentally unhinged as his rule progressed. A large number of statues were set up across the Empire to portray him as Hercules, and he developed a reputation for his fondness for slaying beasts in the arena. As the 'Year of the Five Emperors' approached, these tendencies seemingly increased to megalomaniacal proportions.

In AD 191 Rome had been extensively damaged by a fire that raged for a number of days during which a large number of public buildings (including the Temple of Pax, the Temple of Vesta and some areas of the Imperial Palace) were destroyed. Commodus, in Neronian fashion, sensed this as an opportunity to declare himself a new version of Romulus, ritually refounding Rome and allegedly renaming the city as Colonia Lucia Annia Commodiana. Furthermore all the months of the year were renamed to ensure they corresponded with his now twelve names: Lucius, Aelius, Aurelius, Commodus, Augustus, Herculeus, Romanus, Exsuperatorius, Amazonius, Invictus, Felix, Pius. Next we are told the legions were renamed *Commodianae*, the fleet which imported the grain supply from Egypt and North Africa to Rome the *Alexandria Commodiana Togata*, the Senate the *Commodian Fortunate Senate* and the Imperial Palace and Roman people themselves *Commodianus*, with the specific days on which the reforms were decreed called *Dies Commodianus*. He also had the head of the Colossus of Nero next to the Colosseum at the foot of the Forum replaced with a portrait of himself, equipped with a club and a bronze lion at its feet so as to look like Hercules. This was megalomania writ large, and the elites in the imperial capital at last began to move against the delusional emperor.

In later AD 192 a plot emerged to assassinate Commodus, led by the praetorian prefect Laetus (who had played such a key role in positioning Severus as governor in Pannonia Superior), Eclectus the imperial Chamberlain and Commodus' mistress Marcia. The cabal, casting around for a manageable imperial successor, alighted on Pertinax, who by this time was the urban prefect in Rome and had been chosen by Commodus as his fellow consul that year. All was therefore set, and late on New Year's Eve AD 192 the deed was done, with Marcia initially attempting to kill Commodus with poison. This failed, however, when the emperor vomited up his food and the potion, so a backup plan came into play with one of Commodus' wrestling partners, a man named Narcissus, overpowering him and strangling him that same night (his body was immediately dragged away and cremated). Thus, as AD 193 dawned, all was set for the 'Year of the Five Emperors'.

The first move of the plotters was to establish Pertinax as the new emperor, so he was immediately rushed to the praetorian camp and was proclaimed emperor on New Year's Day – Laetus persuading the unconvinced troops with a promised donative of 12,000 sesterces per man. Pertinax decided to style himself on his role model Marcus Aurelius and quickly set about trying to undo the damage to imperial government by Commodus. Striving to be a worthy emperor, he instituted reforms of the welfare system for the poor, and also of the currency by increasing the silver purity of the denarius. Sadly for him, however, this was not what Laetus had been expecting, and matters swiftly came to a head when the new emperor turned his attention to the Praetorian Guard itself. With relations already poor given their initial reluctance to recognise him, the new emperor then refused to pay them the donative promised by Laetus (one should note here the hardline reputation Pertinax had developed during his experiences in Britain), and a plot to kill him was soon in the offing. One early attempt to replace him with the consul Quintus Sosius Falco three months into his reign failed, but at the end of March one succeeded when 300 angry praetorians forced the palace gates and, despite his desperate attempts to reason with them, eventually killed him. His corpse was swiftly decapitated and the head stuck on the end of a lance to be paraded around the city.

Next up for the imperial throne was the wealthy Didius Julianus, whom we last met when he was the joint consul with Pertinax in AD 175. Clearly no love was lost between them given the speed with which Julianus immediately tried to bribe his way to power, but he was quickly sidelined as three other serious candidates for the imperial throne made their moves. These were Severus, Syrian governor Pescennius Niger (popular with the Roman public) and the British governor Albinus.

It was Severus, poised like a sword of Damocles above Italy in Pannonia Superior, who moved first, and with lightning speed. He had begun his planning to head south as soon as he heard of the death of Pertinax, and by 9 April felt secure enough to make his move. He was declared emperor at

Carnuntum by *legio* XIV *Gemina Martia Victrix*, with contemporary sources saying he tried to decline in the traditional display of reluctance. He was far from it, however, and immediately headed south, *legio* XIV *Gemina* being joined by *legio* I *Adiutrix*, giving him over 10,000 crack troops at his immediate disposal, together with any auxiliaries he could muster. Severus also positioned Pannonia Inferior's *legio* II *Adiutrix* as a strategic reserve, and received pledges of support from the other twelve legions along the Danube and Rhine.

Like a thunderbolt he arrived in Rome, having ignored pleas to negotiate by Julianus. His immediate first action was to confront the Praetorian Guard, who would have been keenly aware they were no match for the military force at Severus' disposal. His response to the disloyalty of the guard was typically robust. Emboldened by the proximity of his own Danubian veterans, he ordered the praetorians to muster in their parade ground and then harangued them at length, saying they deserved to die 1,000 times. Finally he ordered them to strip naked and banished them all to live at least 160 kilometres away from Rome for the rest of their lives (De la Bédoyère 2017, 58). The next day (Hasebroek 1921, 40, suggests 9 June for his physical entry into Rome) he visited a very cowed Senate, which swiftly accepted him as emperor (no surprise given the massive military presence backing him). He trebled the number of *cohorts urbanae* (gendarmes), doubled the number of *vigiles* (city watchmen) and reformed the Praetorian Guard with veterans from his own Danube legions (doubling it in size at the same time). He then held a state funeral for Pertinax, whom he deified. The unfortunate Julianus was then quickly put to death as the new emperor began his eighteen-year reign.

Severus' first priority as emperor was to deal with his remaining rivals, Niger in Syria and Albinus in Britain. The former had by this time already been proclaimed emperor, so ever the pragmatist Severus prioritised his eastern threat. He secured his western flank by proclaiming Albinus his Caesar (junior emperor), then headed east where he fought a year-long campaign against Niger, finally defeating him at the Battle of Issus in May AD 194, where he captured his opponent as he attempted to flee to Parthia to take refuge with its ruler Vologeses V. Niger was beheaded soon after, with Severus making himself even wealthier by personally confiscating Niger's estates and wealth. Having defeated his rival, ever the man of action, Severus turned his attention to the eastern frontier and the Parthians.

The pretext for his first campaign in the east actually came in the form of the Roman vassal states Osrhoene, Adiabene and Hatra, whose rulers used the distraction of Severus' campaign against Niger to massacre the Roman garrisons in key border fortresses, seize them and ultimately besiege Nisibis. They actually claimed allegiance to Severus (their targets had been the troops of Niger) but gave their game away by keeping the territory they had gained, clearly being encouraged to cause trouble by Parthia. Another factor behind the Roman motivation to intervene in Mesopotamia would have been the huge military force that Severus had at his disposal, with his own loyal troops together with those of the defeated Niger. Such an army needed suitable employment to avoid discontent, added to which the ambitious Severus would also have been keen to test himself against the reputation of the likes of Trajan.

War was duly declared and Severus led his first expedition into Mesopotamia, aiming to crack down on the recalcitrant vassal states but also with his eye on glory against Parthia. Unsurprisingly the campaign was successful given the size of force he deployed (a lesson not lost on him in his later campaigns including the *expeditio felicissima Britannica*). Once the siege of Nisibis had been broken, the vassal states were all brought to heel: Osrhoene surrendered straight away; Adiabene was captured; and Hatra conceded, although was not captured. However Severus' plans to use this platform to continue the campaign into Parthia proper were curtailed when news reached him of his next great challenge – the usurpation of Albinus in Britain. Severus therefore rapidly returned to the west with most of his veteran troops.

Herodian (2.15) is explicit that Severus' earlier appointment of Albinus to the rank of Caesar was a ruse to buy himself time, and it seems this was indeed the case. Albinus became increasingly suspicious of the emperor's intentions, especially as Severus had begun to officially favour his sons Caracalla and Geta in public in Rome. He later made Caracalla a joint Augustus in AD 198, while Geta was made a Caesar the same year and a full Augustus in AD 209 (Kean 2005, 115.)

In AD 196 matters with the British governor came to a head, because Albinus was beginning to mint his own coins on which he styled himself a full Augustus. He followed this up by proclaiming himself emperor, by surviving an assassination attempt by Severus (Herodian, 3.5) and by gathering troops from his three legions in Britain for the crossing to Gaul, facilitated by the *Classis Britannica*, a move the British regional fleet was later to regret. This was a sizeable force being carried across the English Channel, and by the time matters reached a climax a year later Albinus had the troops from his three British legions, a Spanish legion, 35,000 auxiliaries and up to 5,000 cavalry

(Moorhead and Stuttard 2012, 150). This large force was a serious symmetrical threat to Severus.

Albinus next defeated the legate Virius Lupus whom Severus had sent to stop his advance in Gaul. The usurper arrived in the south-east, where he set himself up at Lyon, which he declared his capital. Severus, knowing he needed to stamp out this threat quickly, decided to take matters into his own hands and quickly advanced on Albinus, a decisive engagement taking place at the Battle of Lugdunum in February AD 197. The clash, with altogether 150,000 men on the two sides (Birley 1999, 124), was very bloody and certainly a close-run thing. Severus was eventually victorious, with Albinus committing suicide rather than allow himself to be captured. The usurper's head was sent to Rome, displayed on a cross. The *Historia Augusta* (Sev., 11.8) describes the now unchallenged Severus riding over Albinus' body on his own horse – the aim being to ritually trample it. The fortunes of the usurper's troops from Britain who survived the battle aren't known, although given Severus' severe treatment of those who stood in his way their prospects would not have been good.

Some primary sources indicate that Albinus took only some troops from each of his legions, and even if that were the case it is clear (as discussed in Chapter 6) that the garrison in Britain was much depleted and would have taken some time to recover. Severus took a close personal interest in ensuring that this would happen in his name (he would have remembered Pertinax' troubles in Britain a decade earlier, let alone his own personal experiences with Albinus). To that end he set up his trusted supporter Virius Lupus (who had survived his defeat at the hands of Albinus) as the new governor of the province, then sent military commissioners to purge the remaining military leadership in the province of any supporters of Albinus.

These legates made a lasting impact on the Roman presence in Britain: for example, initiating the construction of the land walls of London, clearly aimed at putting the stamp of Severus on the Roman elites there rather than dealing with an external threat. Such a move was a key Severan tactic when reminding his potential opponents who was boss; another example was with his positioning of his arch in the Forum in Rome next to the Senate *Curia* (see p. 110). Furthermore he may also have targeted the regional navies in the west, as an inscription from this period in Rome was interpreted by Frere (1974, 172) as suggesting Severus amalgamated the *Classis Britannica, Classis Germanica, Classis Moesica* and *Classis Pannonica* into one command. Such an assertion is currently unproven, however.

While Britain was being scourged by his legates, Severus turned his attention back to the east – and Parthia – aiming to make his name as a great conquering emperor. Once back in Rome he travelled from Italy by sea, embarking at Brindisi (Roman Brundisium) and landed at Yumurtalık (Roman Aegeae) in Cilicia, from where he travelled to Syria. He immediately assaulted the Parthians.

The war, lasting from AD 197 to AD 198, proved a great success for him. The Parthian capital Ctesiphon was sacked by his legions and the northern half of Mesopotamia was annexed into the Empire – a punishment against the former vassal states for their earlier unsuccessful opportunistic land grab after he had defeated Niger. The only negative aspect of the campaign was his failure to capture the fortress of Hatra again, although he did expand the *limes Arabicus* border defence, in the process constructing new fortifications in the Arabian Desert ranging from Basie to Dumata.

Once the campaign was over, instead of heading back to Rome Severus decided to tour his eastern provinces, a process that was to last four more years. This may have been a deliberate nod to his predecessor Hadrian – Severus losing no opportunity to publicly measure himself against any of his illustrious forerunners. In terms of his route, he went through Egypt (where he viewed the body of Alexander the Great, the Pyramids and the recently repaired Sphinx) and almost certainly Cyrenaica.

Severus returned to Rome in summer AD 202, where he celebrated his *decennalia* with a victory games and oversaw the marriage of Caracalla with Fulvia Plautilla, daughter of Gaius Fulvius Plautianus, the praetorian prefect and fellow Lepcis Magnan. This was a person whom, the primary sources indicate, Severus had started to fall heavily under the influence of from AD 198 – the marriage being the ultimate culmination of this. Kean (2005, 112) says that by this time Plautianus was Severus' closest confidant.

Later in AD 202 Severus returned to Africa Proconsularis and his North African roots, visiting Lepcis Magna, Utica and Carthage. At Lepcis Magna he again displayed his largess by carrying out an energetic building programme. This included a new forum and *basilica*, colonnaded streets and a new harbour. Late in AD 202 he launched a campaign against the Garamantes, who were creating trouble along the *limes Tripolitanus*. The *legio* III *Augusta pia fidelis* under legate Quintus Anicius Faustus had been fighting an intensive, five-year campaign in the region to try to prevent raiding into rich Tripolitania, and steps were already underway to further fortify the border. Typically Severus took matters in hand upon his arrival and launched a campaign far to the south of the *limes*, capturing several significant oasis settlements including Cydamus, Gholaia, Garbia and the Garamantes capital of Garama – the last was more than 600 kilometres south of Lepcis Magna. After incorporating much of this captured territory into Africa Proconsularis (an inscription from AD 202 shows a Roman bathhouse being built at Gholaia), he then further refortified the border as part of his process of significantly investing imperial capital in his homeland. It seems clear from the level of commitment that Severus had brought significant reinforcements with him to join *legio* III *Augusta pia fidelis*, and in retrospect one can almost see this campaign as a dry run for the *expeditio felicissima Britannica*: an aggressive native opponent agitating across an imperial border, with the emperor arriving in person with excessive force to crush them.

The campaign over, Severus continued his travels to the west, spending time in the province of Numidia, which he enlarged through the annexation of the settlements of Vescera, Castellum Dimmidi, Gemellae, Thabudeos, Thubunae and Zabi. Thus, by the time he reluctantly returned to Rome the whole southern frontier of Roman North Africa had been significantly expanded, and then refortified.

Severus was never comfortable back in the imperial capital, and although this is not a biography of him I will briefly touch on his experiences there as this provides insight into why he may have been so keen to launch the *expeditio felicissima Britannica* once the opportunity presented itself.

His relationship with the Senate was never a positive one from the moment he seized power backed by military might, because he viewed them as more of a hindrance than a help and always made sure they were never presented with an easy opportunity to support a potential usurper. Any he suspected of treachery were efficiently executed on charges of conspiracy, ensuring their estates and fortunes joined his own. He then replaced them with his own (often North African) supporters. This was one of the most extreme forms of military dictatorship in the name of the Empire, but he showed none of the signs of megalomania or madness to which such power often led, always endeavouring to keep his feet on the ground and his grasp on reality sound. To that end he always ensured he was popular with the citizenry of Rome once the threat from Niger had been removed, especially after he began stamping out corruption, which had proliferated under Commodus. Whether Severus was as popular elsewhere in Empire (excepting of course in North Africa) is difficult to judge, especially after his institution of the Severan *annona* system.

Finally in this subsection we return to the imperial favourite Plautianus. In typical Roman imperial fashion, things didn't end well for him. Julia Domna and Caracalla (the latter unhappily married to say the least) disliked Plautianus' increasingly excessive power. Caracalla denounced Plautianus in AD 205 for plotting against the emperor and himself, and in the usual Severan fashion the praetorian prefect was rapidly executed.

The primary sources say that Severus' elder brother had similarly warned the emperor of the threat from Plautianus earlier in the year while on his deathbed (the only mention we have of Geta dying). After the execution, Caracalla divorced his wife, who was banished to the Lipari Islands (he had her executed soon after his own father died in AD 211), with her siblings being similarly banished across the Empire.

One other point worth mentioning here is that one of Plautianus' replacements was the famous jurist Aemilius Papinianus (a relative of Julia Domna), who would play a key role as adviser and fellow travelling companion on the *expeditio felicissima Britannica* (see Chapter 6).

The Severans in Rome

Once Severus and his family were installed in the imperial complex in Rome they not only settled in but began to shape the imperial capital in their own image. To that end a number of the key sites in the Forum and on the Palatine Hill were built or reconstructed to the form visible today, while after Severus' death his elder son put his own mark on the urban environment by completing the construction of the enormous Baths of Caracalla, whose design was originated by Severus (and which would have carried the latter's name had he lived, as he planned it to be his ultimate monumental building project).

The Severan Buildings in the southern corner of the Imperial Palace on the Palatine were constructed next to the stadium in the Imperial Palace (a rectangular arena with a viewing stand on one side for the imperial family). They featured huge, arched reception rooms with a platform running across the top, which was designed to give Severus, his family and entourage a fine view of the Circus Maximus below. Along the side of this new set of buildings Severus also constructed a nymphaeum called the Septizodium, which was set on top of a set of terraces cascading down towards the Circus Maximus (although still within the grounds of the Imperial Palace). Severus also rebuilt the palace baths such that they now ran below his new reception rooms and also under the original stadium.

Meanwhile in the Forum itself his wife Julia Domna is credited with rebuilding the Temple of Vesta into the shape visible today (after the fire in AD 191 had burnt down the previous iteration). This building played a key role in the life of the city of Rome, as it was here that the vestal virgins tended the sacred flame, which burnt perpetually to symbolise the city's life force, and the only man able to enter was Severus himself as the *Pontifex Maximus*. The structure built in Julia Domna's name was circular (the traditional shape for such a temple, based on the shape of the ancient huts of Latium) and featured a cylindrical cell decorated with half-columns – the whole surrounded by an external ring of Corinthian columns.

Severus also rebuilt the buildings along the Via Nova – one of the two pre-imperial routeways through the Forum (the other being the Via Sacra). The Via Nova separated the formal buildings in the Forum itself from the imperial structures atop the Palatine. Here, arches evident today spanning the road were erected in the Severan period to carry the upper storeys of shops and houses for those living there or practising commerce.

The most visible Severan structure in the Forum is the triumphal arch that carries his name, planted as outlined in the Introduction in the northwest corner outside the *Curia*, where the Senate met; it was clearly designed to remind them who was the boss. The new arch also encroached on the *Umbilicus Urbis Romae* or *Mundus*, a small monument said to mark the centre of the city of Rome and also believed to be an entrance to the underworld. Typically Severus decided that rather than accommodate the latter as he built his own arch he would rebuild it instead – its remains are the brick structure still visible today.

Monumentalisation writ large, the Arch of Septimius Severus was constructed of white marble, and was dedicated in AD 203 to specifically commemorate Severus' victories when campaigning against Parthia. Caracalla and Geta also originally shared the limelight on the arch, although see below with regard to the younger son.

The arch is twenty-three metres high, built on a raised travertine base, which was originally approached by steps from the Forum. The central archway was spanned by a beautifully coffered, semicircular vault with lateral openings on each side archway. The structure is twenty-five metres in width and almost twelve metres deep. Its three archways rest on piers, to the front of which are composite columns detached on pedestals. On its spandrels (the space between the tip of the arch and the column supports) are carved reliefs of winged victories, while a staircase in the south pier leads to the top, where originally there were statues of the emperor, Caracalla and Geta in a quadriga (four-horse chariot), together with soldiers. Of most interest to this work, however, are the depictions of the Roman military on campaign, as seen on the four relief panels – two on each side of the arch (and elsewhere). These have already been covered in depth in Chapter 2.

The arch has a detailed dedicatory inscription on both sides across the top, which reads:

> To the emperor Caesar Lucius Septimius Severus Pius Pertinax Augustus Parthicus Arabicus Parthicus Adiabenicus, son of Marcus, father of his country, pontifex maximus, in the eleventh year of his tribunician power, in the eleventh year of his rule, consul thrice, and proconsul, and to the emperor Caesar Marcus Aurelius Antoninus Augustus Pius Felix [this is Caracalla], son of Lucius, in the sixth year of his tribunician power, consul, and proconsul (fathers of their country, the best and bravest emperors), on account of the restored Republic and the rule of the Roman people spread by their outstanding virtues at home and abroad, the Senate and the People of Rome (sc. dedicate this monument).

A final noteworthy mention with regard to the arch concerns Geta. As we have seen above, by the time the arch was constructed Severus was ruling jointly as emperor with Caracalla, and he is clearly mentioned in the dedication. Within the latter there is also clearly a parenthesised section in the middle, this being text added to replace the original reference to Geta, chiselled out when Caracalla declared him *damnatio memoriae*. Hence his notable omission above.

Sticking with Severus' elder son, we can look at his baths, which still stand as a remarkable landmark to the Severan dynasty. The Baths of Caracalla, built between AD 212 and AD 217, were the second largest in Rome, and their planning was actually initiated by Severus himself. His idea was to make them one of the first sites in the city visitors saw as they approached along the Via Appia.

Constructing the baths was a huge undertaking, with around 13,000 prisoners of war allegedly being used to level the building site. Furthermore 6,000 artisans and tradesmen were employed every day for the actual construction work, which utilised more than 21 million bricks and tiles. The whole complex was richly decorated in mosaics and fine marble, with some six hundred skilled workers required for the marble work alone, this using 6,300 cubic metres of the fine building stone.

The bathing complex consisted of the huge bathhouse itself and a surrounding park, the latter created by the later Severan emperors Heliogabalus and Severus Alexander. The enormous quantities of water needed were supplied by a new branch of the Aqua Marcia aqueduct, named the Aqua Antoniniana after Caracalla's actual name.

Everything about the baths was monumental. The central building of the bathing complex itself measured 214 metres by 114 metres, and consisted of four levels: two of them above ground and two below. The entrance halls (called the *basilicae thermarum*) in particular were designed to impress. They measured some fifty metres by twenty metres and were in the north-west and south-east corners – the bathhouse being symmetrically built along a north-east to south-west axis. It is estimated that 1,600 people could use the complex at the same time; thus it was the ultimate testament to Severan grandiosity in the Roman built environment.

Having considered Severus' rise to power, his arrival in Rome and his impact on the imperial capital, we can now turn to the *expeditio felicissima Britannica* and his arrival in Britain.

PLATE 1 *The Arch of Septimius Severus, Forum, Rome*

PLATE 2 *Imperial monumentalisation: The Arch of Septimius Severus in the distance, seen through the Arch of Titus*

PLATE 3 *The Arch of Septimius Severus, planted almost atop the Curia Senate House, Forum, Rome. Perhaps Severus was saying to the Senators: 'Behave or else!'*

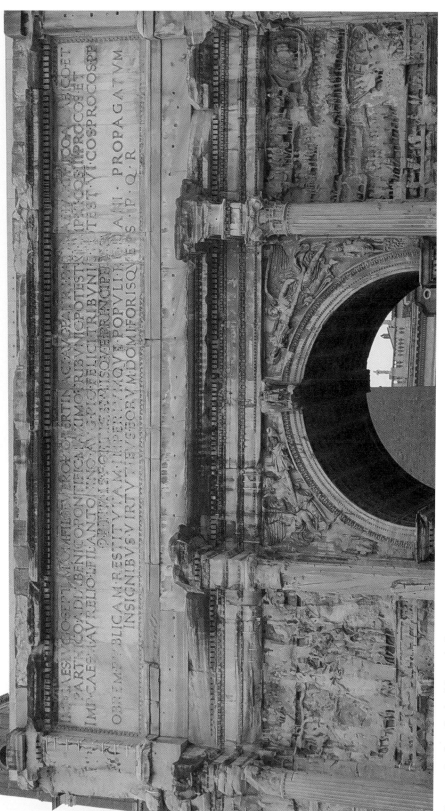

PLATE 4 *Southern façade of the Arch of Septimius Severus, Forum, Rome*

PLATE 5 *Parthian captives on the Arch of Septimius Severus in the Forum, Rome. The sculptures behind are possibly of Caracalla and Geta, although the latter's face was removed in an act of* damnatio memoriae

PLATE 6 *Detail on the Arch of Septimius Severus showing legionaries or* auxilia *in* lorica hamata *chain mail – evidence of changing military technology in the case of the former*

PLATE 7 *Later Roman round body shields on the Arch of Constantine, Rome*

PLATE 8 *Relief from the north facade of the Arch of Septimius Severus, Forum, Rome, showing troops with late Roman body shields – military technology in transition*

PLATE 9 *Logistics is always a key part of military campaigning. Here, wagons carry the supplies for the Severan campaigns against Parthia, as depicted on the Arch of Septimius Severus, Forum, Rome*

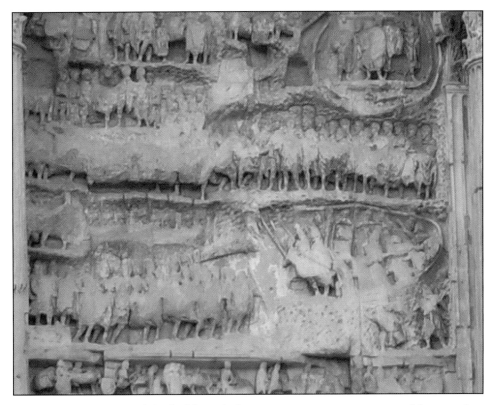

PLATE 10 *Relief from the south facade of the Arch of Septimius Severus, Forum, Rome, with lower panel showing Roman legionaries with full body shields facing Parthian cataphracts*

PLATE 11 *Maritime transport was always the preferred means of transporting heavy goods in the premodern world, hence Severus' use of Brough-on-Humber, South Shields, Cramond and Carpow to support his northern expeditions. This mosaic relief is of a grain supply ship from Ostia Antica*

PLATE 12 *Dacian captive held by a Roman,*
possibly Caracalla, on the Arch of Septimius
Severus, Forum, Rome

PLATE 13 *Legionary, possibly a praetorian, in*
lorica segmentata, *on the Arch of Septimius*
Severus, Forum, Rome

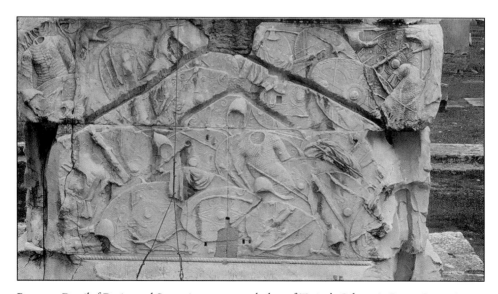

PLATE 14 *Detail of Dacian and Sarmation armour on the base of Trajan's Column in Rome. Sarmation*
armour had certainly influenced cavalry equipment by the time of Severus

PLATE 15 *Panel showing tribute being paid to the emperor, while the guards stand in lorica segmentata, on the Arch of Septimius Severus, Forum, Rome*

PLATE 16 *Roman building stone from the fort, supply base and military harbour at Carpow on the river Tay, providing evidence that at least parts of the structure were stone built. Reused in local wall*

PLATE 17 *Site of the fort, supply base and military harbour at Carpow on the river Tay, as it is today*

PLATE 18 *Barrack block at the fort, supply base and military harbour at Cramond on the Firth of Forth – a key location during the Severan campaigns in Scotland*

PLATE 19 *Enigmatic view of the Highlands from the Gask Ridge, at Muir O'Fauld, Perthshire, where Roman signal stations/watchtowers kept a lookout for trouble at this far northern outpost of the Roman Empire*

PLATE 20 *Site of the Roman Antonine fort at Newstead, Scottish Borders. The huge Severan marching camp was spread across the hillside in the distance*

PLATE 21 *Unusual sequence of five defensive ditches at the Roman fort site at Ardoch, Perthshire. The Severan marching camp was near here*

PLATE 22 *Dere Street, Newstead, Scottish Borders. Agricolan and Antonine Fort to the right, Severan marching camp to the left*

PLATE 23 *Dere Street crossing of the river Esk – the next stop for Severus was Camelon. This medieval structure was built on Roman foundations*

PLATE 24 *Remains of the Temple of Vesta, Forum, Rome, rebuilt by Julia Domna*

PLATE 25 *View of the Circus Maximus as it would have been seen from the viewing platform atop the Severan Buildings in the Imperial Palace on the Palatine Hill, Rome*

PLATE 26 *Reception rooms in the Severan Buildings in the Imperial Palace on the Palatine Hill, Rome. To the right ran the Septizodium*

PLATE 27 *The Baths of Caracalla, seen from the Palatine Hill, Rome. Planning and construction began under Severus*

PLATE 28 *Stone column outside York Minister, originally from the Severan* basilica *of the* principia *in the legionary fortress, York*

PLATE 29 *Multangular Tower, later than the Severan period, and wall of the legionary fortress, York*

CHAPTER 6

Septimius Severus in Britain: Arrival

THIS CHAPTER SETS THE SCENE on the Severan 'shock and awe' campaigns of AD 209 and AD 210 north of Hadrian's Wall as Rome, one last time with this amount of effort, attempted to conquer the far north of the British Isles. It starts with an outline of the region to provide context, and then returns to the narrative story with Severus in Rome, the old warrior about the embark on his last campaigns.

The Region

My review starts with Roman York, the town that became Severus' imperial capital for the last three years of his life and which was the launch pad for his grand incursions into the far north. It then moves north up Dere Street to consider Roman northern Yorkshire, County Durham, Tyne and Wear and Northumberland (noting Severus' campaigning was principally along the east coast), before finally casting a spotlight on that dimmest of Roman border territories and the scene of his final campaigns – Scotland.

Roman York

York was one of the great towns of Roman Britain. Although not as large as London or even some of the bigger *civitas* capitals across the province, it featured its third longest permanent bridge (after that in London and the river Medway crossing at Rochester; Brooks 1994, 4) and was increasingly important as the Roman occupation progressed. Given its importance to the story of Severus and his Scottish campaigns I go into some detail about it here to provide background for what follows.

The town's Roman name of Eboracum is thought to mean 'place of the yews' (Avery 2007). In occupied Britain it was particularly important in a military context (it always anchored the extensive military presence in the north), and also politically. In the latter context, it actually served as the imperial capital during the northern British campaigns of Severus from his arrival in Britain in AD 208 through to his death in AD 211. Shortly after this time, based on Birley's interpretation (2005, 336), York then became an official provincial capital in its own right under Caracalla, when the original province of Britannia was split into two. Thus was created Britannia Superior and Britannia Inferior: the former in the south with London as its capital; and the latter in the north centred on its new capital York.

Later, when towards the end of the third century Britain was declared a diocese as part of the Diocletianic Reformation with now four provinces – Maxima Caesariensis, Britannia Prima, Flavia Caesariensis and Britannia Secunda (White 2007, 37; Jones and Mattingly 1990, 148) – York became the capital for the last. A further province within the diocese called Valentia is later mentioned and is often associated with the north. Some have argued that it saw the division of Britannia Secunda into two along a north–south axis, with York becoming the capital of the new province (although its existence at all – let alone the association with York as its capital – remains problematic). York's political importance in later occupied Britain also developed into it being a centre of religious significance. This was in the context of the growth in popularity of Christianity, such that by the time of the Council of Arles in AD 314 one of the three bishops from Britain present was that representing the Bishopric of York (alongside his counterparts from London and Lincoln) (Mattingly 2006, 348).

York originally owed its existence to the Roman conquest campaigns following the AD 43 invasion, and specifically to Cerialis, one of three great warrior governors – the other two being his governor successors Frontinus and of course Agricola. By the end of the first century AD they had carved out the territory of the province in a form that would be recognisable for much of the rest of the occupation. It had a northern border broadly along the Solway–Tyne Line later to be fortified as Hadrian's Wall.

In AD 71 Cerialis, famous among his contemporaries for the recent putting down of the Batavian Revolt of Julius Civilis in the Rhine delta, was transported across the North Sea to Britain to take up his post as the new governor. Carried on his journey by the newly named *Classis Britannica*, he also bought with him a new legion, the *legio II Adiutrix*. Clearly plans were afoot for renewed campaigning as the territory of the province continued to expand north and west (Elliott 2016a, 126). Cerialis' target was the north, and specifically the Brigantes ('High Ones' or 'Hill Dwellers'), the confederacy of tribes residing in what is now Yorkshire (excepting part of the east coast, the territory of the Parisi), Lancashire, Cumbria, Northumberland and (possibly) south-western Scotland.

This confederation wielded considerable power, its pre-Roman tribal capital being located at Stanwick in north Yorkshire – the site being an enormous hill fort, which enclosed almost 300 hectares, the whole surrounded by nine kilometres of ditches and ramparts (Moorhead and Stuttard 2012, 93). In the period following the Claudian invasion of AD 43 the Brigantes had been Roman allies under their long-standing Queen Cartimandua. Her loyalty had been specifically proven in AD 51, when she had handed over the fugitive native British resistance leader Caratacus after he had fled to the Brigantes following defeat in Wales. This caused a breach with her husband, Venutius, whom she then divorced, and led to a conflict that was to see Rome intervening to save her about AD 57.

Brigantian issues had then been stabilised until the 'Year of the Four Emperors' in AD 69, Venutius using the turbulence back in Rome to revolt again. He was successful this time, deposing the ageing Cartimandua, who once again asked Rome for help (Tacitus, 3.45). This was provided by the governor Marcus Vettius Bolanus, who headed north and was initially successful in fighting the northern confederation. The poet Statius (*Silvae*, 5.2, 53–56) details him campaigning in the 'Caledonian Plains' at this time, indicating that Bolanus had penetrated as far as the Scottish lowlands. Despite this success, however, for some reason matters were not resolved to Rome's satisfaction as the new emperor Vespasian (the ultimate winner in the 'Year of Four Emperors') recalled the governor to Rome in AD 71 – hence the arrival of Cerialis, who (especially after the defeat of Civilis) was one of the emperor's favourites, and a kinsman to boot.

Cerialis was already familiar with Britain, although in a fairly infamous way as, while the legate of the *legio* IX *Hispana*, he had tried to save Colchester during the Boudiccan Revolt. His (admittedly small) army had arrived far too late, and had been decisively defeated by the main British force after which he had fled with his cavalry. This force then remained incongruously besieged in a nearby fort until the governor Gaius Suetonius Paulinus had put down the insurrection. However Cerialis' success in backing the new emperor in his bid for power, and defeating the Batavian revolt, had renewed his reputation by the beginning of the AD 70s – hence his arrival in Britain to take up his governorship.

Equally of note is the new legion which arrived with Cerialis. This was because the *legio* II *Adiutrix* had been created in AD 70 by Vespasian from the marines of the *Classis Ravennas* Ravenna-based regional fleet to fight on his side in the civil war. They were therefore, just like Cerialis, totally faithful to the Flavians, and their deployment to Britain illustrates the importance to the new emperor of the province where he himself had made his name conquering the south-west as legate of the *legio* II *Augusta* after the Claudian invasion.

Tacitus (Agricola, 17) says that Cerialis immediately headed north upon his arrival, to set about the Brigantes, showing that while the campaigns of his predecessor had seen some success matters were far from concluded. In the first instance he ordered the veteran *legio* IX *Hispana* out of its legionary fortress at Lincoln into Yorkshire, where the troops constructed a new fortress (see definitions of fortress size on p. 21) on the northern bank at the point where they crossed the river Ouse. (They had no doubt noted the importance of the regional rivers for lines of supply – the Ouse flowing into the Humber estuary and thence the east coast of occupied Britain and the North Sea.) This was a particularly defensible position as the specific spot chosen was where the tributary river Foss runs into the Ouse, thus providing riverine protection on two flanks. It was here that the legionary *agrimensor* (land surveyors), *librator* (land levellers) and *mensor* (quantity measurers) (Garrison 1998, 75) would have laid out the plan of the new fortress, using their *decempeda* (ten Roman feet graduated measuring rods), *groma* (sighting tools), *chorobates* (spirit levels), *dioptra* (circular measuring tables), *libra* (measuring scales) and *hodometer* (distance measurers). It was this site that would later become York, with an associated *canabae* (a civilian settlement related to a legionary fortress) developing opposite on the south bank of the river. The fact that the *legio* II *Adiutrix* immediately moved into the vacated fortress at Lincoln clearly indicates that the famous ninth legion would not be returning there, and in fact the fortress in York became its permanent base until the early second century.

The original fortress on the site was classically playing-card shaped and very large, enclosing an area of more than twenty hectares and able to host the 5,000 or so men of the legion. Its original defences were a ditch and three-metre-high turf/clay rampart topped by a palisade, with wood-built towers and gates. From around AD 150 (Avery 2007, 7), the whole was replaced by a stone-built structure with a tile bonding layer (common across the Empire and visible as far afield as the fortifications in London, Richborough, Rome and Constantinople). As the occupation progressed the defences increased in sophistication, ultimately featuring a string of defensive towers or bastions such as the Multangular Tower visible today next to the modern Yorkshire Museum in what would have been the west corner of the fortress (its upper section partly rebuilt during the medieval period but still representing in shape the Roman original).

As with other Roman legionary fortresses, that at York existed to provide accommodation for the men and equipment of its legion, in this case initially the *legio* IX *Hispana*. The fortresses's uses were principally to:

- protect the legion if its base was attacked (in fact acting to discourage such an eventuality given the asymmetrical nature of the opposition faced by the forces of Rome for much of the occupation);
- act as a base for the legion (and other military units) to initially suppress and conquer its enemies (the Brigantes at the time York was founded), and later to project power northwards towards Scotland as the occupation progressed (and later along the east coast as that came under threat from Germanic raiding from the mid-third century AD).

Inside the fortress, in all its iterations, was a grid pattern of streets and buildings, which always performed the same function in any similar structure across the Empire. The four corners were positioned at the points of the compass, facing north, south, east and west, hence the playing-card shape. The principal streets within the fortress were called the *via principalis* (main street) and the *via praetoria*. These confuse visitors to the York of today as their line is misaligned with York Minster, which was built atop the remains of the fortress but runs east to west. One of these two roads ran down what is now Stonegate, crossing the bridge and then travelling onto the *canabae*. Meanwhile the four *portae* (gates) to the fortress gave access to the main roads and still correlate with modern entrances to the city. One of the gates gave access from Ermine Street (the great northern road linking London with York), while another gave access to Dere Street (the road north into Scotland).

At the centre of the fortress, dividing the *via praetoria* and with the *via principalis* passing across its front, was the parade ground featuring the *principia* (headquarters building), which housed the senior base commander and his staff. On one side of this parade ground, which was seventy-eight metres wide and perpendicular to the *principia* itself, stood an associated *basilica*. The scale of the latter – certainly from the time of Severus' arrival when other built infrastructure across the region was vastly increased in area – was immense given the size of the single column recovered in 1969 during excavations of the structure. In fact at sixty-eight metres long, thirty-two metres wide and twenty-three metres in height, this *basilica* would have stood just short of the modern height of today's York Minister.

Such a size for the rebuilt *basilica* (the *principia* itself would similarly have been restyled at the same time) would certainly reflect the use of the legionary fortress and its by then extensive *canabae* as an imperial capital while Severus prepared for his assault on the north. From the *tribunal* (podium) at one end of the *basilica* the commanding officer (and indeed later Severus) would have addressed his troops and received visiting dignitaries.

In the *principia* a row of rooms would have been used as offices, with the central one being the *aedes*, which served as the legionary shrine and was the spiritual heart of the fortress (it was here where the legionary standards were kept; see Chapter 2 for discussion on their importance). The *aedes* also had a more practical function in that beneath its floor sat a vault in which was kept the legionary pay chest.

There is no doubt that, even before any Severan expansion, the *principia* with its grand *basilica* at the legionary fortress in York would have been astonishing to the people of the area, a true statement of the power of Rome in the furthest, dark north-west of the Empire. From the time of Severus it would have been even grander. The remains of the *principia* are evident in the undercroft of York Minister, where they are well presented on permanent display, while the recovered column from the *basilica* is visible today to the immediate south of York Minister next to the modern statue of the later emperor Constantine.

Other buildings in close proximity to the *principa* included the *praetorium* (commanding officer's house), which was built in the same manner as a fine town house, this being used by him for business as well as domestic purposes. Illustrating its close proximity to the *principia*, the south-west corner of the *praetorium* at York is thought to be part of the structural remains exposed beneath the Minster (and possibly being the place of origin for the wall paintings on display today).

Also around the central parade ground (and again next to the *principia* to provide ease of access) was the building that housed the legionary supply officer, a character whose role would have dramatically increased in importance as Severus geared up for his advance into Scotland. One can perhaps envision him and those attached to his office by the emperor planning the expansion of the legionary supply bases to support the incursion, working out how to expand the facilities at Corbridge, South Shields, Cramond and Carpow. This individual would have probably been an imperial appointment, replacing the original once Severus had arrived – as we know happened at Corbridge (see below). Meanwhile, opposite this structure across the parade ground was a forum in the York legionary fortress, which was a small duplicate of a classic urban forum acting as a place of business and market for the troops and their suppliers.

The rest of the fortress interior was packed with a wide variety of buildings and structures, some stone built and some wooden, set out in a regular pattern such that any incumbent in the fortress would know as a matter of fact where every amenity was. Such buildings included a large number of barracks to house the troops, granaries to feed them, workshops to manufacture and maintain all their equipment, a hospital and a bathhouse. The last was a very important feature of the Roman cultural experience and served to remind many of the troops of their Mediterranean roots, at least early in the occupation. One can imagine how popular the bathhouse, with its piping-hot steam rooms, would have been in the heart of a northern British winter. The actual legionary bathhouse building itself was located in the southern corner of the fortress during excavations in 1972. These also uncovered an associated Roman sewer, which helped to identify that it occupied an area of 9,100 square metres.

One final comment regarding the legionary fortress here references the unit that garrisoned it. As we have seen, the founding legion was the veteran *legio* IX *Hispana*, which remained here until the early second century. We have direct evidence of those who served in its ranks: for example, through the epigraphy on their tombstones. One such is the standard bearer Lucius Duccius Rufinus, originally from Gaul, whose monumentalised tombstone stands proudly on show today in the Yorkshire Museum. By the time Emperor Hadrian visited York, however, in AD 122 as part of his tour designed to stabilise the troublesome northern border, this legion had left – a last reference to it indicating that it then spent some time in the military camp at Nijmegen in the modern Netherlands. After that it disappears from history, leaving many to speculate as to its fate (although most likely it was simply transferred to another border area of the Empire).

Its replacement was equally famous, the *legio* VI *Victrix*, a military formation with a remarkable fighting history including surviving the siege of Alexandria when under the command of Julius Caesar while protecting the famous Cleopatra. This legion certainly made its roots in York – it remained in place until the end of the Roman occupation. It fought in many campaigns in the north and was certainly gathered by Severus as part of his huge force when he invaded Scotland. Later, and even more famously, it was the soldiers of the *legio* VI *Victrix* who proclaimed Constantine as emperor in AD 306 – an event that continues to resonate to this day given his later championing of Christianity.

The legionary fortress, with fine *principia* and associated *basilica* (the whole designed to emphasise the 'separateness of the garrison'; Gerrard 2013, 128), was of course not the only manifestations of the built environment in Roman York. Just across the river Ouse, directly connected to the legionary fortress by a bridge and the *via praetoria*, was the *canabae*. In it resided all of those who, in a huge variety of ways, supported the military presence of the Roman legionaries there. These civilian residents of Roman York ranged from: the families of the troops across the river (official and otherwise); merchants of all types; those operating the sophisticated transport infrastructure (using not only the road network but also more importantly the region's river systems); those participating in the wide variety of industrial activities not already located within the fortress; and any manifestations the reader can think of for the purveying of entertainment of all types for troops. Later, the population would have been boosted by the local agricultural magnates who provided the grain and other produce to feed the troops and local population. This substantial *canabae* was later to expand in stature to a full-scale *colonia* (probably achieving this status under Caracalla), with the civilian settlement being used to house and settle retired Roman military personnel.

The civilian settlement became a thriving part of Roman York in its own right, ultimately with its own high-quality wall circuit featuring towers, bastions and fortified gateways as sophisticated as those of the legionary fortress. In recent years archaeological excavations, often linked to building work in the area, have uncovered a wealth of data that shows the *canabae* and later *colonia* to have been a bustling, thriving residential and commercial centre. It featured houses of various sizes and levels of prosperity, ranging from roundhouses and small, timber-framed buildings at the lower end of the social scale to large, stone-built, fine-quality town houses with painted wall plaster and elaborate mosaics at the top (the latter perhaps the homes of the agricultural magnates detailed above).

One such grand house at Clementhorpe to the immediate south-east of the *canabae* defensive wall had a room including an polygonal apse that was 71.5 square metres in size, making it the third largest room in a house in Roman Yorkshire (Ottaway 2013, 248). There were also industrial sites and craft workshops (with metalworking and leather manufacturing being particularly evident), civilian bathhouses, a marketplace, shops and even an arena. Meanwhile temples and cemeteries catered for the religious needs of the local population. The temples featured numerous deities that reflected the cosmopolitan nature of Roman society, including one temple dedicated to Isis and another to Mithras, both religions with their roots in the east (Avery 2007, 3). A large number of the finds unearthed during the excavations are now on display in the Yorkshire Museum, while grand sarcophagi from elite burials can be found scattered in the museum garden and behind the Multangular Tower. One of the grave *stelai* is that of Julia Velva, an upper-class lady who died in her fifties. Her fine tombstone is today one of the main attractions in the Yorkshire Museum and shows her living a life of luxury, dining in the grand manner reclining on a couch.

Two further specific examples of funerary practice in Roman York are worthy of note. One is the discovery by York Archaeological Trust (YAT) in 2005 at Driffield Terrace, Holgate of eighty skeletons, thirty of which had been decapitated. Many of these had suffered severe, healed battle injuries, leading to speculation that this was a gladiators' cemetery. The other, at a more mundane level, has been recently detailed by Savine (2017, 46): it is another YAT excavation but this time of a second–fourth century AD, low-status cemetery 300 metres away from the gladiators' cemetery. It featured seventy-five burials where wooden coffins had evidently been used, but no headstones, leading to speculation that it was managed by a community burial club. This was a means where the less well-off in Roman society could pay a regular, small amount into a cooperative fund to ensure that their loved ones were given a fitting burial rather than being laid to rest in an anonymous massed grave.

One interesting point is made by Ottaway in his broad appreciation of Roman Yorkshire, which highlighted that Roman York (and particularly the civilian settlement) does not appear to have been embellished with many grand public buildings in the same way as other provincial capitals: for example, Arles in southern France or Trier in Germany (Ottaway 2013, 247). This is even more surprising given the town's elevation to imperial capital during the Severan visit and campaigns in Scotland, and may reflect its bipolar nature with the very physical distinction between the legionary fortress and the *canabae*. Another factor may have been the military presence itself, because much of the regional economy was always bent towards its exponentially large needs, given the sizeable army presence in the north. In that regard it seems probable that there would have been an ongoing lack of public funds for non-essential capital expenditure projects.

Like much of the rest of the province, York was subject to the vagaries of the political and economic health of the rest of the Empire and equally suffered during periods of decline. This was especially so later in the fourth century AD, when the Western Empire began its terminal decline culminating in its disappearance as a political entity after AD 476. By the early fifth century repeated withdrawals of field army troops from Britain to fight civil wars on the Continent would have had a significant impact on York, given the military nature of the settlement (this despite its later political importance). Avery (2007, 8) paints a particularly grim picture of the end of the Roman town: 'With the withdrawal of the troops and their families, York became a shadow of its former self. Roads became disused, rubbish piled up in the streets, houses fell into decay and the bridge across the river collapsed.'

After the end of the Roman town its walls did remain, however, together with some of the longer-distance road network. Although the town seems to have been abandoned until about AD 600, the roads were to remain a magnet for those who would subsequently occupy the site – initially the Angles (later styled Anglo-Saxons) but later, and much more famously, the Vikings, who as we know called their town Yorvik.

Travelling North

As Severus and his enormous force headed north from York they would have travelled principally along Dere Street, with the east coast being used as a major logistics supply route.

Dere Street (sometimes called Deere Street) is the modern name for the major Roman trunk road that ran to the far north of the province from York. It crossed the Stanegate east–west road, which runs behind Hadrian's Wall

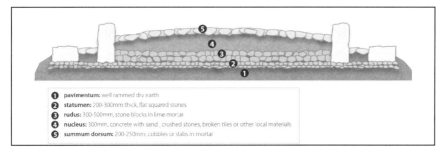

pavimentum: well rammed dry earth
statumen: 200-300mm thick, flat squared stones
rudus: 300-500mm, stone blocks in lime mortar
nucleus: 300mm, concrete with sand , crushed stones, broken tiles or other local materials
summum dorsum: 200-250mm, cobbles or slabs in mortar

Cross-section of a Roman trunk road as built by the Roman military across the Empire, including Dere Street [drawn by Paul Baker]

(which the road predates) at Corbridge, and crossed the wall itself at Portgate immediately to the north. Dere Street then continued into the Scottish Borders and headed further north to the line of the Antonine Wall on the Clyde–Forth Line. It then very likely continued even further north, perhaps to the river Tay, although its route in that regard has been lost to us. It is possible still to trace much of the route south of the border, given that it is still followed by some major modern trunk roads: for example, the A1 to the south of the river Tees; and the A68 as it heads to the north of Corbridge.

The road seems to owe its name to the Anglo-Saxon Kingdom of Deira, which lasted from AD 559 to AD 664 and covered an area ranging from the Humber to the river Tees, and westwards to the Vale of York. The kingdom itself possibly derived its name from the river Derwent. Dere Street corresponds roughly with the first British route identified in the Antonine Itinerary. Intriguingly the Antonine Itinerary actually shows Dere Street heading slightly further south than York, thirteen Roman miles (nineteen kilometres) on to a place called Delgovicia (today unknown), and then a further thirty-six kilometres to a 'Praetorium' (again unknown). As we have seen above, this is the name given to the house of the commander in a Roman fortress, so perhaps this last reference is an intriguing indicator as to the location of a base used by the Roman field army in the north later during the occupation.

The first place of note along Dere Street on the Severan journey north from York is Aldborough (Roman Isurium Brigantum) in north Yorkshire, the *civitas* capital (see Introduction for detail of Roman town types) of the former territory of the Brigantes. The site also featured a fort, one of many scattered across the region dating to the time of Cerialis' campaigns against the Brigantes. This fort guarded the point where Dere Street crossed the river Ure.

The town itself was later walled, to which were added six projecting bastions as the occupation progressed – testament to the ever-present threat from the north (Ottaway 2013, 249).

Heading further north along Dere Street one next reaches Catterick (Roman Cataractonium), again in north Yorkshire, site of the Roman fort guarding the road's crossing of the river Swale (the site also featuring an associated *vicus*). Mattingly (2006, 147) says that this base became the long-term transit camp for those heading to the northern frontier and beyond. Continuing north the next site reached is at Piercebridge, where a Roman presence existed at this Dere Street crossing of the river Tees from AD 70. Continuing onwards, Binchester (Roman Vinovia) in County Durham is the next site, to the immediate north of Bishop Auckland. This was the location of yet another fort (the largest in the county), this time guarding the Dere Street river crossing of the river Wear, and again featuring an extensive *vicus*. Moving on, one next reaches Ebchester (Roman Vindomora) in County Durham, an auxiliary fort protecting the Dere Street crossing of the river Derwent. Finally, just short of Hadrian's Wall, we come to Corbridge in Northumberland at the Dere Street/Stanegate crossing. Corbridge was arguably the most northerly town in the Roman Empire. The site of the Roman settlement was originally a fort established about AD 85, which by the middle of the second century AD had been replaced by a town featuring two walled military compounds.

Before heading north into the Borders, it is important to consider the impact of the *expeditio felicissima Britannica* on the region either side of Hadrian's Wall itself. This was in the form of one of the most striking manifestations of change related to the campaign and is found at the famous fort site at Vindolanda, west of Dere Street. At some stage between AD 208 and AD 211, the Antonine fort structure there was demolished and a new fortlet built to the immediate west at a location previously utilised for extramural occupation. The Antonine fort platform was then reused to build some 250 circular huts laid out back to back in rows of ten, with roads and drains between. The purpose of this dramatic change is unknown to us today, but one might reasonably speculate that the huts were used to house native workers employed in the repair of the wall, or perhaps to provide shelter for any local native population displaced as Severus and his enormous army headed north in Scotland.

Two other occupation-period regional settlements are worth mentioning. One is Brough-on-Humber to the south-east of York on the northern bank of the Humber. Called Petuaria during the occupation, the site was originally a fort founded in AD 70, which was abandoned about AD 125. Its *vicus*, however, developed into a substantial town, later walled, which survived the decline of the fort and is often associated with being the *civitas* capital of the native Parisi tribe. This town featured a substantial port and ferry-crossing – the latter providing a swift link between Lincoln (Roman Lindum Colonia) and York. It would have played a key logistics role during the Severan campaigns as a staging post from the south of the province and the near Continent as the emperor's huge military force gathered around York and then headed north.

The other site of note is South Shields on the south side of the mouth of the river Tyne. It had a vexillation fort and later was massively enlarged by Severus to serve as one of his key logistics bases (see Chapter 2).

Settlement and the Economy in the North

As detailed in Chapter 3, the province of Britannia was very bipolar in nature – those living south and east of a line running from the Severn to the Humber participating in a fully functioning part of the Roman Empire, while with those to the north and west lived in a military border zone. In that regard settlement and the economy in this latter zone was always dominated by the military presence, and exponentially so during times of campaigning north of the border, with the Severan experience being an extreme example. Mattingly (2006, 149) is very specific in this regard:

> A considerable portion of northern England remained under direct military supervision long after the civitas centre of the Brigantes was established at Aldborough. The scale of the garrison was also remarkably static between the first and third centuries: a legionary fortress and over fifty smaller forts spread across the region. The impact of such a large and prolonged garrison on the Brigantes must have been colossal.

Another factor impacting settlement and the economy of the region was the frequent military incursions it suffered, initially from the north over the border and later in the occupation from Ireland down the west coast and from the near Continent north of the *limes Germanicus* down the east. Therefore the landscape that Severus, his entourage and army would have travelled through as it headed north had a particularly unusual militaristic feel to it within the wider province; indeed one might note that the main stops from York through to the border were all fortified in some way, for example. In short, things were grimmer in terms of life experiences for those living in this region than they were to the south.

Ottaway (2013, 181) says that, although there was some redistribution of the native population following the conquest of the Brigantes, the vast majority of the population here seemed to have stayed in their native settlements. The agricultural landscape here at the time was defined by ditch enclosures, with the roundhouse continuing to be the main type of dwelling throughout the occupation. Villa estates did exist, but in diminished numbers compared to the south, with Mattingly (2006, 419) saying that those that are evident are located either in the Vale of York or north of the Humber, with a few also to be found in the broad valleys on the Wolds or on moorland areas. Meanwhile in terms of commerce the regional market centres such as York, Brough-on-Humber and Aldborough were the principal vectors for the flow of capital to the provincial economy (although, given the military presence, the imperial economy here would have been even more dominant than elsewhere in the province).

Agriculture, as elsewhere in the Roman Empire, was the dominant factor in the regional economy, arable production improving as the occupation progressed through the introduction of new technology such as the grain drying kiln – a fine example of which has been found at Crambe near Malton, featuring a limestone flue lining. There was also a new type of plough that featured a coulter – a vertically mounted component that cut an edge ahead of the plough blade itself. In terms of fauna, cattle remained the predominant meat type in evidence, ahead of sheep and pigs.

While less important to the regional economy than agriculture, industry had an important presence here too. One such was pottery manufacturing, where by the middle of the second century AD a transition had taken place from the handmade pottery of the LIA to mass-produced wheel-made vessels of a Roman type (Ottaway 2013, 200), with the military being a major source of demand. Meanwhile metalworking was also an important factor in the economy, especially (and once again) in the context of supplying and maintaining the military presence. This was of course present in a bespoke military context: for example, in the form of the small *fabricae* (industrial workshop) at Corbridge. Here archaeological data including arrowheads, iron scales and iron slag has been found alongside hearths and tempering tanks, resulting in one of the buildings within the Agricolan-period fort being interpreted as a small military manufactory. Outside such direct military control, but still driven by military demand, one also sees in the region civilian industrial metalworking in York (in the *cabana*), Brough-on-Humber and Catterick.

Other goods manufactured in the region included glass (again in York), ceramic building materials, leatherwork and local jewellery. The industrial component of the regional economy was completed by a millstone grit quern manufacturing industry, lead mining, iron manufacturing in east Yorkshire and a quarrying industry that supplied the building stone to urbanise and later fortify the region. The last is interesting in the wider context of the building of grand public buildings in occupied Britain as (even in York with its surprising lack of such structures in any quantity) they are a key feature of the expression by local elites of *Romanitas*. Their fizzling out from the time of the 'Crisis of the Third Century' across the province is often used to illustrate a watershed in the fortunes of Rome. In that regard Pearson (2006, 30) argues that the reuse of materials rather than building with newly quarried stone after this time is a manifestation of the ending of the era of major public building in towns in Britain, excepting some limited activity in Carausian/Allectan London and (surprisingly given their general lack here) in York, where at least one large public building was built in the later third century. This is perhaps indicative of the rise of the new, post-Severan provincial capital whose fortunes waxed while those of other large towns waned.

The Borders and Scotland

Travelling north through the Portgate across Hadrian's Wall, Severus would have exited the Empire and entered a border territory under tight Roman control with outpost forts to the north: for example, at Risingham and High Rochester in Northumberland along Dere Street. Birley (2007, 355) argues that there was no such clear division, with the border actually being more opaque given the military presence to the north of the wall, but for the purposes of this narrative it does provide a defined starting point for the campaign. To the far north of these outposts north of the wall lay a Conradian heart of darkness, as the geographical territory of northern Scotland would have been thought at the time.

Never fully conquered by the world of Rome, frequent military incursions into Scotland (some on a grand scale such as that by Agricola in the late first century AD) must have left a Roman cultural footprint of some kind above the border zone. Indeed it was the presence of Rome south of this that was to osmose the wealth and power northwards that eventually led to a coalescence of power around those favoured by Rome. It was in this context that larger and larger political units began to appear in the far north, which, by the time of the Severan incursions, included his targets the Maeatae and Caledonian confederations (see below for detail). Later, this process of a transference of gifted wealth and power led to the appearance of the Pictish confederation by the late third century AD and the true beginnings of Scottish history as we know it.

Why Rome never conquered Scotland is problematic, with James (2011, 144) making the case that it was because of the failure of the 'open hand alongside sword' strategy that he believes underwrote much of Rome's early imperial growth. This required an elite sophisticated enough in the newly conquered territories to buy into Rome's imperial project once any conquest had taken place. He believes that, despite the repeated attempts to conquer the north of the islands of Britain, such an elite appears to have been singularly lacking in the territories of Scotland (and indeed Ireland). This was certainly the case early in the occupation of the rest of the islands, and even when the larger confederations began to appear later on it may have been a factor given the climate and geography described in Chapter 1. It may also have been the case that the political will to complete the full conquest was more important with regard to Scotland given the difficulties in campaigning so far north, as each incursion (including, particularly, that of Severus) found. Such political will never overcame these difficulties, so Scotland stayed outside the territory of the Empire.

Interestingly in that regard it was important for the Romans to think that they had completed the conquest, at least initially – a grand conceit if you will. This is best exemplified by the building under Domitian of the immense quadrifrons arch at Richborough in Kent in the late first century AD. This structure, acting as the official Imperial Gateway to the province (and through which each new governor had to pass before being allowed to wear his sword of office), was built specifically to commemorate Agricola's successes. We know now of course that this perceived success was far from it, with again a lack of political will after his withdrawal seeing the territories of the far north slip back into the hands of the natives and the line of the northern border settling along the Solway–Tyne Line within a generation. The Richborough arch should therefore be seen for what it really is – a monumental exercise in contemporary public relations. In short Rome never conquered Scotland, and it proved to be a perpetual source of trouble, a world away from the life experiences of those south of the border, even given the grim nature of the north of the province.

There were no towns as such north of Hadrian's Wall excepting the *vicus* settlements associated with the fortifications that tracked the various sporadic Roman incursions into the far north. Prime examples of such fortifications included: the Antonine Wall itself, with its regular sequence of forts of all sizes along its length; the fort and fortified harbours at Cramond and Carpow; the Agricolan legionary fortress at Inchtuthil (on the north bank of the river Tay south-west of Blairgowrie in Perth and Kinross); and the vexillation fort at Newstead (near Melrose in the Borders). The Antonine Wall, Cramond and Carpow have been detailed in Chapter 2, given their importance to this story, but the other two forts mentioned here do provide great insight into the often brief nature of the presence of the Roman military in the north.

The huge fortress at Inchtuthil was constructed in AD 82/83 to serve as the advance headquarters of Agricola during his attempt to conquer Scotland. It was built and occupied by the *legio* XX *Valeria Victrix* and enclosed a total area of 21.5 hectares; it was easily capable of housing the legion's 5,000-plus men. The construction of such a large fortress would have taken up to three seasons, with a temporary camp built nearby to house the troops during the winter months. The fortress formed the hub of a network of smaller forts that were built further north and south at the mouth of each glen; these were known as the Glenblocker forts. This illustrates the strategy that would have been employed had there been the political will to complete the conquest of Scotland – Rome having used a methodology seen in Wales whereby each valley as it was conquered was blocked off by a fortified site to ensure the natives didn't return. Thus gradually the locals were squeezed into a smaller and smaller territory until they had to submit to Rome. As we know, in Scotland this ultimately never happened for the reasons detailed above.

The fortress at Inchtuthil was occupied for only a short time, being evacuated in AD 86/87. It was never reused, even during the Severan incursions in the early third century (possibly showing the rarity of Roman incursions north of the Clyde–Forth Line). Thus it provides one of the most complete plans of a legionary fortress anywhere in the Empire. Its defences consisted of a turf rampart that was faced with stone and a surrounding ditch, and would have been the first phase of a process that would have eventually seen a fully stone-built structure here, as at York. Again as at York, each of the four walls featured a defended gatehouse, and facilities within included a *valetudinarium* (hospital), workshop, baths, sixty-four barrack buildings and the commander's *principia*.

The vexillation fort at Newstead, built on the site of the capital of the native Selgovae (see Chapter 3), once again shows the importance of Dere Street to this story, given that it was built at the point where the road crosses the river Tweed. Again laid out in a standard fashion for a Roman fort of this size, it featured turf-built walls surrounded by four sequential ditches (dating to the later second century AD), with stone-built gateways and possibly towers. Within the walls were workshops, a bathhouse, barracks and a *principia* (smaller than that at Inchtuthil). Walkover surveying of the site has also found *tesserae*, showing that fine-quality flooring was in use here and that the *principia* at least was also stone built. The extensive fort site also included two annexes – one to the north and one to the south – and possibly a *vicus*.

The fort at Newstead is most useful in the context of this work in that it shows the relative frequency of Roman incursions into the Borders (if not further north). Breeze (2000, 25) says that archaeological activity at the site has shown five phases of occupation, broadly fitting into Agricolan (late first century AD) and Antonine (mid-second century AD) phases. Thus the fort was built during Agricola's initial northern campaigns, sometime in the early AD 80s, and was then abandoned and reoccupied on a regular basis with each pulse of Roman activity north until a final abandonment in the early AD 180s. Interestingly, just as at Inchtuthil, the fort site at Newstead was not reused during the Severan invasions. However the Severan marching camp there, as seen in Chapter 2, is just as important as the earlier fort, given its enormous size at sixty-seven hectares (just a little smaller than the biggest at St Leonards Hill). The camp is located just to the south of the fort site and actually intersects its southern annex (Jones 2012, 118). It therefore appears that in the years between the AD 180s' occupation of the fort and the Severan offensive the original structure was slighted to the extent that (even in part) it was not reusable.

Meanwhile in an earlier work (Elliott 2016a, 130) I highlighted the sequence of fortified harbours built by the Romans during their northern campaigning, which were designed to supply the advancing legionary spearheads by sea. These included:

- during the Agricolan campaign, those at Kirkbride, Newton Stuart, Glenluce, Stranraer, Gurvan, Ayr and Dumbarton on the west coast,

and at Camelon on the east coast. The site at Carpow on the Tay may also have been established at this time – the two large enclosures there described in Chapter 2 being attributed to the Flavian period;
- during the Antonine period (and so most likely associated with the advance to, and occupation of, the Antonine Wall), those on the Clyde at Dumbarton on the north shore and Lurg Moor and Bishopton on the south, and on the Forth those at Inveresk, Cramond and Carriden.

As Breeze (2000, 13) highlights, the majority of the physical remnants of the various Roman incursions in the north are in the form of earthworks, typically marching camps. These are detailed in full in Chapters 2 and 7 as they are a key feature of the Severan campaigns and one of the most important pieces of archaeological data used in this research.

In terms of native settlement north of the border around the time of the LIA/occupation-period transition, Mattingly (2006, 422) says that: 'In most areas, social organisation was characterised by dispersed small settlements, suggesting a high degree of social fragmentation into family groups or clan.'

In part the settlement did have distinct similarities (particularly in southern Scotland) to the northern part of the province in the south, although with a particularly regional feel. For example, the roundhouses of south-east Scotland (the most common type of dwelling here, as in the Brigantian south) often used drystone walls in their construction, with an internal ring of posts utilised to support an 'attic' to give extra living space (Kamm 2011, 15). Highlighting the ephemeral nature of security in the north, hill forts featuring many such roundhouses were common in the LIA and into the occupation in southern and central Scotland, with defences including six-metre-high drystone walls and wooden palisades. A good example of such a hill fort was at Burnswark Hill (see Chapter 7), while Mattingly (2006, 423) also mentions them at Traprain Law, Dryburn Bridge and Broxmouth. A number of the forts have stone walls that have been vitrified through the use of fire, and it was previously thought that this was a deliberate measure to strengthen them. Recent research, however, shows it actually weakened the defensive structures and so a modern interpretation sees the vitrification process as a deliberate attempt at slighting the defences (perhaps in the context of Roman offensive operations).

Some other types of settlement and dwelling were unique to Scotland. One example was the wheelhouse found in the exposed coastal areas of the Western Isles. This featured spokes of stone walling radiating out from the centre to support a solid outer wall, with the lower section of the structure sunk down into a pit and an entrance in the form of a tunnel covered in stone and peat slabs. Another example was the crannog – a fortified timber-and-thatch roundhouse built on piles or on an artificial island in a lake (again emphasising the perceived need for security). Also important was the broch, a drystone walled tower common in the north-east of Scotland; with up to four storeys, it was by far the most imposing structure north of the border. More than 500 of these have been found, each set around a central courtyard with a very narrow and easily defendable entrance, and with the inhabitants living in galleries built within. All were erected between 200 BC and AD 150, and their standard design seems to indicate they were built by travelling specialist broch builders.

The economy north of the border was also different to that in the south, although there would have been at least some commonality among the peoples living either side of Hadrian's Wall amid the densest of military presences anywhere in the Empire. The economic differences were most pronounced as one headed into the far north. In his appreciation of the Roman invasions of Scotland, Kamm (2011, 15) says that many of the advances in economic and manufacturing sophistication that were visible across the Roman world by the time of Severan incursions were lacking in Scotland. He adds:

> As crafts became more sophisticated and mass production was introduced, particularly of iron objects and pottery, so trade increased and urban development occurred around centres of industry and commerce. This happened from Spain right across central Europe, and in Britain on the East and South East coasts. Scotland remained largely untouched by such advances until the 13th century AD.

There is some evidence that the coalescence of power through proximity to the Roman world described at the beginning of this subsection was having an economic impact by the time of the Severan incursions, with Mattingly (2006, 423) describing the creation of boundary features and progressive deforestation as more land was cleared for agricultural use. The deforestation in particular would have required substantial societal organisation to be carried out in such an organised manner, and it points to an expanding population. Mattingly (2006, 426) also highlights another manifestation of the impact of Rome from south to north, namely the finding at more than 200 native sites of Roman artefacts. Such data may indicate commercial contact, or may be in the context of conflict, although interestingly there is a blank area in the western borders which probably illustrates the eastern-coast focus of the majority of the Roman campaigns in the north.

In terms of the peoples north of the border, in Chapter 3 I set out the various tribal groupings in Scotland around the time of the conquest in AD 43. However by the time of the Severan incursions (noting the discussion above regarding the coalescence of power) the confederations that we know of are the Maeatae and the Caledonians (the latter a more specific reference to a people by this time rather than the earlier catch-all term for many of the Scottish tribal groupings: for example, the *'Caledoniam incolentes populi'* – the people inhabiting Caledonia – defeated by Agricola at Mons Graupius in AD 83). Both the Maeatae and the Caledonians (in this new context) are first detailed in a late second-century context, with Dio (77.12. 1–4) saying that by this time the names of the other native groupings north of the border had been merged into these two (although it is unclear if this was a matter of fact or a literary device by him to make his narrative easier to follow to a contemporary audience). It is worth quoting Dio in full here, given this is one of the key paragraphs we have in a primary text for the whole of Severus' subsequent campaigns. He says (77.12.1–4):

The Maeatae live next to the cross-wall which cuts the island in half, and the Caledonians are beyond them. Both tribes inhabit wild and waterless mountains and desolate and swampy plains, and possess neither walls, cities, nor tilled fields, but live on their flocks, wild game, and certain fruits . . . their form of rule is democratic for the most part, and they choose their boldest men as rulers. They go into battle in chariots, and have small, swift horses; there are also foot soldiers, very swift in running and very firm in standing ground. For arms they have a shield and a short spear, with bronze apple attached to the end of the spear shaft, so that when the enemy is shaken it may clash and terrify the enemy; and they also have a dagger. They can endure hunger and cold and any kind of hardship; for they plunge into swamps and exist there for many days with only their heads above water, and in forests they support themselves upon bark and roots, and for all emergencies they prepare a certain kind of food, the eating of a small portion of which, the size of a bean, prevents them from feeling either hunger or thirst.

The hunger-preventing food described here has been identified as the heath pea (*Lathyrus linifolius*) by Dr Brian Moffat (2000, 13) of the Soutra Aisle research centre.

This is a fascinating paragraph for many reasons, but in the first instance it shows what a troublesome opponent both confederations would have been for the legions of Rome. This was a very hardy enemy, capable of sustaining military campaigns for a long period in the worst of climatic and geographical conditions. As will be seen in Chapter 7, it seems that both of the Severan incursions in the north were met with intense guerrilla resistance rather than any kind of meeting engagement. However if the quotation above is to be taken even partially at face value, Dio appears to be saying that here was an opponent capable of standing up symmetrically to the world of Rome, with a seemingly steady spear-armed shield wall and an elite aristocracy riding in swift chariots (perhaps they were not as democratic as he describes). The fact that the indigenous Maeatae and Caledonian peoples do not appear to have so stood up en masse against the legions of Rome may indicate, however, that this at least was a literary device (or they were prevented from doing so; see discussion in Chapter 7).

Dio's above account refers to events in the AD 180s but is equally applicable to the Severan period. Although the Antonine Wall had been abandoned by that time and the northern frontier had again been reset along the line of Hadrian's Wall, most interpretations suggest the 'cross-wall' mentioned by Dio was the Antonine Wall and not Hadrian's Wall. This would place the Maeatae either side of the Clyde–Forth Line and perhaps even further north above the river Tay, broadly populating much of the central Midland Valley, with the Caledonians beyond them in the upper reaches of the Midland Valley and into the Highlands.

The names of two hills in this region have in the past been used to show the most northerly and southerly spread of the Maeatae in this interpretation – the former being Dumyat Hill in the Ochils overlooking Stirling (where the remains of a hill fort called Dùn Mhèad in Gaelic is believed to derive from 'hill of the Maeatae') and the latter Myot Hill near Falkirk (Breeze 2000, 111). Kamm (2011, 125) graphically places both confederations even further north: the Maeatae in a line heading south-east to north-west from Stirling up to Aberdeen broadly along the Highland Boundary Fault; and the Caledonians beyond them in the Highlands. Meanwhile an interpretation of the cross-wall as being Hadrian's Wall would place the Maeatae in the Borders and the Caledonians north of the Clyde–Forth Line.

The simple reality, however, is that we don't have the level of definition required to match the literary sources with the archaeological data to allow us to make a reasonable interpretation as to the exact location of both confederations at the time of the campaigns of Severus (or even a guess for that matter). Thus for the purposes of this work I will use the Antonine Wall interpretation as this seems to me the most likely (placing the Maeatae in the central Midland Valley and the Caledonians in the upper Midland Valley and Highlands). In any case, Dio clearly doesn't differentiate them culturally and so from a Roman perspective both would likely have been perceived in the same way – simply as the enemies in the north.

Expeditio Felicissima Britannica

In this section I consider what actually drew Severus to Scotland and his final campaigns there, and then review his initial planning for an operation described by Moorhead and Stuttard (2012, 162) as quite colossal in scale.

Why Did Severus Really Campaign in Scotland?

Back in Rome, Severus was bored. This most military of men was never happy in the imperial capital, with its constant political machinations and temptations. In Britain there was clearly renewed friction across the northern border and Severus, brooding in the Imperial Palace, was apparently angry that the governor in the province – Lucius Alfenus Senecio (Birley 2005, 191) – was winning wars there while he himself was tied down defeating the banditry rising of one Bulla and his 600 followers (Dio 76.10.6). He was further displeased by the way his sons Caracalla and Geta were behaving in Rome, indulging in a lifestyle of luxury clearly at odds with the old warrior's martial nature. When Senecio wrote to him in AD 207 in some degree of alarm, Severus therefore jumped at the chance for action. Herodian (3.14.1–2) says the letter explained that:

> . . . the governor of Britain [had] informed Severus by dispatches that the barbarians there were in revolt and overrunning the country, looting and destroying virtually everything on the island. He told Severus that he needed either a stronger army [usually interpreted as a request for more troops] for the defence of the province or the presence of the emperor himself. Severus was delighted with this news: glory-loving by nature, he wished to win victories over the Britons to add to the victories and titles of honor he had won in the East and the West.

Given Herodian's known inaccuracies in his life of Severus, the veracity of this account and the very existence of Senecio's letter needs in the first instance to be challenged. Birley (1999, 172) highlights that the classical historian was well known for the use of the rhetorical *topos* – a stock formula such as a pun, proverb, cause-and-effect or a comparison. We have two specifically relevant instances of this where Herodian utilised the existence of a letter similar to Senecio's from other provincial governors in his later work to justify imperial expeditions. These were with regard to Syria and Mesopotamia, and to Illyria. In the case of the former, the dramatic events described in the letter requiring the emperor's attention actually date to five years earlier than the communiqué – one of the facts that leads Birley to reject Herodian's narrative regarding Senecio's letter as pure invention (Birley 1999, 172).

If we were to take Herodian's story factually, then context is very important as we consider this famous request, given it is so often the starting point for narratives of the Severan *expeditio felicissima Britannica*. After a period following the Albinus usurpation attempt, when the new governor had weathered severe agitation along the northern border through buying off the invaders with huge subsidies (see Chapter 3), Rome was again starting to assert its authority in the north of Britain. For example, we do know that earlier in the decade in which the contested letter was sent, Senecio had started the restoration of a number of the installations along Hadrian's Wall, with auxiliaries being used to build a granary at Birdoswald (and possibly being active in this regard further south at Corbridge; Frere 1974, 171), and also to restore buildings at Chesters and Housesteads. Meanwhile a victory dedication by the *Ala* I *Asturum* under Senecio's governorship at Benwell indicates military success on his part, thought to be related to events in AD 206 when Dio (77.10.6) references victories in Britain (the source of Severus' irritation detailed above). However all of this positive activity seems to have changed in a very short space of time with some kind of military crisis in the north (and further to the south if we take Herodian's interpretation of Senecio's request at face value). Given that we have no data to allow us to interpret what this crisis in AD 207 actually was, the request and the emperor's very rapid, seemingly over-the-top response require further consideration.

The reference to the emperor's 'delight' in the Herodian quote seems pretty clear-cut at first glance, especially in the context of his concerns with the behaviour of his sons in Rome. A blunt reading of the primary sources would seem to indicate that the threat was sudden, very real, and that when presented with the opportunity to intervene Severus couldn't wait to get stuck in.

Others, however, have raised issues with taking Herodian at face value, over and above Birley's wider reticence regarding the letter. Wilkes (2005, 213), for example, has questioned why Severus would trouble himself with a disturbance on the fringes of Rome's most remote province for the last three years of his life (given the primary sources also tell us that the emperor didn't think he would return alive once he committed to the expedition). Rankov (2009, 170) suggests one of the reasons was that Severus was actually far more concerned with re-establishing his authority over the military in Britain since it had been the seat of Albinus' earlier attempt at usurpation. Note here also Severus' experiences in the later AD 180s witnessing the troubles of British governor Pertinax with the military when he himself was governor of Gallia Lugdunensis, a province that also interestingly quickly supported Albinus. In that regard Rankov says: '. . . the expedition [was] . . . as much concerned with re-establishing the loyalty of the army as with dealing with barbarian incursions or the conquest of Scotland for its own sake.'

In this interpretation the letter from Senecio (if it existed) might therefore have been part of a plan concocted to give Severus an opportunity to carry out an expedition he wouldn't normally have had the motive for. This is an interesting argument given that he had already sent his legates to Britain in the immediate aftermath of his victory over Albinus, and had also seemingly gone to the length of temporarily breaking up the regional fleets of the north-west of the Empire (see Chapter 3). Furthermore it was almost certainly under his legates that building had started of the land walls of Roman London (which would certainly have reminded the province's elite in its capital who the boss was). Matters must have become very strained indeed if all of the above had failed to the extent that Severus had to come up with some kind of diplomatic ploy.

Perhaps Hodgson (2014, 35) is correct in saying: 'If the loyalty of the British Army was really the only issue, one wonders why Severus left it so long: he was freed up from his eastern wars by AD 201. Rankov may be right to sense Severus' long-standing fear of disloyalty in Britain, but wrong to dismiss the seriousness of the "barbarian incursions".' He goes on to speculate that perhaps the legates had failed to overcome problems that originated with the weakening of the British garrison after Albinus had taken his best army troops to their defeat at Lugdunum in AD 197. Given the size of the losses it would certainly have taken time to rebuild the military strength of the recalcitrant province, although another factor may have been Severus responding to his own near usurpation by deliberately leaving the garrison undermanned (and the province thus inadvertently vulnerable). Perhaps one can see the building of the Severan walls of London in this light also (noting Herodian in his contested letter saying that the 'barbarians' were destroying everything on the island, no matter how far-fetched this sounds if it existed).

Meanwhile Bidwell (2012) has carried out an examination of the archaeological data regarding the garrisons in the northern forts of the province in the final years of the second century AD and also the beginning of the third. He concludes that evidence at Bainbridge, South Shields and Bowes does seem to show the military there below full strength both in terms of numbers and its cadre of commanders (Bidwell 2012, 69), even though as we have seen above the rebuilding of physical military structures was taking place under Senecio. Following this narrative, Severus' concerns about Britain being a continuing hotbed of potential revolt may in fact have led to a situation where the Maeatae and Caledonians sensed an opportunity, their appetites already whetted by their being bought off with massive bribes during their previous incursions. As Hodgson (2014, 36) says: 'The silver denarius subsidy hoards, evident in the archaeological as well as the literary record, are a clear enough attestation of how seriously Rome took her northern neighbours in Britain, and the expense to which she was prepared to go to manage them.'

Such hoards persisted longer in the far north of Britain than on the Continent, where they generally ceased about AD 194, after Severus' elevation to emperor. This shows that even though reconstruction had begun along the northern frontier under Senecio (or even earlier under his predecessor Gaius Valerius Pudens – new barracks being constructed at Bainbridge in early AD 205), the Empire at this time still found it easier to buy off their troublesome northern neighbours. Thus with the northern frontier still denuded of an appropriate garrison (even as the infrastructure was being rebuilt to accommodate newcomers) the Maeatae and Caledonians may have seen an irresistible opportunity for easy pickings.

We are therefore left with a broad range of factors which may have been behind Severus' *expeditio felicissima Britannica*:

- Severus, whether Senecio's letter existed or not, was itching to get away from Rome and return to the field. He was a warrior bored in the capital and concerned about his sons' behaviour. He may therefore have been looking for an opportunity for martial endeavour, and in the most extreme interpretation manufactured one. In this context, while clearly Britain was very remote from Rome, one should not forget that it was always a magnet for those looking for military prowess within the imperial system, its north truly the Wild West of the Empire.

- The need for a legacy for the leading soldier of his age. A long-term sufferer from chronic rheumatic gout, Severus was not a well man by this time (and indeed, as detailed above, did not expect to return from his British expedition), and would not have wanted to leave unfinished business in the form of unrest in Britain. In that regard, all Roman emperors (no matter how successful) knew they would be judged against the glory of the first emperor Augustus, and Severus would have been keenly aware of the words of the late first century BC poet Horace that his emperor (then Augustus) would only be judged a god if the Britons and Parthians were defeated. In that context, from Severus' perspective, he had dealt with the Parthians. All that was left were the troublesome northern Britons.

- All was not well with the garrison in Britain, even after the attentions of the emperor's legates. Rebuilding of infrastructure was taking place, but was evidently still undermanned. It is unclear whether this was a deliberate ploy by Severus, who feared an internal threat there rather than an external one from the north, or was simply a natural outcome of the difficulties in rebuilding a garrison force much denuded by Albinus. (It is noteworthy that some of the later Latin chroniclers such as Orosius speak of the trouble described by Senecio as a rebellion.)

- The motivations and behaviour of the protagonists – a factor much overlooked by many commentators. The Maeatae and Caledonians had already been heavily engaged along the border throughout the previous generation at various times from the AD 180s, and had been bought off with enormous quantities of portable wealth in the AD 190s. That in itself must have caused enormous friction among their own elites, already coalescing into larger and larger political units through the cultural impact of the close proximity of the Empire to the south. It may therefore have been the case that their leaders, now permanently on the lookout for a military distraction to the south, saw the opportunity for a profit-making raid to keep their warriors occupied.

- A possible harvest shock (crop failure) in the early third century in Scotland. Given the emergence of the two confederations detailed above in the late second century, it seems reasonable to suggest that the population in the region was growing and there were more mouths to feed. We also know (see Chapter 1) that the weather at the time of the two Severan campaigns north was unusually poor. We might therefore speculate that the latter could have impacted crop yields, leading to a need for the native leaders north of the frontier to head south to feed their growing populations.

My view is that we are looking at a combination of factors, presenting all of those involved with a unique set of circumstances which together led to what followed. The warrior confederations north of the border were getting a taste for vast wealth and looking for an opportunity for easy plunder (and may have been hungry), the northern border for some reason was undermanned, and the emperor was on the prowl for war and mindful of his legacy. Whether triggered by the arrival of Senecio's letter or provincial news in another form (real or engineered), the scene was therefore set for imperial shock and awe writ large, possibly the most devastating campaign ever fought on British soil.

Planning the Campaign

Whatever the reason behind the emperor's reaction to the news from Britain, Severus didn't need a second invitation and jumped at the chance to take the field one last time. Birley (1999, 175) enigmatically describes Severus' first action as the gathering of anyone in imperial circles with knowledge of Britain to his side for close counsel. Such individuals would have included Virius Lupus (the trusted first governor he had installed in Britain following the defeat of Albinus' revolt) and Pudens (now likely back in Rome after his stint as governor following Senecio's promotion). Other candidates would have been Gaius Julius Asper (patron of the province of Britannia in Rome) and Polus Terentianus (Severus' ally back in the 'Year of the Five Emperors' in AD 193, when Polus was the governor of Dacia, who had also been the legate of the *legio* II *Augusta* in Caerleon). Another former legate of this elite legion close to hand was Silius Plautius Haterianus (a fellow Lepcitane of the emperor, who might have mentioned to him the temperature differential between a North African summer and a British winter), while another candidate would have been Antius Crescens Calpurnianus. Calpurnianus was a *quindecimvir sacris faciendis* (responsible for the maintenance of temples) at the time and a former *iuridicus* (legal expert and key member of a governor's *officium consularis*) in Britain, who was briefly the acting governor in the province under Commodus.

As the year progressed the emperor began the detailed logistical planning for his *expeditio felicissima Britannica*. The first step was to bring together the key leaders and advisers who would accompany him. Birley (1999, 175) says there is no evidence that he took any of those with whom he initially sought counsel, perhaps preferring a younger team to join him on what he knew would be an arduous expedition. Those we do know accompanied him in his senior team included two senatorial *comites* (imperial companions): Julius Avitus Alexianus (the brother-in-law of the empress) and C. Junius Faustinus Postumianus (the recent governor of Moesia Inferior and another fellow North African who would take over as governor in Britain upon the expedition's arrival – an interesting appointment, perhaps reflecting Senecio's fall from grace after his urgent request for help). Others who joined the top team for the expedition included Sex. Varius Marcellus of Apamea, the new procurator in Britain, this appointment again indicating that all was not well in the province. Marcellus was another safe pair of hands from a Severan perspective, being the son-in-law of Julius Avitus Alexianus, married to Julia Domna's niece Julia Soaemias (they were the parents of the future emperor Elagabalus). Meanwhile also accompanying the emperor was the Praetorian Guard prefect Aemilius Papinianus, one of the replacements for Plautianus in AD 204 (see Chapter 5 for detail). We also know of two others named in the senior team from inscriptions regarding their job titles but whose actual names are now lost to us: one was on a buff sandstone altar found at Corbridge and he was assigned the key role of managing the granaries and logistics base there; and another (in Rome) whose role is very illuminating indeed, being assigned the task of leading the *Classis Britannica*. The same person is mentioned in Chapter 5 as possibly commanding an amalgamated *Classis Britannica*, *Classis Germanica*, *Classis Moesica* and *Classis Pannonica,* because he is referenced in the same inscription commanding the Rhine and Danubian regional fleets (Frere 1974, 172). If true, this could be yet another sign that all was not well with the military in Britain.

Overall the emperor's team to lead the expedition would have been huge, the appointment of the logistics manager at Corbridge detailed above showing the scale of pre-planning. This is a key individual in our story as it is in the context of his inscription (RIB 1143) that we get the reference to the contemporary description of the campaign as the *tempore expeditionis felicissi(mae) Britannic(ae)*.

In full, this important text reads: '[. . .]*norus* [. . . *pr*]*aep*(*ositus*) *cur*(*am*) *agens horreorum tempo*[*r*]*e expeditionis felicissi*(*mae*) *Britannic*(*ae*) *v*(*otum*) *s*(*olvit*) *l*(*ibens*) *m*(*erito*).' This translates as: '[. . .]*norus* . . ., officer in charge of the granaries at the time of the most successful expedition to Britain, gladly and deservedly fulfilled his vow.'

Severus knew he would be away for years (and again, thought he would not return), so not for him the sixteen-day visit of Claudius in AD 43. There was a clear commitment to smash the opposition once and for all, and to award the ageing emperor with a last set of victory laurels. As Birley points out (1999, 175), given this commitment in time, while he was away the whole process of running the Empire would have to take place from Britain (and, as we detail above and below, specifically York – that most unlikely of imperial capitals). With that in mind, Severus would also have gathered other key members of the *Consilium Principis* (main council), including his *ab epistulis* (head of secretariat), to join him; he was nothing if not thorough, in fact taking his entire imperial court with him. Even more importantly, we also know that Severus brought with him the *fiscus* (imperial treasury) and the *rationalis* (high-ranking financial officer) who ran it.

To this would have been added his own retinue including large numbers of imperial freed men and slaves from his *familia Caesaris*, of whom we specifically know of two. These were Castor (the court chamberlain) and Euodus (who had previously been Caracalla's tutor). The emperor was also joined by his close family including Julia Domna, Caracalla and Geta – the last two probably the first on his list of attendees given his keenness to remove them from the sensual diversions of Rome. Key senators who were not already part of his inner circle also came along – and all of this before the military leadership for the expedition was set in place.

The emperor's next step was to ensure stability in Rome and throughout the whole breadth of the huge Empire while he was away at its most north-westerly tip (especially given his hostile relationship with the Senate). We have some detail here, and although we lack a complete picture Severus' planning seems to have had a rather North African feel to it, with key provinces in the hands of his kinsmen, supporters and friends. For example, Pannonia Superior was under the governorship of Egnatius Victor, while Germania Superior was being ruled by Aiacius Modestus Crescentianus – both being North African natives – while the legionary legate in the key Danubian frontier province of Pannonia Inferior was Septimius Castinus, likely a family member. Other key postings were allocated to trusted former military colleagues: for example, the vital province in the east of Coele Syria (Severus having divided the province of Syria into two military/administrative units) was being governed by another probable North African, Marius Maximus, who had been a legionary legate under Severus' brother Geta when the latter was governor of Moesia Inferior in AD 193. Severus' plans were clearly meticulous given that, even after his death in AD 211 in York, the Empire within and outside its borders remained remarkably quiet (despite Caracalla's purge of his father's inner circle as soon as the latter had passed away and his later 'terror' in Rome).

As AD 207 slipped into AD 208 Caracalla and Geta were both appointed as consuls in Rome, holding office for the third and second time, respectively. Caracalla now equalled Severus' three years in that post. By this time Caracalla had been 'joint' emperor for a decade, while Geta remained as the junior 'most noble Caesar'. Coins were then minted showing the emperor riding off to war, though we know from the primary sources that he was actually carried in his litter for most of his journey because of the gout he was suffering from. The sources indicate that his two sons reached the continental coast before him, probably with their own entourage. The majority of the huge imperial party would have taken things more slowly given the enormous baggage train travelling with the emperor.

The orders for the mobilisation of the military units making up Severus' force would actually have been sent out across the Western Empire some time in AD 207, using the *cursus publicus*, such that the military components were all ready to move early in AD 208 to coincide with Severus' departure from Rome. It is in this context that we can see the northern regional fleets (under their single unnamed commander) gathering off the major ports on the continental coast of Gaul (principally Boulogne) and modern Belgium and the Netherlands, ready to start ferrying the troops to Britain. This would have commenced from spring AD 208, with many being sent direct to the north of the province through Brough-on-Humber from where they headed to York to await the emperor. Others would have landed further north at Wallsend and South Shields, either making camp there or travelling back south to York, while still more troops would have sailed through the then Great Estuary in East Anglia to Caistor St Edmunds (Roman Venta Icenorum), *civitas* capital of the Iceni in north Norfolk, or travelled down the Thames Estuary before beginning the long march north along Ermine Street.

Severus and his large entourage would certainly have entered Britain through the Imperial Gateway at Richborough in Kent, however. This was essential given that he would have wanted to put his stamp on the formerly recalcitrant province from the start. The image of the ageing and ailing emperor (he was sixty-three by this time) being carried through Domitian's quadrifrons arch in a sedan chair is an enigmatic one, although one wonders if he might have made the effort to hobble through under his own power because of the importance of the expedition to him. Either way, he had arrived and the *expeditio felicissima Britannica* was under way.

CHAPTER 7

Septimius Severus in Britain: On Campaign

THIS CHAPTER DESCRIBES THE TWO campaigns of Severus in Scotland in AD 209 and AD 210 as the emperor attempted to finally stamp out the threat to his province from the far north. The first campaign seems to have met enough objectives for he and his sons to officially celebrate a victory while in the second one he ordered his troops to commit a genocide. Many have commented in the past that there is little in the primary sources to enable a full picture of these campaigns to be set in place, but I believe that there is now sufficient data from the archaeological record and from analogy (in association with the primary sources) to do this. In that regard I have found my academic background invaluable, which combined both the study of warfare in all its forms (with a focus on the classical world) with that of archaeology (I remain an active archaeologist).

To enable me to present my interpretation of the two Severan campaigns in Scotland, I begin with a brief analysis of the enormous force that Severus led into the far north in his 'shock and awe' campaign. I then set the scene as Severus established his imperial capital in York, before getting into the detail of the two campaigns, by looking at the overall strategy and the routes taken (including a new interpretation of the use made of the *Classis Britannica* based on my PhD research) and then by describing the experience of battle as faced by all concerned – it being universally grim. Finally I assess the two campaigns against the earlier analyses and place them within my proposed chronology.

Severus' Military Force

We can determine the composition of the 'Severan surge' by cross-referencing the various units known or inferred to have participated by the primary sources, archaeological data and informed commentators. For example, given that one of the prefects of the Praetorian Guard, Aemilius Papinianus, was part of the Severan leadership team for the expedition, it seems highly likely that at least part (and probably a significant portion) of this elite fighting force participated. Severus would certainly not have travelled without his own guard, and it should be remembered that by this time the praetorians were composed of veterans from the Danubian frontier after the emperor had reformed the body shortly after becoming emperor. The *equites singulares Augusti* (imperial guard cavalry) – doubled in size by this time following the pattern set when Severus reformed the Praetorian Guard – would also have participated, while another ready source of troops close to hand in Italy while he planned his campaign was the *legio* II *Parthica* based near Rome, many of whose legionaries would also have joined him in his *expeditio felicissima Britannica* (Birley 2005, 200). In addition it has been speculated that one of the urban cohorts of Rome may have joined Severus' force.

Other units receiving notification in AD 207 to prepare to journey to Britain would have been the troops based along the northern frontiers of the Empire. According to Birley (1999, 175): 'The Rhine and Danube armies will also, it is clear, have contributed to the expedition . . . It may well be that several whole legions were sent, although it is more probable that vexillations only were detached.'

Given the size of Severus' eventual force it seems probable that the legions along the Rhine and Danube were stripped down to the bare minimum to hold the frontier. One can imagine large amounts of tribute being paid to the tribal confederations north of the border to encourage their peaceable intentions while the emperor was in Britain.

Once in Britain these legionaries would have been joined by those of the three British legions based there: *legio* II *Augusta* based at Caerleon (under new leadership since it had played a prominent role in the usurpation attempt by Albinus in the previous decade); *legio* VI *Victrix* at York; and *legio* XX *Valeria Victrix* at Chester. The British legions seem to have performed well during the Severan campaigns: for example, *legio* VI *Victrix* was awarded the commemorative title *Britannica Pia Fidelis* (based on tile stamps from Carpow);

and *legio* **XX** *Valeria Victrix* was similarly styled *Antoniniana* by Caracalla after the death of his father.

To this elite force of troops we can add the auxiliaries, still a prominent component of the Principate armies of this period (see Chapter 2). Either based in Britain, or being ordered to the province to accompany the Severan expedition, Moorhead and Stuttard (2012, 162) estimate their numbers at a huge 35,000. We know specifically of one of the units engaged in this regard – the *cohors* V *Gallorum* – whose presence has been identified at South Shields and Cramond.

This gathering of military units from across the west implies a total force of around 50,000 frontline troops being mustered for the campaigns in the north of Britain. This figure corresponds to the calculation referenced by Moorhead and Stuttard (2012, 162) that the granaries at South Shields could hold enough grain to feed 50,000 men for two months, and also the seemingly random figure chosen by Dio (77.12.2) when describing casualties in the campaign. As set out in Chapter 2, the gathering together of such an enormous force was a dramatic undertaking by the emperor; he effectively created (given the wide origins of the forces engaged) what would later in the Empire be called a field army for his *expeditio felicissima Britannica*.

To this figure of 50,000 we can then add the 7,000 naval *milites* of the *Classis Britannica*. Despite still seemingly being under a joint command structure with its Rhine and Danubian counterparts, they would have played a vital role controlling the littoral flank of the campaign (including along the river networks encountered), scouting ahead of the legionary spearheads, patrolling once territory had been pacified and (perhaps most importantly) transporting men and supplies (see detail below).

Severus in His Imperial Capital, York

Severus and his entourage would have arrived in York in late spring AD 208, no doubt finding the key town in the north of Britain surrounded by vast encampments of troops gathering from across the west of his Empire to participate in his *expeditio felicissima Britannica*.

The primary sources say that either on his journey to (or through) Britain, or when he arrived in York, his native opponents in the far north tried to sue for peace. If true this is not surprising given the overwhelming force they would by now have been aware he was about to unleash upon them. Their spies and other sources in the south would also have told the native leaders about Severus' grim reputation when dealing with his enemies – and even friends when it suited him. Given the size of military force he had gathered, the emperor was in no mood for compromise, as it was not a realistic option for him even if he was minded to consider it. Herodian (3.14.4) says that instead he wanted to 'prolong his time in Britain and not return hurriedly to Rome, while entertaining his ambition to add to his victories and titles by a campaign against the British, so he sent the delegates away empty-handed, and put everything in order for war'.

This also fits in well with the analysis in Chapter 6 regarding his motives for his *expeditio felicissima Britannica*, which included a desire to get out of Rome and also his mindfulness of legacy. Thus, whatever his opponents in the north hoped to achieve in trying to negotiate, they failed, and an apocalypse was set to descend on them.

Now settled in York, Severus set about establishing the civil administration of the Empire in a town that was to become the imperial capital for three years. He probably felt more at home than expected because a temple to the Graeco-Egyptian deity Serapis had recently been erected there by Claudius Hieronymianus, the legionary legate of *legio* VI *Victrix*. As detailed in Chapter 6, the legionary fortress was likely to have been significantly improved during Severus' stay, with the *principia* becoming the Imperial Palace for him and his immediate family, and its attached *basilica* monumentalised. In the latter regard it seems highly probable that the large column on display outside York Minster today dates to this period. Meanwhile his *Consilium Principis* and military leadership would have been housed close by, perhaps in the *praetorium*.

One can imagine the chaos in the *cabana*/civilian settlement across the river Ouse when word reached the local populace that the emperor was on his way with an enormous entourage in tow. Thus merchants from far and wide (selling the widest range of goods imaginable) arrived to make the most of this once-in-a-lifetime opportunity. One thing we can be sure of – as the merchants arrived they would have found the whole region under military lockdown as the army swelled slowly but inexorably to 50,000 men.

We have our best insight here into the workings of the Severan imperial administration in York not in the context of the emperor himself but through his younger son Geta. This is because when Severus left his new imperial capital to campaign in the north with Caracalla, it was Geta who was left behind down south to run the Empire (his mother Julia Domna staying behind too, always on hand to provide wise counsel). Geta is specifically recorded (with his brother) on an inscription from Aenus in Thrace, which says that on 12 September during one of the years the imperial family were in York he heard an embassy from the town. If Caracalla was present too, this would have been AD 208 or early AD 209, while if the mention of Caracalla was just a literary device then it would have been later AD 209 because September would have been at the height of the campaigning season in the north. The embassy, led by Diogenes (son of Theocharis), seems to have been successful given that the event was recorded on fine white marble in the Thracian town (presumably copied from the original recording of the event in the imperial *commentarii*).

The imperial presence in York is also traceable through archaeological data of another kind – this time face pots for creams. Moorhead and Stuttard (2012, 163) say that such cosmetic containers dating to this period have been found during excavations in York decorated with female figures with Julia Domna's famous crimped coiffure hairstyle. They argue that it is evidence of her 'dazzling the locals with . . . sophisticated continental fashions'.

One other event could supply an even more unique insight into the activities of Geta while running the imperial administration for his father. This is with regard to the martyring of St Alban – one of the most famous events in the history of the Christianity in the British Isles. The basic story here involves a Christian priest arriving in the Roman town of Verulamium (modern St Albans), during a time when the religion was being persecuted, and finding shelter with the man later to be sainted as St Alban (Lambert, 210, 6). According to the story, the latter was moved by the priest's constant vigil and prayer and so renounced paganism, then received Christian instruction. The hiding place of the priest became known, however, and to protect him St Alban put on the priest's cloak of office and surrendered himself instead. Questioned by a judge, St Alban announced himself a Christian and refused to make the required sacrifice to the pagan gods. He was then flogged but still refused, after which he was executed on a hill above the town on 22 June in an unknown year, and it is here that the tale crosses the path of Severus' *expeditio felicissima Britannica*. This is because of an obscure reference (based on a late hagiographical source published by a German scholar in 1904) to a 'most Impious Caesar' ordering persecutions in Britain to cease. This Morris (1968, 1) argues dated the event to AD 209 because of the difference between an Augustus (full emperor) and Caesar (junior emperor, as Geta was at this time). Given the specific location in Britain of the event, and the timeframe, this gives only two candidates for such a Caesar. The first, remarkably, is Geta himself (who wasn't made a full Augustus until later AD 209), while the other points to the later third/early fourth centuries AD in the form of Constantius Chlorus (father of Constantine, whose statue today sits outside York Minister), who performed the junior emperor role in north-western Europe under Diocletian. Birley (1999,180) suggests that Chlorus can be ruled out, given the protection he already afforded the religion. This leaves the Severan candidate as our likely Caesar, although clearly this is currently unprovable (and has a very tight time window in AD 209, from the time when the emperor and Caracalla went out on campaign to when Geta was elevated).

Strategy and Route

In this section I analyse the overall strategy of the Severan campaigns in Scotland, paying particular attention to the specific routes taken (based on the archaeological evidence) and also to the key military (as well as transport and supply) role played by the regional navy.

The logistics chain, which underpinned the campaigns, was crucial for keeping such a huge military force in the field in enemy territory. To that end the eastern maritime flank was essential, with a never-ending conveyor heading north from South Shields with food and supplies. Along the route it stopped off at Cramond on the Forth and Carpow on the Tay as required. The carried materials where possible were then trans-shipped to smaller riverine vessels to transport their goods to the troops on the front line and in the rear. The vessels would then return with any booty, prisoners soon to be slaves, and the wounded (of which there were many in these two campaigns), before the whole process started again.

The overall strategy employed seems to have been simple but brutally effective. The 'Severan surge' crossed the frontier and headed north along Dere Street in spring AD 209 (the second campaign in AD 210 is considered later in the chapter), hammering into the Scottish Borders as one massive homogeneous force along the route north. It cauterised all before it (and in its immediate vicinity), and the local tribes sued for peace as quickly as possible given the obvious asymmetry in size and military capability. As the Roman force advanced with the emperor and Caracalla as well as with an enormous supply train, outriders from the *alae* (auxiliary cavalry) would have ranged far and wide to protect the flanks of the advance and provide a scouting function

– no doubt raiding recalcitrant native settlements wherever possible. Light and medium artillery pieces would have been in the supply train but not the larger siege engines (as used in the east) – Severus knew that he wouldn't be needing them for this expedition. At the end of each day's march a huge sixty-seven-hectare marching camp (detailed in Chapter 2) was built, making the Roman force effectively untouchable. Soon the Scottish Borders (at least in the east) were completely subdued and the Forth reached, with Dere Street then turning west and crossing over the river Esk at Inveresk.

At some point on the south shore a bridge was built to allow the force to cross the Forth, while the former Antonine Wall from the Forth in the east to the Clyde in the west was in part repaired and remanned, with a view to protecting the rear once the Roman force advanced further north. As to the crossing, the exact location has never been found and there is some debate about where this would have been, and of what kind the crossing took. What we can say definitively is that a bridge crossing did take place.

The principal data used here to determine the bridge type (and that later discussed for the Tay) is based on contemporary coin evidence. Robertson (1980, 137) definitively identifies these coins as a gold aureus, bronze asses and bronze medallions of Severus from AD 208, which all feature an image of a permanent monumental bridge, and a small coin or medallion of Caracalla dated to AD 209 featuring a bridge of boats. Although he misdated it to AD 208, Reed (1975, 92) earlier describes the Caracallan coin, saying that it '. . . shows a bridge of boats (with Caracalla and his father marching over it) with the legend Traiectus underneath, [it being] similar to a bridge on coins of Marcus Aurelius of AD 172, showing his crossing of the Danube'.

One of the locations suggested by this coin would have been a crossing of the Forth at South Queensferry near Edinburgh, divided in the middle by Inch Garvie, where the Forth Railway Bridge now stands. Reed (1975) goes on to make the case that a bridge of boats up to two kilometres in length (possibly up to 500 boats, impressive considering the overall size of the *Classis Britannica* was 900 vessels) was constructed under Caracalla's authority – hence it being on his coin. He says that archaeological data emerging at the time of his writing also supported his hypothesis, arguing that the location of the twenty-five-hectare marching camp at Auchtermuchty in Fife on a line from North Queensferry to Carpow indicates a road on that line (see below for discussion). Reed (1975) cites Dio (77.40) as a primary source when he details: '. . . as he advanced through the country he experienced countless hardships in cutting down the

forests, levelling the heights, filling up the swamps, and bridging the rivers
. . .' Reed chose to interpret this in the context of a road-building exercise
northwards along this line in Fife (and onwards to Carpow and the river Tay
crossing), an interesting idea given the continued discussion on strategy below.

South Queensferry is also close to the important fort, supply base and
fortified harbour of Cramond to its east on the line of Dere Street. Heading
even further east one gets to the Dere Street crossing of the river Esk at
Inveresk, another local site of major Roman provenance. Other options have
been suggested for the Forth crossing: for example, further upriver north-east
of the Antonine Wall fortress of Camelon (on the river Carro, a Firth of Forth
tributary); another near Alloa; and even at Stirling. However Reed's earlier
hypothesis does make sense given the strategy I propose below.

Having crossed the Forth I believe the huge force then divided into two
legionary spearheads: a larger one comprising two-thirds of the troops
available (likely with the three British legions, used to campaigning in this
theatre) under the fitter Caracalla; and a smaller one featuring the Praetorian
Guard, other guard units and the *legio* II *Parthica,* all under the ailing Severus.
The other units in the overall force – for example, the *auxilia* – would have
been divided between the two as required.

Caracalla led his larger force in a blitzkrieg lightning strike south-west
to north-east along the Highland Boundary Fault, building the sequence of
fifty-four-hectare marching camps as he went along, to seal off the Highlands
from the Maeatae and Caledonians living in the Midland Valley and to prevent
any Caledonian reserves from emerging into the campaigning theatre from
the Highlands themselves. As such, each marching camp (actually in this
interpretation more like an embryonic version of the permanent fortresses
detailed in the Introduction) and any ancillary fortifications would have been
built to deliberately cut off the glens leading into the Highlands.

A further hypothesis here sees the Gask Ridge system of watchtowers
and signal stations at least in part brought out of retirement to again act as a
link between the marching camps and any other scouts on the Highland Line
and reserves to the south. However there is currently little evidence of this,
although the site of the fort of Ardoch at its south-western end was certainly
reused as a fifty-four-hectare marching camp site.

Meanwhile in short order and after very tough fighting (see following two
sections) Kair House was reached with the marching camp built there on the
Bervie Water, thirteen kilometres south-west of Stonehaven on the coast and

with the Highland Line visibly converging with the sea. Thus the Highlands and the route northwards to the Moray and Buchan Lowlands beneath the Moray Firth had been sealed off – such a move being possible only given the enormous force at the disposal of the Roman invaders. An interesting aside here is that, given his smaller force in the late first century AD, Agricola wasn't able to do this; he had to pursue his Caledonian opponents even further north along his string of forty-four-hectare marching camps up to Muiryfold north of the Grampians (although note there is some debate that camps of this group such as Kintore could also have been reused by Severus).

Before addressing the direction taken, and the role, of the second legionary spearhead, I firstly turn to the role played by the *Classis Britannica* regional navy in this campaign, as it directly complements that of the first spearhead along the Highland Line under Caracalla. In the first instance, the fleet would have carried out the vital transport and supply roles, using the network detailed above operating out of the fortified harbours at South Shields on the Tyne, Cramond on the Forth and Carpow on the Tay. However it is with regard to its combat roles in the Severan campaigns that I here present a new hypothesis for the first time, based on my PhD research and also my recently published work on the regional navy (Elliott 2016a).

The principal combat roles of the *Classis Britannica* in this campaign would have been littoral control (of both the coast, to which the term refers, and also along the river networks), as well as scouting, patrolling and reconnaissance. There would have been no requirement for activity in the oceanic blue water zone given the lack of any symmetrical threat, and the desire of any premodern navy to operate within sight of the coast if possible. I therefore now consider activities in the littoral zone as it is here that the *Classis Britannica* played its greatest role in a military context during the Severan campaigns in Scotland.

Littoral naval action differs in a number of ways from open ocean warfare, with Vego (2014, 30) emphasising that most military activity here is tactical in nature, with decentralised command and control being the key to success given the rapidity with which a tactical and operational situation can change. A classic example of this is in the context of Caesar's 55 BC first incursion into Britain, when he reports (Julius Caesar 4.25) that the standard bearer of *legio* X (later *Fretensis*) had to leap ashore to encourage his fellow legionaries to follow him, they being surprised to find their landing zone opposed by native British chariots and foot soldiers.

Naval military operations in the littoral zone also required a different mix of platforms and capabilities to those required in the oceanic zone, and to this end the platforms available to the *Classis Britannica* during the Severan campaigns would have been ideal. Specifically, as detailed in Chapter 2, these were the fast and nimble *liburnae* (bireme galleys) armed with ballista, as well as *myoparo* and *scapha* (cutters and skiffs). All three types would have been ideal platforms with which to engage enemy forces in the littoral zone, where they would have carried out coastal raiding to degrade the regional economies of the Maeatae and Caledonians. The importance of being able to engage in combat in this littoral zone is self-evident when one considers that today 95 per cent of the world's population is settled within 600 miles of the coast, and 80 per cent of the world's nations actually border the sea. Things would have been no different during the Roman occupation of Britain. Vego (2014, 31) provides additional insight here regarding the economic importance of the littoral zone, highlighting that all seaborne trade begins and ends there.

For background when considering naval activity during Severus' *expeditio felicissima Britannica*, the specific characteristics of carrying out military operations in the littoral zone include:

- restricted space for manoeuvring. One should note here how many naval battles in the premodern era took place because one side was trapped against the coastline: for example, the key naval battles of Carteia and the Ebro river and in the Second Punic War (Pitassi 2012, 6);
- the dangerous marine environment for warships along a given coastline, when a sudden change in the weather could prove fatal – as evidenced by the loss of twenty-seven Roman warships off Cape Palinuro in southeastern Italy in 254 BC in the First Punic War (Polybius 1.39);
- the inherent difficulty in staying undetected by the enemy given the proximity of the coast and the associated reduction in warning time to respond to enemy aggression.

For an excellent example of the last point we can look to the Battle of Lilybaeum in 217 BC in the Second Punic War again, when a tip-off from Hiero of Syracuse led to the Roman interception of a Carthaginian naval raiding force and the capture of seven ships and 1,700 prisoners (Briscoe 1989, 66). It may well be, however, that during the Severan campaigns in Scotland one of the desired outcomes was actually the opposite of this – the aim here being for the native Britons of the far north to actually see the navy in action to damage local morale. We certainly have references to this during Agricola's late first century AD activities in the same region.

In terms of the *Classis Britannica*'s experiences of littoral warfare during the Severan campaigns, this would have been part of a wider strategy to seal off the coastal regions of the Midland Valley up to the point where the Highland Line met the North Sea around Stonehaven, and perhaps even further north up to the Moray Firth. As such the Maeatae and Caledonians (at least those in the Midland Valley) would have been completely trapped in this lowland region by Caracalla's legionary spearhead driving north-eastwards along the Highland Line and the *Classis Britannica* along the coast. Furthermore the regional navy would have provided direct support to the ground forces by deploying up the navigable sections of the regional river systems – for example, the Tay – from where they would have provided direct support to the second legionary spearhead (detailed below). Additionally along the coast itself the fleet would have forged ahead of the ground troops of this second spearhead (again see below) to seize any natural harbours and build fortified supply bases to ensure that as the legionaries and *auxilia* arrived along this coastal route provisions were available to maintain the lightning campaign speed the following day. This was a technique perfected in Britain during the campaigns of conquest in the first century AD: for example, that of Vespasian in the south-west in the mid-AD 40s (Elliott 2016a, 119). The presence of the regional fleet would have also ensured that the native Britons had no chance whatsoever to mount any maritime raids to the coastal flank and rear of the advancing Roman land forces.

Having considered the littoral activities of the *Classis Britannica*, we can next examine the scouting, patrolling and reconnaissance functions performed by the regional fleet. Given its mix of vessel types and capabilities as set out above, it was ideally poised to provide the military moving into Scotland along its two axes with intelligence about what to expect along the line of advance in waters it knew very well. In that regard one can imagine the *Classis Britannica* as being the eyes and ears of the legionary spearheads on the maritime flanks of the army, whether along the coast or down the major river networks. The fleet's hard work was clearly noticed by Severus and Caracalla, as coins featuring both Neptune and Oceanus were minted in AD 209 and have been interpreted as referencing the activity of the *Classis Britannica* (Reed 1975, 97). Also some of silver and bronze coins minted between AD 208 and AD 210 show a galley with its stern adorned with standards, as previously used on imagery dating to Trajan's Dacian campaigns. Furthermore Reed argues that Frere's (1974, 172) suggested amalgamation of the commands of the regional navies of Britain, the Rhine and Danube was specifically to facilitate the Severan Scottish campaigns given the size of the force deployed.

Having set out the land (through Caracalla's force) and maritime (through the *Classis Britannica*) advances used by Severus to isolate the native Britons in the central and northern Midland Valley, I now detail the second legionary spearhead's line of advance. This was under the emperor himself with (as set out above) one-third of the land forces available, heading directly north from the Forth and then crossing through Fife. This region is thought to have been heavily settled by the Maeatae, whom the emperor would have taken time to subjugate. Two marching camps – at Auchtermuchty and Edenwood (both of twenty-five hectares, reflecting the smaller size of this force) – help track this campaign.

It seems likely this was a short exercise, considering the asymmetry of the forces involved. Severus would have quickly reached the river Tay at Carpow, where the later of two enclosures here is related to his arrival. This temporary fortification was quickly superseded by the fort, supply base and fortified harbour detailed in Chapter 2.

The key to this location was not this structure, however, but another bridge. Reed (1975) argues that the Severan coins and medallions featuring a permanent monumental bridge and dated to AD 208 (see p. 151) could be related to a new stone-built crossing here, but this view was later rebutted in detail by Robertson (1980, 137). I agree with the latter interpretation, because this was far too early in the campaign to build such a structure. It might therefore refer either to a pre-existing stone-built bridge (Flavian or Antonine, very unlikely) or more likely relate to the bridge over the river Ouse at York or the river Tyne crossing at the Pons Aelius Roman fort (now modern Newcastle), if this bridge is in Britain at all. My preference here at Carpow is yet another bridge of boats, as argued by Robertson (1980, 137) for this location, in addition to that across the Forth. In this context the Caracallan coin of AD 209 then references both, possibly in a generic context for all major river crossings associated with the campaign.

As detailed above, Reed (1975, 95) suggested that in order to link the Forth and Tay crossings a road was built through Fife. He argues that this ran from North Queensferry (the northern footing of his Forth bridge of boats) to Auchterderran (where he cites antiquarian reports of a marching camp and the finding of a coin of Pertinax – if the latter is correct then clearly it is post

Flavian and Antonine). From there the road went to the east of Loch Leven (where 600 coins dating from Galba to Severus were found in 1851 at Portmoak) and finally onwards to the known marching camp site at Auchtermuchty and thence Carpow. To be clear, no road has actually been found to date along this route, and it may well be – given the often marshy nature along its proposed length – that it was to here that the primary-source references to log-built roads being constructed refer.

By the time the bridge at Carpow was ready for use by the Severan legionary spearhead its larger counterpart under Caracalla had already sealed off the Highlands, while the *Classis Britannica* was protecting the coast. Therefore all within the Midland Valley who hadn't been able to escape west or north were now trapped and at the mercy of the Romans.

Severus then struck north across the Tay bridge into the soft underbelly of native resistance. He followed a coastal route initially before driving hard to meet up with the larger force under the emperor's son, perhaps at Inverbervie (Kamm 2011, 126) on the coast near the marching camp site at Kair House. Such a strategy may explain the brutality of this campaign, because the natives had literally nowhere to run when the Romans ravaged the whole of the Midland Valley. In such circumstances the native Britons had no chance to coalesce into a single homogeneous fighting force, and the resistance to the Romans was reduced to localised, vicious guerrilla warfare as the only means of defence, and that is very evident here. According to Faulkner (2001, 120) the experience of Roman conquest was of robbery with violence writ large, very evident here. Most primary sources state that there was no single meeting engagement (see below), yet we know from the primary sources commented upon in Chapter 6 (see p. 133) that the native Britons were known to be capable of fighting in line of battle if necessary.

Having set out the strategy and route of the AD 209 campaign (which would have been replicated in AD 210, but with even more brutality) I now detail the experiences of battle as suffered by all concerned, before turning to a chronological narrative for the AD 209 and AD 210 campaigns.

The Experience of Battle

The Severan campaigns of AD 209 and AD 210 were grim for all the protagonists. The weather seems to have been worse than usual, even for the far north of the islands of Britain, and the terrain proved particularly difficult for the Romans.

Our best account comes from Dio (76.13) regarding the AD 209 campaign, which is set down in full below given the amount of information it provides (with my comments in square brackets):

> . . . as he [Severus] advanced through the country he experienced countless hardships in cutting down the forests, levelling the heights, filling up the swamps, and bridging the rivers; but he fought no battle and beheld no enemy in battle array. The enemy purposely put sheep and cattle in front of the soldiers for them to seize, in order that they might be lured on still further until they were worn out; for in fact the water caused great suffering to the Romans, and when they became scattered, they would be attacked. Then, unable to walk, they would be slain by their own men, in order to avoid capture, so that a full fifty thousand died [clearly a massive exaggeration, but indicative of the difficulties the Romans faced]. But Severus did not desist until he approached the extremity of the island.

Herodian's account (3.14) also highlights the difficulty in pinning the Britons down to enable an engagement to take place: '. . . frequent battles and skirmishes occurred, and in these the Romans were victorious. But it was easy for the Britons to slip away; putting their knowledge of the surrounding area to good use, they disappeared in the woods and marshes. The Romans' unfamiliarity with the terrain prolonged the war.'

The reference to battles in the Herodian quote has been interpreted by most as indicating small engagements, in the context of the subjugation of the Midland Valley. In fact only one primary source seems overtly to detail major engagements, with Orosius (VII.17) in his brief reference to the campaign speaking of 'great and serious battles'. Of all of these voices Dio is the clearest and most relevant (Orosius, for example, was writing in the early fifth century AD), and it is Dio's insistence that Severus 'fought no battle and beheld no enemy in battle array' that I choose here to follow. As Moorhead and Stuttard (2012, 164) argue, a century of studying the tactics of the Romans had taught the native Britons to avoid a formal engagement if at all possible, with Herodian (3.14) saying the tactics '. . . told against the Romans and prolonged the war'.

The nature of the opponents also counted against the Romans, as evidenced by the Dio quote in Chapter 6 regarding the hardiness of the Maeatae and Caledonians (see p. 133). They were clearly far more experienced to a life of living rough in their indigenous terrain when required, with Herodian (3.14) saying they dispensed with breast plates and helmets 'which would impede their movement through the marshes'. All these references illustrate the guerrilla warfare nature of the native British opposition.

It is perhaps useful here to look elsewhere chronologically and geographically for analogies to see how the legionaries, *auxilia* and naval *milites* of Rome would have responded. The Roman military was well experienced in fighting such campaigns, particularly in Britain given the asymmetry when comparing their own forces to those of the native northern Britons (this was not the situation against the Parthians, for example). This would also have been the case for Severus in North Africa earlier in his reign when he engaged the Garamantes, who were similarly symmetrically disadvantaged against the Romans, and this previous campaign would certainly have made an impression on the emperor, the lessons learned later being deployed in Scotland. Roman military textbooks also detailed how to conduct such a specialist style of warfare: for example, former British first century AD governor Frontinus (1.6.3) explained in his *Strategemata* (Stratagems) how to deal with ambushes using classical world examples:

> When Iphicrates was leading his army in Thrace in a long file on account of the nature of the terrain, and the report was brought to him that the enemy planned to attack his rearguard, he ordered some cohorts to withdraw to both flanks and halt, while the rest were to quicken their pace and flee. But from the complete line as it passed by, he kept back all the choicest soldiers. Thus, when the enemy were busy with promiscuous pillaging, and in fact were already exhausted, while his own men were refreshed and drawn up in order, he attacked and routed the foe and stripped them of their booty.

What seems clear from all the above primary sources is that, despite the difficulties pinning down their opponents (clearly fighting for survival), the Romans adapted to the tactics being used against them, even if at great cost. Goldsworthy (2003, 168) in his detailed analysis of the Roman Army on campaign is clear in his view that such adaption to the circumstances was one of the great characteristics of the Roman military:

> It is certainly a mistake to claim the professional Roman Army was unsuited to fighting enemies who waged guerrilla warfare and avoided open battle. In time, the Romans were always able to adapt to the local situation. The sophisticated structure, training and well organised supply system (very evident in Severus' *expeditio felicissima Britannica*) gave them advantages in all levels of warfare.

Thus, while things were grim for the Romans, they overcame the adversity and ensured that the discomfort felt by all levels of native northern British society (whose local economy was destroyed in the first year of campaigning) was far more brutal. The 'Severan surge' in that sense achieved its objective.

Finally in this section I will use one final analogy to illustrate what being on the receiving end of such close Roman military attention was like. This is in the context of recently published research regarding the seven-hectare hill fort site at Burnswark in Dumfriesshire in the Scottish Borders. Here a debate has taken place as to whether data previously considered (from antiquarian and 1960s' archaeological excavations) showed a Roman siege at the site (either Hadrianic or early Antonine in date) or whether the site was actually an example of a Roman siege training exercise. The key items of interest in that regard were the north and south Roman siege camps, and also a plethora of ballista bolts and balls and lead slingshots found at the site.

To reach a conclusion either way the Trimontium Trust recently carried out a review of the existing research and also secured fresh data – the latter based on a systematic, metal-detecting survey to identify more lead slingshots (with a view to plotting their scatter) and also experimental archaeology regarding the use of slings in siege warfare (Reid 2016, 22). The results of this research suggest yet another grim interpretation for the activities of the Romans north of the frontier, with the two camps now being seen as a real-world tactical response to the topography in the context of a full siege, and the widespread scatter of slingshots and other missiles (and their quality) suggesting deadly intent. As Reid (2016, 26) says, the evidence shows that:

> . . . there was a massive missile barrage at Burnswark. This was not just restricted to the gateways, but extended along a full half kilometer of native rampart. The simplest explanation for this distribution is that the defenders on the hilltop were suppressed by a hail of sling bullets with an accurate range of 120m and the stopping power of a modern handgun, as well as ballista bolts, and arrows. This presumably covered an attacking force sweeping out the three huge gateways and storming the hilltop. Such a combination of missile troops and conventional infantry is likely to have been brutally effective.

There we have yet again the use of the word brutal with regard to Roman activity in the far north of Britain.

One other factor adds even more insight into the awful experience of the native Britons on the receiving end of this devastation. Some of slingshots had a four-millimetre hole through their centre, which was designed to make a screeching noise when slung. This is an early example of psychological warfare on the battlefield, bringing to mind the screaming sirens of diving Junkers Ju-87 Stukas during the blitzkrieg early in Second World War, adding to the misery of those on the receiving end.

The Two Campaigns of AD 209 and AD 210

Having set out the strategy and route of the Severan campaigns in Scotland, and discussed the experiences of those involved in the conflict, I now use this knowledge to build out a chronology for the two incursions. Both Dio and Herodian indicate throughout their accounts of Severus in the north of Britain that there were specifically two campaigns, and there has been much debate about which years these were in – the only firm date we have is of the emperor's death in AD 211. Reed (1975, 99), for example, comes up with a very detailed chronology, which I summarise here:

AD 207   Caracalla campaigns in Britain with the three British legions up to the Forth, with Severus arriving in Gaul.

AD 208   Severus arrives in Britain, then campaigns with Caracalla through Fife, with the bridges built at South Queensferry over the Forth and Carpow over the Tay.

AD 209   Caracalla advances north along the old route taken by Agricola in the Flavian period up to Keithock, while Severus heads north over the Tay bridge.

AD 210   All forces advance to Inveresk on the Forth, building the sixty-seven-hectare sequence of marching camps in the Scottish Borders, with Caracalla then moving up the Highland Line to Kair House near the coast. Later in the year, after a negotiated peace with the Caledonians making concessions, the Maeatae revolt, followed by the Caledonians after Severus orders his genocide.

There are many issues with this chronology and it is best to counter some of the suggestions through the use of a knowledge of military campaigning and simple common sense. Firstly there is no evidence of campaigning in AD 207, and it is in that year that I believe Severus received his news from the province (by letter from Senecio or in another form) requesting imperial assistance in

Britain. Secondly Reed's (1975) reference to Severus and Caracalla campaigning in Fife in AD 208 is clearly a device to allow him to claim that the AD 208 Severan coin showing a permanent bridge refers to the river Tay crossing at Carpow. As I have set out above, this is far more likely to refer to a bridge at York or Newcastle (if in Britain at all). Thirdly this chronology significantly underestimates the time it would have taken to gather and then provision an invasion force of 50,000 men for such an arduous campaign. Finally there is no data to support the suggested chronology of the various marching camp sequences. Therefore, taking into account my own extensive research as set out above including the use of the most up-to-date data, I believe that the following is a far more likely chronology regarding the two campaigns:

AD 207   News from the province arrives in Rome (in Senecio's letter or another form), and planning for the campaign begins immediately. Orders are dispatched to the various military units that will participate in the campaign to begin their preparations to travel to Britain.

AD 208   The invasion force gathers in York and the north of the province, ultimately numbering 50,000 men. Severus establishes York as his imperial capital.

AD 209   First campaign, with the whole force traversing the Scottish Borders along Dere Street, the Forth then bridged, after which Caracalla (with two-thirds of the force) drives a legionary spearhead up the Highland Boundary Fault line to Kair House. From there he seals off the Highlands from the central and northern Midlands Valley, constructing the fifty-four-hectare marching camp sequence. At the same time the *Classis Britannica* seals off the coast up to the same point, trapping the Maeatae and Caledonians. Finally Severus leads the remaining one-third of the force through Fife, crosses the river Tay at Carpow and then ravages the Midland Valley there. The native Britons sue for peace, territory is ceded and the campaign ends. At this point key elements of the defensive network built by the Romans for the campaign remain garrisoned (for example, Carpow), although much of the force including the emperor and his son withdraw south to York before the onset of winter.

AD 210   The Maeatae (and later the Caledonians) revolt, and the
            previous year's campaign is repeated, although this time with
            Severus' direction to commit genocide. The emperor is too ill to
            join the campaign himself so the whole force is led by Caracalla.
            Success of some kind is achieved given the subsequent lengthy
            peace in the region (see Chapter 8).

AD 211   Severus dies in York in February, and Caracalla and Geta swiftly
            withdraw to Rome.

There is a simple elegance to this chronology within which sits comfortably
all the principal elements of the story as noted by the primary sources, and
the subsequent gathering of archaeological data. In particular, there would
have been no chance that the full force of 50,000 men would have been left in
place in the far north during a regional winter, if only because of the immense
difficulties keeping such a force supplied in the front line given the likely
weather conditions. In normal circumstances, for example, the regional fleet
would avoid all but the most vital activities at sea during the winter months.

Having set out a usable chronology, we can now briefly look at the two
campaigns in turn. In terms of the first campaign, Dio (76.13) says that once
Severus had reached the most northerly point of advance he:

> . . . observed most accurately the variation of the sun's motion and the length
> of the days and the nights in summer and winter respectively. Having thus been
> conveyed through practically the whole of the hostile country (for he actually
> was conveyed in a covered litter most of the way, on account of his infirmity),
> he returned to the friendly portion, after he had forced the Britons to come to
> terms, on the condition that they should abandon a large part of their territory.

We have little insight here as to the exact detail of the specific events of the
AD 209 campaign, and Dio and Herodian would certainly have had none of
the motivation to write positively about Severus as Tacitus did with his father-
in-law Agricola. Thus we can be fairly certain that if the campaign had been
a disaster then we would known about it. To that end therefore it seems that,
despite the grim nature of the campaign, its size and rapidity were successful
and the enemy defeated, and Hodgson (2014, 48) argues that those parts of
Scotland reached by Severus' forces would have been terribly damaged. The
Romans would have been keen to wrap up events at this point given the cost
to the imperial *fiscus* of keeping such a huge force in the field. Meanwhile the

steady stream of casualties (note Dio's improbable figure of 50,000) from guerrilla activity would also have begun to tell on the morale of troops by the end of the campaigning season, if not earlier. Additionally the ageing emperor (being carried in his litter and in pain from his affliction with gout) would have been exhausted by this point, and so decided to agree terms with his equally exhausted enemy. This may actually have been unpopular with his military leadership and some of the troops, as Dio (76.14) next tells the famous tale of an attempted imperial patricide. This passage is important enough to be presented in full, with my comments in square brackets:

> Antoninus [Caracalla] was causing him alarm and endless anxiety by his intemperate life, by his evident intention to murder his brother if the chance should offer [this is further considered in Chapter 8], and, finally, by plotting against the emperor himself . . . [thus] when both were riding forward to meet the Caledonians [and presumably Maeatae], in order to receive their arms and discuss the details of the truce, Antoninus attempted to kill his father outright with his own hand. They were proceeding on horseback, Severus also being mounted, in spite of the fact that he was weakened by infirmity in his feet, and the rest of the army was following; the enemy's force were likewise spectators. At this juncture, while all were proceeding in silence and in order, Antoninus reined in his horse and drew his sword, as if he were going to strike his father in the back. But the others who were riding with them, upon seeing this, cried out, and so Antoninus, in alarm, desisted from his attempt. Severus turned at their shout and saw the sword, yet he did not utter a word, but ascended the tribunal [where the peace was to be signed], finished what he had to do, and returned to headquarters. Then he summoned his son . . . ordered a sword to be placed within easy reach, and upbraided the youth for having dared to do such a thing at all and especially for having been on the point of committing so monstrous a crime in the sight of all, both the allies and the enemy. And finally he said: 'Now if you really want to slay me, put me out of the way here; for you are strong, while I am an old man and prostrate. For, if you do not shrink from the deed, but hesitate to murder me with your own hands, there is Papinian, the [praetorian] prefect, standing beside you, whom you can order to slay me; for surely he will do anything that you command, since you are also emperor.' Though he spoke in this fashion, he nevertheless did Antoninus no harm . . . on the present occasion he allowed his love for his offspring to

outweigh his love for his country; and yet in doing so he betrayed his other son, for he well knew what would happen (once he himself was dead).

If this isn't a literary device by Dio, who was very critical of Caracalla later as emperor, then the narrative seems pretty clear that Severus here only just survived an assassination and usurpation attempt. The peace was signed nevertheless, and on terms favourable to Rome, with the native Britons ceding plentiful territory to the Empire (perhaps up to the Antonine Wall line, and even Fife given Carpow's evident ongoing use with its inscription to Caracalla, as detailed in Chapter 2). Severus next proclaimed a famous victory, with he and his two sons being given the title *Britannicus* and with celebratory coins being struck to commemorate this. Campaigning, at least for the short term, was over, and to apparent imperial satisfaction. Dio (76.16.5) even adds an anecdote here about Julia Domna, saying that after the peace had been agreed she had a conversation with the wife of a Caledonian leader named Argentocoxus in which they compared the sexual customs of their cultures.

As always in the Roman experience north of the provincial border (at least up to this point), such a state of comparative calm was not to last. Severus, Caracalla and the military leadership wintered in York and still seem to have been there in May 210, as Birley (1999, 185) highlights a letter sent in their names in response to an inquiry by a lady called Caecilia dated the 5th of that month. However clearly the terms that had so satisfied the Romans in AD 209 were not so agreeable to at least the Maeatae (probably the recipients of the most extreme experiences of the AD 209 campaign) because in AD 210 they revolted again. Birley (1999, 186) suggests one reason was that one of the tribal centres may have been near the later Pictish (he says that they could in fact be considered 'proto-Picts') capital site at Abernethy, very close to the Roman site and bridge at Carpow, and it may latterly have dawned upon the native Britons here that the Romans in the region were determined to stay for the long term, settled in the Maeatae heartland.

One can only guess at the sad fate of the Roman garrisons in the region as the revolt gathered pace, and Severus once more determined to march north and this time finish the job. His ill health got the better of him, however, so the ensuing campaign (a replica of the first) was led by the apparently forgiven Caracalla. The emperor was less forgiving to the natives, especially when the Caledonians soon predictably joined in. At this point he issued the genocidal order to kill all the Britons the Romans came across (Southern 2013, 248), apparently in response to the natives' rough treatment of the invading Romans, although it may well have been that the order was actually given after the initial Maeatae revolt. (This genocide was the starting point for this book.) The new campaign seems again to have been successful from a Roman perspective as commemorative coins of Caracalla and his brother Geta celebrating victory in Britain were minted in Rome in AD 212 (Mason 2003, 139). As usual, however, nothing was to remain as Severus had intended, because in February AD 211 he died in the freezing cold of a northern British winter.

CHAPTER 8

Septimius Severus in Britain: Aftermath and Conclusion

I N THIS FINAL CHAPTER I consider the legacy of the Severan *expeditio felicissima Britannica*, taking a view about whether the 'shock and awe' strategy employed by the emperor in the form of his 'Severan Surge' was ultimately worth the enormous effort. I also consider the impact of the genocide ordered by Severus in his second year of campaigning, looking to see if there is any evidential data to support Dio's claim. Finally I conclude by setting his legacy, including that of his campaigns in Britain, into the context of the wider narrative of the Roman Empire in the West.

To achieve these aims I first examine what happened from the point the emperor died, and then the subsequent and dramatic developments in Rome. I then consider the implications of his death for the Roman presence in Britain (with a specific focus on the campaigning region north of the border). I next revisit the possible aims of Severus' campaigns in Britain, as set out in Chapter 6, before reviewing what was actually achieved here considering in detail the allegations of genocide. Having looked at the legacies of this campaign, I then see how they fit in with Severus' reputation as a great warrior emperor.

What Happened Next

Severus died aged sixty-five on 4 February 211 in York after what appears to have been a long illness – the primary sources often referring to his infirmity later in life. The *Historia Augusta* (22.4–7), perhaps pandering to his known superstitious nature, here suggests four near-contemporary omens which foreshadowed the event:

- A dream by the emperor regarding his own deification.
- An episode at a games in honour of victory in the north, which Birley (1999, 184) suggests may have been at Carpow. Here three plaster figures of the goddess Victory were set up, one each for Severus (in the centre, carrying a globe inscribed with his name), Caracalla and Geta. That of the emperor was unceremoniously blown over by a gust of wind.
- Another episode, this time on the return south after the campaigning season, was detailed in the *Historia Augusta* and has become an important component in the debate about ethnicity within the Roman military. It is therefore worth recording in full here:

> On another occasion, when he was returning to his nearest quarters from an inspection of the wall at Luguvalium [Carlisle] in Britain, at a time when he had not only proved victorious but had concluded a perpetual peace, just as he was wondering what omen would present itself, an Ethiopian soldier, who was famous among buffoons and always a notable jester, met him with a garland of cypress-boughs [sacred to Pluto, God of the underworld]. And when Severus in a rage ordered that the man be removed from his sight, troubled as he was by the man's ominous colour and the ominous nature of the garland, the Ethiopian by way of jest cried, it is said, 'You have been all things, you have conquered all things, now O conqueror, be a God'.

Birley (1999, 184) suggests the location of the wall section visited by Severus here was the fort at Aballava (Burgh-by-Sands) to the west of Carlisle, as we know there was a Moorish auxiliary unit based there in the third century AD called the *numerus Maurorum Aurelianorum* (Fryer 2010, 2).

- The final episode also relates to the issue of colour (this time sacrificial animals) and again is worth detailing in full from the *Historia Augusta*:

> And when finally reaching the town [either Carlisle itself or perhaps York] he wished to perform a sacrifice, in the first place, through a misunderstanding on the part of the rustic soothsayer, he was taken to the Temple of Bellona [a Sabine goddess of war], and, in the second place, the victims provided him were black. And then, when he abandoned the sacrifice in disgust and betook himself to the palace [supporting

the York interpretation], through some carelessness on the part of the attendants the black victims followed him up to its very doors.

As to the nature of the fatal illness itself, modern narratives most often refer to gout, hence Severus' need for a litter as he seems to have been unable to walk. Other commentators have argued that his illness might have been chronic arthritis. Neither would have been a primary cause of his death, so might be interpreted as symptoms of some more serious affliction: for example, Herodian (3.15.1) talks of a 'more prolonged illness'. Modern commentators, however, attribute Severus' death to natural causes, although the primary sources are more nuanced as to whether Caracalla played some part. For example, Dio (76/77.15.2) says: '. . . his disease carried him off . . . with some assistance from Antoninus [Caracalla] as well, it is said.' Herodian (3.14.1–3) goes further regarding Caracalla's intent:

> [Caracalla] . . . began to persuade them [the army] to look to him alone, and was canvassing for the position of sole ruler by every means [note by this time Geta had also been elevated to an Augustus, in addition to Severus and Caracalla], slandering his brother. But his father, ill for a long time and being slow to die, seemed to him a burden and a nuisance. He tried to persuade both his doctors and attendants who were caring for him to mistreat the old man, so as to be rid of him sooner. But finally, though slowly, Severus, for the most part destroyed by sorrow [because of his elder son's treachery] did expire, having had a life of greater distinction, as far as warfare is concerned, than all other emperors.

Both authors wrote very negatively about Caracalla and can be expected not to reflect positively on his intentions with regard to his ailing father, but there is no smoking gun here either – even if there was a likely intent, and indeed opportunity. In that regard, on balance it seems most likely that Severus died of natural causes, carried off by the cold of a bitter winter at the northern extremity of his Empire (especially given Caracalla's subsequent treatment of his father's doctors).

Severus was succeeded by his two sons as joint Augusti. His body was cremated in York, where his ashes were placed inside an urn of 'purple stone' (Dio, 76.15.4). This had been ordered before his death (it is not clear if from Britain, which is very unlikely, although Birley 1999, 256, says it could have been Derbyshire 'Blue John') or if it had travelled with him from Italy. This urn shows a degree of foreknowledge on his part that he wouldn't return from the province. From this description the urn was probably made from porphyry – a rare and very hard volcanic rock consisting of quartz, feldspar and mica; its name means purple, so was a fitting resting place for the ashes of an emperor.

Caracalla and Geta then made quick preparations to return to Rome to secure their respective power bases, with the former taking the lead in agreeing a hasty and new settlement with the Maeatae and Caledonians (this 'new' peace would have been over and above whatever official ending there had been to the AD 210 campaign). Birley (1999, 188), interpreting the primary sources, highlights the withdrawal of the Roman troops from enemy territory and the abandoning of the forts. While as with AD 209 the full 50,000 troops wouldn't have wintered in the far north after the conclusion of the AD 210 campaign, the garrisons left behind at key sites such as Ardoch, Carpow, the Antonine Wall (possibly) and Cramond would have been larger given the trouble after the first peace treaty.

We have little insight into this new peace treaty following Severus' death, other than the fact that the northern frontier was once again set on the Solway Firth–Tyne Line of Hadrian's Wall (now substantially repaired). Note that none of the primary sources mentions the state of the native Britons in the far north by this time, especially in the context of the evident devastation of the AD 210 campaign and its apparent genocide. It does seem likely that Caracalla's settlement would have been particularly one-sided.

Relations between the two brothers, never good, deteriorated rapidly in York. Severus may have wanted the two to rule in tandem, as with Marcus Aurelius and Lucius Verus in the second century AD, but Caracalla certainly didn't see it that way (note how he led the negotiations to agree the withdrawal from the north). In fact his first actions can be seen in a 'like father like son' light because he quickly dismissed the Praetorian Guard prefect Papinianus (we should remember he was actually Caracalla's relative on his mother's side, and some of the primary sources say Severus had trusted the prefect with the brother's welfare). He also executed some of his father's most devoted freed men (including Castor the court chamberlain and Euodus, his own former tutor), men whom Severus would have tasked with trying to keep the imperial family together. The order would also have been sent out at this time to execute Caracalla's former wife, the unfortunate Plautilla. He also apparently had put to death Severus' court doctors who had refused to act against the old man at his suggestion prior to the emperor's death. Caracalla then seems to have tried to get the army to recognise him as sole emperor (perhaps even plotting to kill his younger brother), but failed because apparently Geta actually looked like his father, which made him popular with the troops.

Early in the spring of AD 211 the imperial party made ready to leave for Rome, with Julia Domna and the imperial *comites* making a final concerted effort in Britain to reconcile her sons, to which Caracalla responded positively with a public display of affection for Geta. This wasn't to last, however, with the brothers having separate quarters on their journey home – Kean (2005, 115) says that they hardly spoke. Kean adds that one of the key factors here was Geta's refusal to behave as a junior to his elder brother (even though they were both Augusti), as Lucius Verus had done in a similar situation with Marcus Aurelius. Both brothers had their own court factions, all jockeying for favour and position in whatever form the new regime took.

Once back in Rome matters worsened again, with perhaps the final event the brothers jointly participated in as Augusti being the burial of Severus in the Mausoleum of Hadrian. From this point the imperial government, its key officials hoping to bed in a new regime with a smooth handover from Severus to the two brothers, instead ground to a halt because of their constant bickering over every policy decision or appointment. Even today you can imagine the machinations of all concerned played out in the vast complex of fine rooms, apartments and undercrofts, if you stand in the Severan Buildings in the Imperial Palace on the Palatine.

Some primary sources say there was talk for a short while of the brothers dividing the Empire between them – Geta taking control of the east. Even if this was true the solution quickly fell through, apparently at the instigation of Julia Domna (Scarre 1995b, 139). After this, things soon came to a head, with Caracalla's closest supporters urging him to have Geta murdered, especially as the Senate (never supporters of Severus) were apparently supporting the younger brother (Birley 1999, 189). Scarre (1995b, 139) also says Geta had made a concerted attempt to get the support of the literary men of Rome, and so was receiving a better press, which generated stronger public support. At this point Caracalla finally gave into his supporter's demands and ordered the fratricide, with a first assassination attempt being made around the time of the festival of Saturnalia in mid-December AD 211, although it failed. A second on 26 December ultimately succeeded (Birley 1999, 189).

This plot seems to have involved the tempting of Geta to 'peace talks' with his brother on neutral territory, specifically their mother's private quarters in the Imperial Palace. Geta unwisely took the invite at face value and attended without his bodyguard, thereby walking into a trap and being stabbed by soldiers loyal to his brother. As the story goes, he apparently ran to his mother, dying in her arms, with Caracalla either actively participating in his murder or being present to urge his soldiers on.

Papinianus, the former praetorian prefect, was beheaded shortly afterwards and his body dragged through the streets of Rome. A 'terror' then seems to have followed in the imperial capital, with up to 20,000 viewed as aligned with either Severus or Geta executed. Notable unfortunates here included the son of Pertinax, a sister of Commodus and a cousin of Caracalla (also called Septimius Severus). Meanwhile Caracalla ensured that, at least in an official sense, his brother would 'disappear' by declaring a *damnatio memoriae* (translated as condemnation of memory) against him. This led to many images of the brothers having Geta's portrait defaced, and inscriptions mentioning him being similarly destroyed. These are still visible: for example, on the Arch of Septimius Severus. The character of Caracalla and his role in the overall Severan legacy is considered at the end of this chapter.

I now turn to what happened next following Severus' death in the province of Britain broadly, and specifically in the far north. It is very clear from the above that, without Severus' willpower to drive the difficult and expensive campaigns in the north onwards, neither Caracalla nor Geta had the slightest inclination to continue military activity there (the actual aims of Severus are considered again below). Furthermore, given what appears to have been a scouring of the Midland Valley of all opposition and native British economic activity in the AD 210 campaign, there was perhaps no need for a significant Roman military presence there excepting the garrisons at key sites. Thus we are presented with a picture of a controlled disengagement by the army, those garrisons left after the AD 210 campaign withdrawing one by one. The Rhine and Danubian vexillations returned to their continental bases and the two British legions from further south went back to Caerleon and Chester. *Legio* VI *Victrix* remained in place in York, its legate no doubt pleased to have his by now substantially aggrandised *principia* and *praetorium* back. Meanwhile the Praetorian Guard and troops of the *legio* II *Parthica* would have travelled back to Rome.

The archaeological data available gives some insight into this process of disengagement in the far north and withdrawal to the line of Hadrian's Wall. Hodgson (2014, 46) says an absence of coins later than AD 207 from the fort, supply bases and fortified harbour at Carpow, and AD 209 from its counterpart at Cramond, has convinced some numismatists and archaeologists that this data implies their abandonment immediately after the death of Severus in AD 211. Other commentators using the same data argue an even earlier abandonment. The number of Severan coins from Carpow and Cramond on which these conclusions have been based is very small (at the time of writing, eleven at Carpow and nineteen at Cramond), and so it could be argued that at present the numismatic evidence from both sites cannot safely be used to suggest total abandonment after Severus' death. It might even allow the possibility that these sites were held for some years after AD 211 as maritime outposts north of Hadrian's Wall, especially noting the Caracallan gateway inscription at Carpow (likely the key port of evacuation for the withdrawing troops in the far north, as I suggest in Chapter 2).

If this system of coastal outposts in the far north was one of the main legacies of Severus' *expeditio felicissima Britannica*, it was short-lived. For example, the bathhouse at Carpow did not display the alterations to be expected if used for a significant period of time, and the site also featured a restricted range of pottery types, which indicates a short time span of occupation (Hodgson 2014, 47). Cramond, further south on the Forth, may have been occupied later than this, with Hodgson saying that the expansion of the fort site at South Shields to accommodate the whole of *cohors* V *Gallorum* in the AD 220s could indicate the end of that unit's association with Cramond – it being linked with both sites during the Severan campaigns (see Chapters 2 and 7).

The Aims of Severus' Campaigns

Before reviewing what was actually achieved by the enormous lengths Severus went to in order to defeat the Maeatae and Caledonians in modern Scotland, I first revisit the potential factors behind his *expeditio felicissima Britannica* set out in Chapter 6 to allow us to make a judgement. These were:

- Severus was eager to escape from Rome, the warrior emperor bored and also worried about the lavish lifestyles being led by his two sons.
- He was concerned with his legacy as a great soldier, and wanted one final chance to gain a conquest never before achieved by Rome.
- In the wake of Albinus' late second-century usurpation attempt, all was not well with the garrison in Britain. The province was thus vulnerable.

- In that regard, the final and most obvious reason behind his *expeditio felicissima Britannica* was to counter the aggression of the Maeatae and Caledonians. At a time when their populations were growing following the coalescence of power through contact with Rome, they may have been suffering a harvest shock given the poor weather recorded in the province at this time. Thus the native Britons of the far north had three potential causes to head south: opportunity (given the province's vulnerability); the need to keep a growing warrior class busy; and potential starvation.

As I concluded in Chapter 6, it was probably a combination of all of these factors that drew Severus to Britain at the end of his life for one final campaign, and from these four we can extract two that allow us to measure how successful Severus was in his campaigns. These were his desire for one final conquest, and his need to counter the aggression of the Maeatae and Caledonians. These are now considered in detail.

What Did the *Expeditio Felicissima Britannica* Achieve?

Severus certainly deployed enough troops in the two campaigns of AD 209 and AD 210 to secure (at least) the Scottish Borders and the central and northern Midland Valley (including Fife) as part of the province. Note here he had already initiated the process that was to divide Britannia in half so if he had followed through on any such intention the conquered areas would have become part of Britannia Inferior. However a lively debate continues to take place about whether Severus actually wanted the full presence of Rome to stay north of the border after his campaigns, or if he simply wished to smash the Maeatae and Caledonians and then leave. Reed (1975, 99), for example, compares Severus' campaigns with those of Agricola, who he believes certainly expected (until his recall by Domitian) to stay in the north given the building of the full-size legionary fortress at Inchtuthil. He says that one could interpret Severus' construction of the full-size fort, supply base and fortified harbour at Carpow in the same light, and concludes that Severus certainly intended to occupy Fife (and so by definition the Scottish Borders given that these lay further south). Reed adds that one interpretation of the very high frequency of coins from AD 209 and AD 210 showing *annona* payments might actually be a reference to corn now being supplied as tribute by the Maeatae. In arguing for such an intended occupation, however, he set himself against the likes of Frere (1974, 176), who argues that there was no intention to occupy the conquered territory.

The difficulty we face here in ascertaining who is correct among the various voices on both sides of this debate is that, while the archaeological data certainly shows the presence in the far north of the *expeditio felicissima Britannica*, it is silent regarding the emperor's ultimate intentions. We are therefore reduced to taking an informed view based on the limited data, analogy and anecdote – the last two based on Severus' activities elsewhere, both chronologically and geographically, once emperor. Using such sources I therefore conclude that Severus did intend to incorporate the Scottish Borders and certainly Fife – if not the whole central and northern Midland Valley – into the new province of Britannia Inferior. The commitment of such a vast force against what, at face value, would have been such an inferior opponent speaks to this level of territorial commitment, as does the deliberate sealing off of the Highlands by Caracalla, driving his legionary spearhead along the Highland Boundary Fault in AD 209 and AD 210. Furthermore, after his successful campaigns in the east and North Africa, Severus certainly set about reordering the regional *limes* to incorporate newly conquered territories, and it would be odd indeed if this great, ageing warrior, obsessed with legacy, hadn't planned to do the same in Scotland. Thus we have to judge if he succeeded in this aim, and the answer has to be a definitive 'no'. This is fully understandable because the whole plan was based on his own vision and drive, which his sons completely lacked once he was dead. Given the levels of depopulation in the region after the AD 210 campaign (see below), there seems no doubt that had he lived a significant portion of modern Scotland would have been taken into the Roman Empire, perhaps with new stone-built settlements emerging, and with the story of modern Scotland and the emergence of the Picts significantly changed.

As to whether Severus successfully countered the Maeatae and Caledonians, there is no doubt in my mind that in this he was absolutely successful. Their ability to cause trouble south of the border was significantly depleted and the regional economy destroyed. A number of factors have been used by a variety of commentators to prove this to be the case, and especially the effects of the genocide Dio says was ordered in AD 210. Hodgson (2014, 48), for example, says there is a long historical tradition of viewing Severus' *expeditio felicissima Britannica* as successful given the peaceful state of the province in the third century AD, while Frere (1974, 176) highlights the fact that the northern frontier remained at peace until AD 296 – probably the longest period that this occurred until the premodern era. Hodgson (2014, 48) tests this view, saying that this 'third century peace' might actually be the result of the silence of the literary sources about the provinces of Britain at the time. The primary sources would certainly have had plenty of other things to write about during the 'Crisis of the Third Century', which enveloped the whole Empire from the death of Severus Alexander in AD 235 until the accession of Diocletian in AD 284, with Britain reverting to its more traditional role as a backwater frontier zone. Hodgson goes on to say that the strength to which the outpost forts north of Hadrian's Wall were held in the earlier part of the third century shows how necessary a system of early warning against incursion from Scotland remained (although this again might be a hangover from the pre-Severan situation – the Romans taking no chances given what had happened previously). Hodgson (2014, 48) adds: 'If Scotland had been pacified, what was a vexillation of *legio* VI (Victrix) doing on the main route north, at Piercebridge on the Tees, in AD 217, accompanied by legionary detachments from both Upper and Lower Germany?'

Fortunately we have other hard evidence here to back up the general view that lowland Scotland was significantly depopulated after the campaigns of AD 209 and 210 (and particularly the latter). For example it seems likely that as part of the Maeatae and Caledonian surrender of AD 210, or the settlement made by Caracalla after his father's death in AD 211, both confederations supplied recruits to the Roman military (through enforced conscription) to be formed into units for deployment to the continental provinces. Evidence of this is seen in an inscription of AD 232 from Upper Germany at the fort at Walldurn, which mentions *Brit(tones) dediticii* (Caracalla himself campaigned here in AD 213), while a Caledonian named Lossio Veda, grandson of Vepogenus, appears in Colchester far to the south in the reign of Severus Alexander.

Meanwhile woodland regeneration in the campaigning region during the Roman occupation, detected by pollen analysis, has also been linked to the Severan genocide story of AD 210, with the agricultural land going uncultivated for a number of generations and thus indicating a significant depopulation event. Furthermore archaeological research between 1996 and 2005 by the Ben Lawers Historic Landscape Project (Atkinson 2016) may actually show the physical evidence of this depopulation. This work was carried out around Loch Tay in the Central Highlands and shows that a healthy Iron Age settlement pattern of hut circles, homesteads and crannogs flourished until the end of the second century, after which all the sites were abandoned with no trace of human activity for another 250 years (excepting perhaps one crannog, which might have been reoccupied by AD 420). This location would have been on the western periphery of the campaigning area and would certainly have supplied troops to fight with the Maeatae or Caledonians. They clearly did not return, given this level of abandonment. Roman troops perhaps crossed the Highland Boundary Fault into the Highlands in AD 209 or AD 210 to raid the settlements there, although there is no evidence of this.

Taken all together, the above evidence does indicate strongly that the genocide suggested by Dio at some level did take place, with the campaigning region ravaged; in fact it is surprising that Caracalla could find any elites left with whom to make a settlement in AD 211. As Southern (2013, 251) suggests, this indicates that the 'slash and burn' policy of the AD 210 campaign really did lead to severe depopulation in the region, which took several generations of peaceful coexistence to overcome. Those comparatively few Maeatae and Caledonians left after peace was settled faced the prospect of enforced conscription and removal to the Rhine or Danube frontiers, or enslavement and a slow and painful death.

The Severan Legacy and the Role of His Scottish Campaigns Therein

Severus has a strong legacy among his fellow pantheon of Roman emperors, as a driven and successful warrior once in power who thrived when on campaign and who left his mark in both the imperial capital and across the Empire. In that regard, although his military expenditure placed a great strain on the imperial *fiscus* and the wider imperial economy, Severus is best remembered as a strong and able ruler. His enlargement of the territory brought within the *limes Tripolitanus* during his North African campaign (surely a dry run for what would later take place in Scotland) secured Africa as the key agricultural base of the Empire alongside Egypt, while his victories over the Parthian Empire were decisive during his own lifetime (and indeed monumentalised on his arch in the Forum in Rome). In fact it could be said that a status quo of Roman dominance in the east following his late second-century campaigns lasted until AD 251.

Severus was also distinguished in his own lifetime for his building works, because he knew that this would be one of the ways his legacy would be best remembered. Apart his triumphal arch, he also erected the Severan Buildings in the Imperial Palace on the Palatine (including the installation of the Septizodium nymphaeum), shaping this grandest of residences to his own needs. He also, as detailed in Chapter 6, greatly enriched his native city of Lepcis Magna, which featured a further triumphal arch to commemorate his visit of AD 203.

We do of course have to balance this legacy with what I hope has been shown convincingly in this book – that in his campaigns in Scotland in AD 209 and AD 210 Severus brutalised the local population, perhaps to the point of near annihilation through the order of his genocide. Such was the lot for the emperors of Rome and their opponents, however, classical warfare often being a zero sum game which the loser lost dramatically.

Severus paid for any success he achieved in his own lifetime, by dying a miserable death in great pain as far from the centre of his Empire as he could get, in the freezing cold of a northern winter and in the almost certain knowledge that once he was gone the two sons he had favoured so much would devour each other in their quest to be sole ruler (definitely, in the case of Caracalla). His rule also proved to be the highpoint of the Severan dynasty he founded, with all his successors meeting an untimely end: the unfortunate Geta; the increasingly psychotic Caracalla, who was driven to cruelty by guilt and insecurity (Scarre 1995b, 147); the bizarre Elagabalus; and the weak Severus Alexander (with the interlude of Macrinus between Caracalla and Elagabalus). In fact it was at the point that Severus Alexander was assassinated in AD 235 that the 'Crisis of the Third Century' began, its fuse lit much earlier as Severus pondered what he knew would be a troubled succession as he lay dying in AD 211.

What we are then left with is the story of one of the great campaigns of the ancient world, a fantastical military adventure at the furthest northern extremity of the Roman Empire in the west, with all concerned enduring great hardship (particularly the Maeatae and Caledonians), and all on an epic scale to rival anything written by Tolkien or featuring more recently in popular culture. Ultimately, despite Severus clearly securing peace in the north of the islands of Britain for four generations, the far north of the region there went unconquered and was to remain so throughout the Roman occupation of Britain.

Timeline of Roman Britain

THIS TIMELINE SHOWS KEY EVENTS in the story of the Roman occupation of Britain. It is designed to allow the events of Severus' *expeditio felicissima Britannica* to be set into a firm chronological context.

Date	Event
Date	*Event*
58 BC	Caesar begins his conquest of Gaul.
57 BC	Veneti submit to Caesar.
56 BC	Rebellion of the Veneti; Battle of Morbihan.
55 BC	First Roman invasion of Britain; Caesar's first incursion.
54 BC	Second Roman invasion of Britain; Caesar's second incursion.
44 BC	Caesar assassinated in Rome.
27 BC	The conquest of north-west Spain begins; Octavian becomes Augustus.
AD 9	Varus' three legions, together with nine auxiliary units, destroyed in Teutoburg Forest, Germany by the Cherusci tribe and others.
AD 40	Caligula's planned invasion of Britain aborted.
AD 43	Third, and successful, Roman invasion of Britain under the emperor Claudius, with the troops commanded by Aulus Plautius.
AD 44	Future emperor Vespasian successfully campaigns in the south-west of Britain, leading the *legio* II *Augusta*.
AD 47	New governor Publius Ostorius Scapula campaigns in north

	Wales, subdues the first revolt by Iceni tribe in the north of East Anglia.
AD 48	First revolt of the Brigantes tribe in northern Britain.
AD 49	*Colonia* for veterans founded at Colchester, with the *legio* XX *Valeria Victrix* moving to Gloucester; Scapula campaigns in Wales.
AD 50	Construction begins of first forum in the new-found city of London.
AD 51	Leader of the British resistance to Roman rule, Caratacus, captured by the Romans after being handed over to them by the Brigantian queen Cartimandua.
AD 52	Silures tribe in southern Wales pacified by Governor Didius Gallus.
AD 54	Claudius poisoned to death; Nero becomes emperor.
AD 57	Quintus Veranius becomes the governor, dying in office; Rome intervenes in favour of Queen Cartimandua in a dispute over the leadership of the Brigantes.
AD 58	Gaius Suetonius Paulinus becomes governor.
AD 59–60	Initial subjugation of the Druids in the far west of Britain, and initial invasion of Anglesey by Governor Gaius Suetonius Paulinus; the campaign is cut short by the Boudiccan Revolt.
AD 60–1	Boudiccan Revolt takes place, featuring the destruction of Colchester, St Albans and London; the revolt is defeated by Gaius Suetonius Paulinus, and is followed by the suicide of Boudicca.
AD 61–3	Publius Petronius Turpilianus becomes governor, followed by Marcus Trebellius Maximus.
AD 68	Nero overthrown; Galba becomes emperor.
AD 69	'Year of Four Emperors'; in Britain Cartimandua, queen of the Brigantes and ally of Rome, is overthrown by former husband Venutius; Marcus Vettius Bolanus is governor.
AD 70	The *Classis Britannica* regional navy in Britain is named for the first time in the context of the Batavian Revolt of Civilis on the river Rhine.
AD 71	Vespasian orders new British governor Quintus Petillius Cerialis to campaign in the north of Britain; the Brigantes are defeated, with Venutius captured and killed.

AD 74	Sextus Julius Frontinus appointed as the new governor in Britain; further campaigning in Wales follows, and Chester is founded.
AD 77	Gnaeus Julius Agricola becomes governor in Britain; Wales and western Britain are finally conquered.
AD 78	Agricola consolidates the Roman control of Brigantian territory.
AD 79	Agricola begins his campaign to subdue the whole of the north of Britain, including Scotland; the emperor Vespasian dies and is replaced by his son Titus.
AD 80	Agricola continues his campaigning in Scotland.
AD 81	Death of Titus, who is succeeded by Domitian.
AD 82	Agricola continues campaigning in Scotland.
AD 83	Agricola brings the combined Caledonian tribes to battle at Mons Graupius in the Grampians, south of the Moray Firth (or possibly even further north); the *Classis Britannica* circumnavigates northern Scotland; the conquest of Britain is declared 'complete', with construction beginning of a monumental arch at Richborough in modern Kent to commemorate the event.
AD 87	Roman troops are withdrawn from the far north of Britain because of pressures elsewhere in the Empire; Inchtuthil in Tayside is abandoned.
AD 90	Lincoln becomes a *colonia*.
AD 96	Domitian assassinated, bringing to an end the Flavian dynasty; he is succeeded by Nerva; Gloucester becomes a *colonia*.
AD 98	Death of Nerva, who is succeeded by Trajan; in Britain, Publius Metilius Nepos is the governor, followed by Titus Avidius Quietus.
AD 100	Trajan orders the full withdrawal of Roman troops from Scotland, and then establishes a new frontier along the Solway Firth–Tyne Line; all defences north of this line are abandoned by AD 105.
AD 103	Lucius Neratius Marcellus is governor.
AD 115	Marcus Atilius Bradua is governor.
AD 117	Death of Trajan, who is succeeded by Hadrian; this coincides with major disturbances in the north of the province.

AD 122   Hadrian visits Britain, initiating the construction of Hadrian's Wall on the Solway Firth–Tyne Line; Aulus Platorius Nepos is the governor.

AD 126   Lucius Trebius Germanus is governor.

AD 131   Sextus Julius Severus is governor.

AD 133   Publius Mummius Sisenna is governor.

AD 138   Death of Hadrian, who is succeeded by Antoninus Pius; Quintus Lollius Urbicus is the governor in Britain.

AD 142   Military engagement north of Hadrian's Wall continues under Quintus Lollius Urbicus, on the orders of Antoninus Pius, in an attempt to subdue the tribes of northern Britain and southern Scotland – the latter region being conquered again; construction begins of the Antonine Wall along Clyde–Forth Line, the new northern frontier.

AD 145   Gnaeus Papirus Aelianus is governor.

AD 155   Central St Albans is destroyed by fire.

AD 157   Gnaeus Julius Verus is governor.

AD 161   Antoninus Pius dies, and is succeeded by Marcus Aurelius.

AD 162   Marcus Statius Priscus is governor of Britain, followed by Sextus Calpurnius Agricola; the Antonine Wall is evacuated, with the northern border once again moving south to the line of Hadrian's Wall.

AD 169   More trouble in northern Britain.

AD 174   Caerellius is governor.

AD 175   5,500 Sarmatian cavalry sent to Britain.

AD 178   Ulpius Marcellus is governor.

AD 180   Marcus Aurelius dies, replaced by Commodus.

AD 182   The tribes either side of Hadrian's Wall start raiding along and across the border, with Roman troops responding with counter-raids; towns far to the south of the wall begin constructing the first earth-and-timber defence circuits, indicating that tribal raiding penetrated far into the province.

AD 184   Commodus receives his seventh acclamation as imperator, taking the title Britannicus.

AD 185   Some 1,500 picked troops from Britain travel to Rome with a petition for the emperor Commodus, asking that he dismisses the praetorian prefect Perennis; the new governor in Britain is the future emperor Publius Helvius Pertinax.

AD 191/192 Decimus Clodius Albinus becomes governor in Britain.

AD 193 The 'Year of the Five Emperors', with Septimius Severus emerging the victor.

AD 196 British governor Albinus invades Gaul and is proclaimed emperor by the legions from Britain and Spain.

AD 197 Albinus is defeated by Severus at the closely fought Battle of Lugdunum (modern Lyons) and is killed; planning begins to divide the province of Britain into two – Britannia Superior and Britannia Inferior (although see p. 22); Virius Lupus is the new governor.

AD 197–198 Severus sends military commissioners to Britain aiming to quickly suppress the supporters of Albinus; Roman troops rebuild parts of Hadrian's Wall (some of which may have actually been destroyed) and other parts of the northern defences, which had been damaged by an increase in tribal raiding after Albinus had travelled to Gaul with his troops; construction also starts at this time of the land walls of London; Severus begins his reforms of the military, while he himself campaigns in Parthia for two years.

AD 202 Caracalla marries Fulvia Plautilla; Severus campaigns in North Africa; Gaius Valerius Pudens is governor in Britain.

AD 205 Lucius Alfenus Senecio is governor in Britain.

AD 207 News arrives in Rome from Britain (perhaps the letter from Senecio detailed by Herodian) asking Severus for urgent assistance in the form of the emperor himself or more troops.

AD 208 Severus arrives in Britain with the imperial household and additional troops, after planning a major campaign against the Maeatae and Caledonian tribal confederations north of Hadrian's Wall.

AD 209 The first Severan campaign in Scotland.

AD 210 The second Severan campaign in Scotland, led by Caracalla; genocide ordered by Severus.

AD 211 Severus dies at York, with his sons Caracalla and Geta becoming joint emperors; the campaign in the north of Britain is suspended and the brothers return to Rome; Caracalla murders Geta; Britain is later officially divided into two provinces –

	Britannia Superior and Britannia Inferior.
AD 216	Marcus Antonius Gordianus is governor of Britannia Inferior.
AD 222	Tiberius Julius Pollienus Auspex is governor of Britannia Superior.
AD 223	Claudius Xenophon is governor of Britannia Inferior.
AD 224	Ardashir I of Persia defeats his Parthian overlords over a two-year period, bringing the Sassanid Persian Empire into being.
AD 225	Maximus is governor of Britannia Inferior.
AD 226	Calvisius Rufus becomes governor of Britannia Inferior, being followed by Valerius Crescens and then by Claudius Appellinus.
AD 235	Assassination of Severus Alexander, beginning the 'Crisis of the Third Century'; Maximinus Thrax becomes emperor.
AD 237	Tuccianus becomes governor of Britannia Inferior.
AD 238	Marcus Martiannius Pulcher becomes governor of Britannia Superior; Maecilius Fuscus becomes governor of Britannia Inferior, quickly followed by Egnatius Lucilianus.
AD 242	Nonius Philippus becomes governor of Britannia Inferior.
AD 244	Aemilianus becomes governor of Britannia Inferior.
AD 249	The last potential mention of the *Classis Britannica* regional fleet, on epigraphy commemorating Saturninus, ex-captain in the British fleet.
AD 250	Irish raiding takes place along the west coast, with Germanic raiding along the east coast; the first use of the term Pict to describe the confederation of tribes in northern Scotland.
AD 253	Desticius Juba becomes governor of Britannia Superior.
AD 255	London's wall circuit is completed with the building of the river wall and bastions.
AD 260	The 'Gallic Empire' is declared by Postumus, splitting Britain, Gaul and Spain away from the Empire for fourteen years.
AD 262	Octavius Sabinus becomes governor of Britannia Inferior.
AD 268	Postumus is murdered by his own troops.
AD 274	The emperor Aurelian defeats the 'Gallic Empire', with Britain, Gaul and Spain rejoining the Empire.
AD 277	Vandals and Burgundian mercenaries are settled in Britain, with Victorinus defeating a British usurpation.
AD 284	Diocletian becomes emperor; beginning of Diocletianic reforms

of the military; end of the 'Crisis of the Third Century'.

AD 287   The usurpation of Carausius, which splits Britain and northern Gaul away from the Empire.

AD 293   Western Caesar Constantius Chlorus recaptures northern Gaul from Carausius, who is then assassinated by Allectus, the latter then taking over control from his former master in Britain.

AD 296   The fourth Roman invasion of Britain, with Constantius Chlorus invading to defeat Allectus, the western Caesar then returning the two provinces to the Empire; around this time Britain is declared a diocese as part of the Diocletianic Reformation, with the four provinces of Maxima Caesariensis, Britannia Prima, Flavia Caesariensis and Britannia Secunda.

AD 306   Constantius Chlorus campaigns in the north of Britain, then dies in York; his son Constantine is proclaimed emperor by the troops.

AD 312   Constantine becomes sole emperor in the west, with his military reforms beginning around this time.

AD 313   Constantine and Licinius agree to end the persecution of Christians.

AD 314   Three British bishops attend the Council of Bishops at Arles.

AD 324   Constantine becomes the sole emperor of the whole Empire.

AD 337   Constantine prepares for war with Persia but falls ill in Nicomedia and dies.

AD 343   The emperor Constans makes a winter crossing of the English Channel to Britain following the defeat of his brother Constantine II three years earlier, possibly in the context of a military emergency in the north of the island.

AD 350   The military leader Magnentius (born in Britain) usurps power in Gaul, with the provinces in Britain and Spain quickly supporting him, and ultimately the whole of the Western Empire.

AD 351   Magnentius defeated by the eastern emperor Constantius II at the Battle of Mursa Major, and then retreats to Gaul; Magnentius is defeated again at the Battle of Mons Seleucus, after which he commits suicide; Constantius II sends Paul 'the chain' to Britain to purge the aristocracy after the revolt of Magnentius; the *vicarius* of the diocese, Martinus, commits

	suicide rather than face trial.
AD 358	Alypius becomes *vicarius* of the diocese.
AD 359	British bishops attend the Council of Rimini; the emperor Julian builds 700 ships to transport grain from Britain to feed his Rhine army.
AD 367	Civilis becomes the *vicarius* of the diocese; the 'Great Conspiracy' of Picts from Scotland, Attecotti from the Western Isles, Irish and Germanic raiders attack Britain, overwhelming the frontier defences.
AD 369	Count Theodosius arrives in Britain to suppress the revolt and restore order, with Magnus Maximus serving under him; the northern frontier is rebuilt yet again.
AD 383	Magnus Maximus (now the British military commander, and possibly the *vicarius* of the diocese) campaigns against Pictish and Irish raiders; he is proclaimed emperor by his troops and invades Gaul, which declares its support for him, as does Spain.
AD 387	Magnus Maximus invades Italy, where he ousts the emperor, Valentinian II.
AD 388	Magnus Maximus is defeated and executed by Theodosius I, emperor in the East.
AD 391	Theodosius I bans pagan worship, although the practice still continues in Britain.
AD 395	Chrysanthus becomes *vicarius* of the diocese.
AD 400	The Western Empire *magister militum* Stilicho campaigns in Britain and defeats Pictish, Irish and Germanic raiders; he then withdraws many troops from the diocese to help defend Italy against the Goths, with Britain left dangerously exposed to further attack; Victorinus becomes the new *vicarius*.
AD 402	Last import of base coins into Britain takes place.
AD 405	Heavy Irish raiding on the south-western coast of Britain occurs, this being a possible date for the capture of St Patrick.
AD 406	Vandals, Burgundians, Alans, Franks and Suevi overrun the *limes Germanicus* near Mainz and invade Gaul.
AD 407	In swift succession the military in Britain declare Marcus, then Gratian and finally Constantine III to be the emperor; the last crosses to Gaul with the remaining *comitatenses* field army troops from Britain, setting up his capital at Arles.

AD 409	The British aristocracy throw out their Roman administrators, with the diocese cut adrift from the remaining parts of the Western Empire.
AD 410	The western emperor Honorius allegedly tells the Britons to look to their own defences (note here the debate about the accuracy of this).
AD 411	Constantine III is captured and executed on the orders of Honorius.
AD 429	St Germanus visits Britain to debate with the Pelagian Christians there; further conflict with the Picts and Irish.
AD 430	Effective end of coin use in Britain.
AD 454	The Britons appeal to the *magister militum* Flavius Aetius by letter in 'the groans of the Britons' request for military assistance, but no troops are available to help.
AD 476	The last western emperor, Romulus Augustulus, is deposed; end of the Roman Empire in the West.

References

Ancient Sources

Julius Caesar (1951) *The Conquest of Gaul*. Handford, S. A. (ed.). London: Penguin.

Cassius Dio (1925) *Roman History*. Cary, E. (ed.). Cambridge, MA: Harvard University Press/Loeb Classical Library.

Sextus Julius Frontinus (1990) *Strategemata*. Ireland, R. I. (ed). Ann Arbor, MI: University of Michigan Press.

Herodian (1989) *History of the Roman Empire*. Whittaker, C. R. (ed.). Cambridge, MA: Harvard University Press/Loeb Classical Library.

Historia Augusta (1921) Magie, D. (ed.). Cambridge, MA: Harvard University Press/Loeb Classical Library,

Homer, *The Iliad* (1950) Rieu, E. V. (ed.). London: Penguin.

Paulus Orosius (1936) *Seven Books of History Against the Pagans*. Woodworth, R. I. (trans.). New York: Columbia University Press

Pausanias (1979) *Guide to Greece: Central Greece*. Levi, P. (ed.). London: Penguin.

Pliny the Younger (1963) *Epistularum Libri Decem*. Mynors, R. A. B. (ed.). Oxford: Clarendon Press/Oxford Classical Texts.

Polybius (1979) *The Rise of the Roman Empire*. Scott-Kilvert, I. (ed.). London: Penguin.

Strabo (2014) *The Geography*. Roler, D. W. (ed.). Cambridge: Cambridge University Press.

Cornelius Tacitus (1970) *The Agricola*. Mattingly, H. (ed.). London: Penguin.

Publius Flavius Vegetius Renatus (1993) *Epitoma Rei Militaris*. Milner, N. P. (trans.). Liverpool: Liverpool University Press.

Modern Sources

Atkinson, J. A. (2016) 'Ben Lawers: An Archaeological Landscape in Time', *Scottish Archaeological Internet Results*, vol. 62. Retrieved from: http://archaeologydataservice.ac.uk/archiveDS/archiveDownload?t=arch-310-1/dissemination/pdf/2056-7421_62_Ben_Lawers.pdf [accessed 16 November 2017].

Avery, A. (2007) *The Story of York*. Pickering: Blackthorn Press.

Bidwell, P. (2007) *Roman Forts in Britain*. Stroud: Tempus.

Bidwell, P. (2012) 'The Roman Fort at Bainbridge, Wensleydale: Excavations by B. R. Hartley on the *principia* and a summary account of other excavations and surveys', *Britannia*, vol. 43, 45–113.

Birley, A. R. (1999) *Septimius Severus: The African Emperor*. Abingdon: Routledge.

Birley, A. R. (2005) *The Roman Government of Britain*. Oxford: Oxford University Press.

Birley, A. R. (2007) 'The Frontier Zone in Britain: Hadrian to Caracalla'. In: de Blois, L. and Lo Cascio, E. (eds), *The Impact of the Roman Army (200 BC– AD 476)*. Leiden: Brill, 355–70.

Bonifay, M. (2014) 'Africa: Patterns of Consumption in Coastal Regions Versus Inland Regions. The Ceramic Evidence', *Late Antique Archaeology*, vol. 10, no. 1, 529–66.

Breeze, D. J. (2000) *Roman Scotland*. London: Batsford Ltd/Historic Scotland.

Breeze, D. J. and Dobson, B. (2000) *Hadrian's Wall*. London: Penguin.

Briscoe, J. (1989) 'The Second Punic War'. In: Astin, A.E. (ed.), *The Cambridge Ancient History – Volume 8*. Cambridge: Cambridge University Press, 44–80.

Brooks, N. P. (1994) 'Rochester Bridge AD 43 to 1381'. In: Yates, N. and Gibson, J. H. (eds), *Traffic and Politics – The Construction and Management of Rochester Bridge AD 42–1993*. Woodbridge: Boydell Press, 1–35.

Burgess, R. W. (1993) 'Principes cum Tyrannis: Two Studies on the Kaisergeschichte and Its Tradition', *The Classical Quarterly*, vol. 43, 491–500.

Connolly, P. (1988) *Greece and Rome at War*. London: Macdonald.

Cornell, T. J. and Matthews, J. (1982) *Atlas of the Roman World*. Oxford: Phaidon Press.

Cowan, R. (2003a) *Roman Legionary, 58 BC–AD 69*. Oxford: Osprey.

Cowan, R. (2003b) *Imperial Roman Legionary, AD 161 – 284*. Oxford: Osprey.

D'Amato, R. (2016) *Roman Army Units in the Western Provinces (1)*. Oxford: Osprey.

De la Bédoyère, G. (2017) 'The Emperors' Fatal Servants', *History Today* (March), 58–62.

Elliott, P. (2014) *Legions in Crisis*. Stroud: Fonthill Media.

Elliott, S. (2016a) *Sea Eagles of Empire: The* Classis Britannica *and the Battles for Britain*. Stroud: The History Press.

Elliott, S. (2016b) 'The Sea Eagles: The *Classis Britannica* and the Roman Conquest of Britain', *Military History Monthly*, vol. 75, 18–41.

Elliott, S. (2017) *Empire State: How the Roman Military Built an Empire*. Oxford: Oxbow.

Ellis Jones, J. (2012) *The Maritime Landscape of Roman Britain*. Oxford: BAR/ Archaeological and Historical Associates.

Erdkamp, P. (2005) *The Grain Market in the Roman Empire: A Social, Political, and Economic Study*. Cambridge: Cambridge University Press.

Faulkner, N. (2001) *The Decline and Fall of Roman Britain*. Stroud: Tempus.

Fields, N. (2003) *Hadrian's Wall AD 122–410*. Oxford: Osprey Publishing.

Finley, M. (1999) *The Ancient Economy*. Berkeley, CA: University of California Press.

Frere, S. (1974) *Britannia: A History of Roman Britain* (3rd edn). London: Routledge.

Fryer, P. (2010) *Staying Power: The History of Black People in Britain*. London: Pluto Press.

Garrison, E. G. (1998) *History of Engineering and Technology: Artful Methods*. Boca Raton, FL: CRC Press.

Gerrard, J. (2013) *The Ruin of Roman Britain: An Archaeological Perspective*. Cambridge: Cambridge University Press.

Goldsworthy, A. (2003) *The Complete Roman Army*. London: Thames & Hudson.

Goldsworthy, A. (2014) *Augustus: From Revolutionary to Emperor*. London: Weidenfeld & Nicolson.

Golvin, J. C. (2003) *Ancient Cities Brought to Life*. Ludlow: Thalamus.

Grainge, G. (2005) *The Roman Invasions of Britain*. Stroud: Tempus.

Hasebroek, J. (1921) *Untersuchungen zur Geschichte des Kaisers Septimius Severus*. Heidelberg: J. Winters.

Haverfield, F. (1906, reprint 2009) *The Romanization of Roman Britain*. New York: Cornell University Press.

Hingley, R. (1982) 'Roman Britain: The Structure of Roman Imperialism and the Consequences of Imperialism on the Development of a Peripheral Province'. In: Miles, D. (ed.), *The Romano-British Countryside: Studies in Rural Settlement and Economy*. Oxford: BAR/Archaeological and Historical Associates, 17–52.

Hingley, R. (2005) *Globalizing Roman Culture – Unity, Diversity and Empire*. London: Routledge.

Hodgson, N. (2007) 'Arbeia Roman Fort – South Shields', *Current Archaeology*, vol. 19, no. 133, 24–42.

Hodgson, N. (2014) 'The British Expeditions of Septimius Severus', *Britannia*, vol. 45, 31–51.

Hopkins, K. (1985) *Death and Renewal*. Cambridge: Cambridge University Press.

Hornblower, S. and Spawforth, A. (1996) *The Oxford Classical Dictionary*. Oxford: Oxford University Press.

James, S. (2011) *Rome and the Sword*. London: Thames & Hudson.

Jones, A. H. M. (1953) 'Inflation under the Roman Empire', *Economic History Review,* vol. 5, 293–318.

Jones, B. and Mattingly, D. (1990) *An Atlas of Roman Britain*. Oxford: Oxbow.

Jones, R. (2011) *Roman Camps in Scotland*. Edinburgh: Society of Antiquaries of Scotland.

Jones, R. (2012) *Roman Marching Camps in Britain*. Stroud: Amberley.

Kamm, A. (2011) *The Last Frontier: The Roman Invasions of Scotland*. Glasgow: Tempus.

Kean, R. M. (2005) *The Complete Chronicle of the Emperors of Rome*. Ludlow: Thalamus.

Keppie, L. (2015) *The Legacy of Rome: Scotland's Roman Remains*. Edinburgh: Birlinn.

Kulikowski, M. (2016) *Imperial Triumph: The Roman World from Hadrian to Constantine*. London: Profile.

Lambert, M. (2010) *Christians and Pagans*. New Haven, CT, and London: Yale University Press.

Levick, B. (2007) *Julia Domna: Syrian Empress*. London: Routledge.

Mason, D. J. P. (2003) *Roman Britain and the Roman Navy*. Stroud: The History Press.

Mattingly, D. (2006) *An Imperial Possession: Britain in the Roman Empire*. London: Penguin.

Millett, M. (1990) *The Romanization of Britain*. Cambridge: Cambridge University Press.

Millett, M. (2015) 'Broader Perspectives on Past Lives'. In: Halkon, P., Millett, M. and Woodhouse, H. (eds), *Hayton, East Yorkshire: Archaeological Studies of the Iron Age and Roman Landscapes. Volumes 1 and 2*. Yorkshire Archaeological Report no. 7. Leeds: Yorkshire Archaeological Society, 542–58.

Moffat, B. (2000) 'A Marvellous Plant: The Place of the Heath Pea in Scottish Botanical Tradition', *Folio*, vol. 1, 13–15.

Moorhead, S. and Stuttard, D. (2012) *The Romans Who Shaped Britain*. London: Thames & Hudson.

Morris, J. (1968) 'The Date of St Alban', *Hertfordshire Archaeology and History*, vol. 1, 1–8.

Oleson, J. P. (2009) *The Oxford Handbook of Engineering and Technology in the Classical World*. Oxford: Oxford University Press.

Ottaway, P. (2013) *Roman Yorkshire*. Pickering: Blackthorn Press.

Parfitt, K. (2013) 'Folkestone During the Roman Period'. In: Coulson, I. (ed.), *Folkestone to 1500: A Town Unearthed*. Canterbury: Canterbury Archaeological Trust, 31–54.

Pearson, A. F. (2006) *The Work of Giants: Stone Quarrying in Roman Britain*. Stroud: Tempus.

Pitassi, M. (2012) *The Roman Navy*. Barnsley: Seaforth.

Platnauer, M. (1918) *Untersuchungen zur Geschichte des Kaisers Septimius Severus*. Oxford: Oxford University Press.

Pollard, N. (2000) *Soldiers, Cities and Civilians in Roman Syria*. Ann Arbor, MI: University of Michigan Press.

Rankov, B. (2009) 'A Secret of Empire (imperii Arcanum): An Unacknowledged Factor in Roman Imperial Expansion'. In: Hanson, W. S. (ed.), *The Army and Frontiers of Rome: Papers Offered to David J. Breeze on the Occasion of his Sixty-Fifth Birthday and His Retirement from Historic Scotland*. Portsmouth, RI: Journal of Roman Archaeology Supplementary Series, vol. 74, 163–72.

Reed, N. (1975) 'The Scottish Campaigns of Septimius Severus', *Proceedings of the Royal Society of Antiquaries of Scotland*, PSAS 107 (1975–6), 92–102.

Reid, R. (2016) 'Bullets, Ballistas and Burnswark: A Roman Assault on a Hillfort in Scotland', *Current Archaeology*, vol. 27, no. 316, 20–6.

Robertson, A. S. (1980) 'The Bridges on the Severan Coins of AD 208 and 209'. In: Hanson, W. S. and Keppie, L. J. F. (eds), *Roman Frontier Studies*. Oxford: BAR/Archaeological and Historical Associates, 131–40.

Savine, B. (2017) 'The Burial Club: Excavating Eboracum's Common People', *Current Archaeology*, vol. 28, no. 331, 46–50.

Scarre, C. (1995a) *The Penguin Historical Atlas of Ancient Rome*. London: Penguin.

Scarre, C. (1995b) *Chronicle of the Roman Emperors*. London: Thames & Hudson.

Southern, P. (2013) *Roman Britain*. Stroud: Amberley.

Speidel, M. A. (1992) 'Roman Army Pay Scales', *The Journal of Roman Studies*, vol. 82, 87–106.

Temin, P. (2012) *The Roman Market Economy*. Princeton, NJ: Princeton University Press.

Vego, M. (2014). 'On Littoral Warfare', *Naval War College Bulletin*, vol. 68, 30–67.

Warry, J. (1980) *Warfare in the Classical World*. London: Salamander.

White, R. (2007) *Britannia Prima – Britain's Last Roman Province*. Stroud: Tempus.

Wilkes, J. J. (2005) 'Provinces and Frontiers'. In: Bowman. A. K., Garnsey, P. and Cameron, A. (eds), *The Cambridge Ancient History vol. XII, The Crisis of Empire, AD 193–337*. Cambridge: Cambridge University Press, 212–68.

Willis, S. (2008) Review of 'An Imperial Possession: Britain in the Roman Empire', *The American Journal of Archaeology*, vol. 112 (online). Retrieved from: http://www.ajaonline.org/online-review-book/587 [Accessed 10 January 2017].

Windrow, M. and McBride, A. (1996) *Imperial Rome at War*. Hong Kong: Concord.

Further Reading

Ancient Sources

Marcus Cato (1934) *De Agri Cultura*. Ash, H. B. and Hooper, W. D. (eds).
  Cambridge, MA: Harvard University Press/Loeb Classical Library.
Sextus Julius (1969) *Frontinus, Strategemata*. Bennett, C. E. (ed.). Portsmouth,
  NH: Heinemann.
Quintus Horatius Flaccus (Horace) (2008) *The Complete 'Odes' and 'Epodes'*.
  West, D. (ed.). Oxford: Oxford Paperbacks.
Pliny the Elder (1940) *Natural History*. Rackham, H. (ed.). Harvard, MA:
  Harvard University Press/Loeb Classical Library.

Modern Sources

Burnham, B. C. and Davies, J. L. (2010) *Roman Frontiers in Wales and the
  Marches*. Aberystwyth: Royal Commission on the Ancient and Historical
  Monuments of Wales.
Cornell, T. J. (1993) 'The End of Roman Imperial Expansion'. In: Rich,
  J. and Shipley, G. (eds), *War and Society in the Roman World*. London:
  Routledge, 139–70.
Cowan, R. (2002) 'Aspects of the Roman Field Army: The Praetorian Guard,
  Legio II *Parthica* and Legionary Vexillations'. Unpublished PhD thesis:
  University of Glasgow.
Cowan, R. (2015) *Roman Legionary* AD *284–337*. Oxford: Osprey.
Cunliffe, B. (1988) *Greeks, Romans and Barbarians: Spheres of Interaction*.
  London: Batsford.

D'Amato, R. (2009) *Imperial Roman Naval Forces 31 BC–AD 500*. Oxford: Osprcy.

D'Amato, R. and Sumner, G. (2009) *Arms and Armour of the Imperial Roman Soldier*. Barnsley: Frontline.

Elliott, S. (2011) 'The Medway Formula'. Unpublished MA dissertation: University College London.

Elliott, S. (2013) 'A Roman Villa at Teston', *British Archaeology*, vol. 133, 40–6.

Elliott, S. (2014a) 'The Medway Formula – A Search for Evidence that the Roman Authorities Improved the River's Navigability to Facilitate their Extensive Ragstone Quarrying Industry'. *Archaeologia Cantiana*, vol. 135, 251–60.

Elliott, S. (2014b) 'Britain's First Industrial Revolution', *History Today*, vol. 64, no. 5, 49–55.

Elliott, S. (2014c) 'The Mystery of the Medway Stones', *Current Archaeology*, vol. 25, no. 298, 11.

Elliott, S. (2016) 'When Britannia Ruled the Waves', *The Story of Roman Britain*. BBC *History Magazine Special Edition*, 38–43.

Erdkamp, P. (2013) 'The Food Supply of the Capital'. In: Erdkamp, P. (ed.), *The Cambridge Companion to Ancient Rome*. Cambridge: Cambridge University Press, 262–78.

Esmonde Cleary, A. S. (1989) *The Ending of Roman Britain*. London: Batsford.

Esmonde Cleary, A. S. (2013) *The Roman West AD 200 – 500*. Cambridge: Cambridge University Press.

Fields, N. (2006) *Rome's Saxon Shore*. Oxford: Osprey.

Fleming, R. (2010) *Britain After Rome*. London: Penguin.

Fuhrmann, C. J. (2011) *Policing the Roman Empire: Soldiers, Administration and Public Order*. Oxford: Oxford University Press.

Gardner, A. (2007) *An Archaeology of Identity*. Walnut Creek, CA: Left Coast Press.

Gardner, A. (2013) 'Thinking about Roman Imperialism: Postcolonialism, Globalisation and Beyond?', *Britannia*, vol. 44, 1–25.

Goldsworthy, A. (2000) *Roman Warfare*. London: Cassell.

Gradoni, M. K. (2013) 'The Parthian Campaigns of Septimius Severus: Causes, and Roles in Dynastic Legitimation'. In: De Sena, E. C. (ed.), *The Roman Empire During the Severan Dynasty*. Piscataway, NJ: American Journal of Ancient History/Gorgias Press.

Greene, K. (1986) *The Archaeology of the Roman Economy*. Berkeley and Los Angeles, CA: University of California Press.

Halkon, P. (2011) 'Iron Landscape and Power in Iron Age East Yorkshire', *The Archaeological Journal*, vol. 168. 134–65.

Hall, J. and Merrifield, R. (1986) *Roman London*. London: HMSO Publications for the Museum of London.

Halsall, G. (2013) *Worlds of Arthur*. Oxford: Oxford University Press.

Hanson, W. S. (1996) 'Forest Clearance and the Roman Army', *Britannia*, vol. 27, 354–8.

Hingley, R. (1989) *Rural Settlement in Roman Britain*. London: Seaby.

Higgins, C. (2013) *Under Another Sky: Journeys in Roman Britain*. London: Jonathan Cape.

Hingley, R. (2007) 'The Roman Landscape of Britain: From Hoskins to Today'. In: Fleming, A. and Hingley, R. (eds), *Prehistoric and Roman Landscapes*. Oxford: Windgather Press, 101–12.

James, S. (1999) 'The Community of the Soldiers: A Major Identity and Centre of Power in Roman Britain'. In: Baker, P., Jundi, S. and Witcher, R. (eds), *TRAC 98: Proceedings of the Eighth Annual Theoretical Roman Archaeology Conference, Leicester (1998)*. Oxford: Oxbow, 14–25.

Kiley, K. F. (2012) *The Uniforms of the Roman World*. Wigston: Lorenz.

Kolb, A. (2001) 'The Cursus Publicus'. In: Adams, C. and Laurence, R. (eds), *Travel and Geography in the Roman Empire*. London: Routledge, 95–106.

Le Bohec, Y. (2000) *The Imperial Roman Army*. London: Routledge.

Lemak, J. (2006) Review of 'The Grain Market in the Roman Empire: A Social, Political, and Economic Study' (online but no longer available).

McGrail, S. (2014) *Early Ships and Seafaring: European Water Transport*. Barnsley: Pen & Sword Archaeology.

Manley, J. (2002) AD *43: The Roman Invasion of Britain*. Stroud: Tempus.

Margary, I. D. (1967) *Roman Roads in Britain*. London: John Baker.

Mason, D. J. P. (2001) *Roman Chester: City of the Eagles*. Stroud: Tempus.

Mattingly, D. (2009) 'The Imperial Economy'. In: Potter, D.S. (ed.), *Companion to the Roman Empire*. Hoboken: Wiley-Blackwell.

Mattingly, D. (2011) *Imperialism, Power and Identity – Experiencing the Roman Empire*. Princeton, NJ: Princeton University Press.

Merrifield, R. (1965) *The Roman City of London*. London: Benn.

Miles, A. (1972) 'Romano-British Buildings at The Mount, Maidstone', *Archaeologia Cantiana,* vol. 87, 217–19.

Millett, M. (1990) 'Introduction: London as a Capital'. In: Watson, B. (ed.), *Roman London: Recent Archaeological Work*. Portsmouth: Journal of Roman Archaeology Supplementary Series, no. 24, 7–12.

Millett, M. (1995) *Roman Britain*. London: Batsford.

Millett, M. (2007) 'Roman Kent'. In: Williams, H. (ed.), *The Archaeology of Kent to 800 AD*. Woodbridge: Boyden Press and Kent County Council, 135–86.

Milne, G. (2000) 'A Roman Provincial Fleet; The Classis Britannica reconsidered'. In: Oliver G., Brock, R., Cornell, T. and Hodgkinson, S. (eds), *The Sea in Antiquity*. Oxford: BAR/Archaeological and Historical Associates, 127–31.

Moorhead, S. (2014) *A History of Roman Coinage in Britain*. Witham: Greenlight.

Mould, Q. (2010) 'Military Equipment'. In: Bennett, P., Ridler, I. and Sparey-Green, C. (eds), *The Roman Watermills and Settlement at Ickham, Kent*. Canterbury: Canterbury Archaeology Trust, 141–8.

Parker, P. (2009) *The Empire Stops Here*. London: Cape.

Pearson, A. F. (2002) *The Roman Shore Forts*. Stroud: Tempus and Oxford: BAR/Archaeological and Historical Associates.

Pearson, A. F. (2003) *The Construction of the Saxon Shore Forts*. Oxford: BAR/Archaeological and Historical Associates.

Rae, A. and Rae, V. (1974) 'The Roman Fort at Cramond, Edinburgh: Excavations 1954–(1966)', *Britannia*, vol. 5, 163–224.

Reece, R. (1980) 'Town and Country: The End of Roman Britain', *World Archaeology*, vol. 12, no. 1, 77–92.

Reece, R. (1981) 'The Third Century, Crisis or Change?'. In: King, A. and Henig, M. (eds), *The Roman West in the Third Century*. Oxford: BAR/Archaeological and Historical Associates.

Rickman, G. (1980) *The Corn Supply of Ancient Rome*. Oxford: Oxford University Press.

Robertson, A. S. (1974) 'Romano-British Coin Hoards: Their Numismatic, Archaeological and Historical Significance'. In: Casey, J. and Reece, R. (eds), *Coins and the Archaeologist*. Oxford: BAR/Archaeological and Historical Associates, 12–36.

Rodgers, N. and Dodge, H. (2009) *The History and Conquests of Ancient Rome*. London: Hermes House.

Rogers, A. (2011) *Late Roman Towns in Britain: Rethinking Change and Decline*.

Cambridge: Cambridge University Press.

Salway, P. (1981) *Roman Britain*. Oxford: Oxford University Press.

Sheldon, H. (2010) 'Enclosing Londinium', *London and Middlesex Archaeological Society Transactions*, vol. 61, 227–35.

Southern, P. (2016) *Hadrian's Wall: Everyday Life on a Roman Frontier*. Stroud: Amberley.

Starr, C. G. (1941) *The Roman Imperial Navy 31 BC–AD 324*. New York, NY: Cornell University Press.

Tomlin, R. S. O. (2016) *Roman London's First Voices*. London: Museum of London Archaeology.

Warry, P. (2010) 'Legionary Tile Production in Britain', *Britannia*, vol. 41, 127–47.

Whitby, M. (2002) *Rome at War AD 293 – 696*. Oxford: Osprey.

Willis, S. (2007) 'Roman Towns, Roman Landscapes: The Cultural Terrain of Town and Country in the Roman Period'. In: Fleming, A. and Hingley, R. (eds), *Prehistoric and Roman Landscapes*. Oxford: Windgather Press, 143–64.

Wilson, P. (2002) *Roman Catterick and its Hinterland Volume 1*. York: Council for British Archaeology.

Index